METAPHYSICS

Other interview books from Automatic Press ♦ VIP

Formal Philosophy
edited by Vincent F. Hendricks & John Symons
November 2005

Masses of Formal Philosophy
edited by Vincent F. Hendricks & John Symons
October 2006

Political Questions: 5 Questions for Political Philosophers
edited by Morten Ebbe Juul Nielsen
December 2006

Philosophy of Technology: 5 Questions
edited by Jan-Kyrre Berg Olsen & Evan Selinger
February 2007

Game Theory: 5 Questions
edited by Vincent F. Hendricks & Pelle Guldborg Hansen
April 2007

Philosophy of Mathematics: 5 Questions
edited by Vincent F. Hendricks & Hannes Leitgeb
January 2008

Philosophy of Computing and Information: 5 Questions
edited by Luciano Floridi
Sepetmber 2008

Epistemology: 5 Questions
edited by Vincent F. Hendricks & Duncan Pritchard
September 2008

Mind and Consciousness: 5 Questions
edited by Patrick Grim
January 2009

Evolutionary Theory: 5 Questions
edited by Gry Oftedal et al.
November 2009

Epistemic Logic: 5 Questions
edited by Vincent F. Hendricks and Olivier Roy
August 2010

See all published and forthcoming books in the 5 Questions series at
www.vince-inc.com/automatic.html

METAPHYSICS
5 QUESTIONS

edited by

Asbjørn Steglich-Petersen

Automatic Press ♦ $\frac{V}{I}$P

Automatic Press ♦ $\frac{V}{I}$P

Information on this title: www.vince-inc.com/automatic.html

© Automatic Press / VIP 2010

This publication is in copyright. Subject to statuary exception and to the provisions of relevant collective licensing agreements, no reproduction of any part may take place without the written permission of the publisher.

First published 2010

Printed in the United States of America
and the United Kingdom

ISBN-10   87-92130-30-5   paperback
ISBN-13   978-87-92130-30-3   paperback

The publisher has no responsibilities for
the persistence or accuracy of URLs for external or
third party Internet Web sites referred to in this publication
and does not guarantee that any content on such
Web sites is, or will remain, accurate or appropriate.

Typeset in $\LaTeX 2_\varepsilon$
Cover design by Vincent F. Hendricks

Contents

Preface   iii

Acknowledgements   v

1   Lynne Rudder Baker   1

2   Helen Beebee   11

3   Thomas Hofweber   19

4   Hugh Mellor   35

5   Peter Menzies   39

6   Stephen Mumford   53

7   Daniel Nolan   63

8   Eric T. Olson   75

9   L. A. Paul   85

10   Lorenz B. Puntel   91

11   Gonzalo Rodriguez-Pereyra   103

12   Gideon Rosen   109

13   Jonathan Schaffer   123

14   Peter Simons   135

15   Barry Smith   145

16   Michael Tooley   161

17   Peter van Inwagen   179

18 Dean Zimmerman	197
About the Editor	225
Index	226

Preface

Metaphysics has always occupied a special place in philosophy. For those attracted to it, metaphysics is the discipline where we are allowed to concentrate on the most basic and exciting questions that can be asked – questions that, according to its practitioners, are often presupposed by other fields of philosophical and scientific inquiry. But metaphysics is also the most notorious subject of philosophy, and when philosophy from time to time is derided as obscure guesswork and idle speculation, metaphysics is usually first in the line criticism.

After a period in disrepute in the last century, it seems that metaphysics is once again entering a golden age. Rather than withering away, metaphysics has emerged from the purgatory of logical positivism and ordinary language philosophy as a more disciplined and focused field of inquiry than ever. New formal tools and methods of analysis are brought to bear on the ancient questions, in a pace that makes it difficult to keep abreast with all the exciting developments.

―――――――――――― ♦ ――――――――――――

Metaphysics: 5 Questions is an attempt to record some of these developments in a somewhat more personal and informal manner than that found in conventional academic papers. The volume is a collection of interviews with some of the most eminent and influential metaphysicians of the last few decades. Each contributor has been asked to answer the following five questions, pertaining both to their personal path through the world of metaphysics, and to their views on the status and methodology of metaphysics as it is practiced today:

1. Why were you initially drawn to metaphysics (and what keeps you interested)?

2. What do you consider to be your most important contributions to metaphysics?

3. What do you think is the proper role of metaphysics in relation to other areas of philosophy and other academic disciplines, including the natural sciences?

4. What do you consider the proper method for metaphysics?

5. What do you consider to be the most neglected topics in contemporary metaphysics, and what direction would you like metaphysics to take in the future?

The questions, particularly the ones concerning the methodology and relation of metaphysics to other scientific fields, are far from easy. Indeed, one may be excused for thinking that a book of this format is an inappropriate venue for the proper consideration of such weighty issues. Nevertheless, I hope that the reader will find that the informal and candid style of the interviews helps to demystify somewhat how metaphysical research is actually done, or at least how its most eminent practitioners take themselves to be doing it. The personal accounts of the contributors' way into metaphysics, and their estimation of the importance of their own work in the field, may also contain important lessons, or at least encouragement, particularly for those on their way into the world of metaphysics. Whatever you take away from them, I hope that you will find the interviews as enjoyable and stimulating as I have.

Aarhus, February 2010
Asbjørn Steglich-Petersen
Editor

Acknowledgements

I am particularly grateful to the contributors for devoting time to writing such erudite, enlightening, and often thought-provoking interviews, and grateful to the philosophical community in general for showing interest in this project. In addition, I would like to thank editor-in-chief Vincent F. Hendricks, managing editor Rasmus Rendsvig and asssistant editor Henrik Boensvang of **Automatic Press ♦ $\frac{V}{I}$ P**. Finally, I am grateful to the Danish National Research Council for Culture and Communication for financial support.

Aarhus, February 2010
Asbjørn Steglich-Petersen
Editor

1
Lynne Rudder Baker

Distinguished Professor of Philosophy
University of Massachusetts Amherst, USA

Why were you initially drawn to metaphysics (and what keeps you interested)?

In mid-career, I was inexorably drawn to metaphysics by questions that arise in the philosophy of mind. Beliefs, it seems to me, are not entities in the head; they are not entities at all. 'Belief' is just a nominalization of 'believes'. Beliefs (and other attitudes) are properties of persons—whole persons. This view immediately raises the question: What are persons? With that question, I was launched into metaphysics.

Some of the most brilliant and most thoughtful philosophers I know are in metaphysics, and they say some very peculiar things—that chairs don't exist, or even that you and I don't exist. Or that the apparent variety of things in the world is really only a variety of concepts of things that are fundamentally alike. We apply different concepts to, say, walnuts and screwdrivers, but in reality they are both sums of temporal parts. I could go on.

The brilliant metaphysicians have tended not to take an ontological interest in the objects that we interact with in everyday life. To treat ordinary objects with ontological seriousness is to be willing to consider them in basic ontology: on standard views, roses, persons, and electron microscopes do not belong in basic ontology. Rather, such things may be treated linguistically. Many metaphysicians are willing to say that sentences like 'The roses are in bloom' or 'I have never seen an electron microscope' are true. But, they contend, the truth of such sentences does not require that a full description of reality mention roses or electron microscopes. Alternatively, they may take medium-sized objects to be just sums of particles.

I found myself responding to what the brilliant metaphysicians said with what David Lewis (himself a brilliant metaphysician) called the 'incredulous stare'. So, I wanted to toss another view into the arena, one that I could bring myself to believe. The differences between roses and electron microscopes are ontological: a rose is of a fundamentally different kind from an electron microscope, and both belong in any complete inventory of what exists. That is, an ontology that mentioned particles but not electron microscopes would be incomplete.

Yes, I agree that microphysical particles make up every particular object in the natural world. But it does not follow that, ontologically speaking, medium-sized objects are reducible to microparticles, nor does it follow that the realm of ordinary medium-sized objects that we encounter and interact with is in any way inferior to the realm of microphysical particles. I set out to make sense of the idea that the world that we interact with is as real as the microparticles that make it up. But, then, how should ordinary objects—persons, artifacts, artworks—be understood if not as collections of atoms (or something similar)? That question grabbed me. I set out to give a metaphysical underpinning—as rigorous as those of other philosophers—to ordinary phenomena with which we are all familiar.

What keeps me interested in metaphysics is the profound satisfaction of getting clear (or trying to) about reality in terms that make our experience of it intelligible. Most of my efforts have been directed toward the world of everyday life—the world that we live and die in, the world that surprises or bores us, the world that we cannot get away from.

In short, I was drawn to metaphysics in a natural transition from the philosophy of mind. What I found in the brilliant metaphysicians made reality too thin. They had to go through contortions to connect what they considered real with the world familiar to all of us. So I set out to develop a unified view of the world that we all interact with, and to give a general account of its inhabitants.

What do you consider to be your most important contributions to metaphysics?

'Contribution' may be an overstatement. What I have tried to do has met with with varying degrees of success. My aim in metaphysics has been to give an ontological account of things in the everyday world—people, organisms, artifacts, molecules—and of the ways that they are related to each other. The account is relentlessly nonreductive: each thing is constituted by things on lower levels, but is not reducible to, nor identical to, anything on a lower level. For example, a mallet is constituted by the sum of a wooden rod and a cylinder, which is constituted by sums of celuose molecules, which is constituted by..... Or a particular salt molecule is constituted by the sum of a sodium atom and a chlorine atom, which in turn is constituted by a sum of subatomic particles.... Or a human person is constituted by a human animal, which is constituted by a sum of organs, which is constituted by a sum of cells....

But the mallet is neither identical to, nor reducible to, the sum of the rod and cylinder that constitute it. First, the identity of a constituted thing (like a mallet) may depend on relational properties, even intentional properties, but the identity of a sum depends only on the existence of its mereological parts. For example, something's being an automobile depends not only on the relation of the engine, drive train, wheels, brakes etc. to each other; nothing is an automobile in the absence of economic practices, and beings with desires and intentions. Something that looked like a '57 Chevy that spontaneously coalesced in outer space would not be an automobile. It's not just that we wouldn't call it an 'automobile'. It would not *be* one.

One of the discoveries that this constitution view has led to is that constitution is not composition. Composition is cheap: any things have a mereological sum. A mereological sum is just a collection or aggregation of objects. Any aggregation, (e.g., my left eyeball and the *Mona Lisa*) has a sum, but sums are just that: sums. No sum is identical to any material object. A sum is ontologically redundant; given its proper parts, the sum automatically exists. Material objects are not ontologically redundant. So, material objects cannot be identical to mereological sums. But this raises the question: what is the relation between my desk and the physical particles that make it up at this time? Well, the physical particles that make up my desk now automatically have a mereological sum, and that sum constitutes my desk now. Constitution is the ontological glue between sums of particles and material objects.

The Constitution View allows that an object may be constituted by different things at different times; it may change its parts without going out of existence. Scratch my desk, and *it* (the very same desk) is constituted by a different sum of microphysical particles. Replace a light bulb and the lamp survives. The Constitution View also allows that the things we interact with—each other, our tools and natural environment—have as great ontological status as we do or as microphysical particles do.

One application of the Constitution View that I take to be a valuable contribution is its account of human persons. A human person (i.e., a human being) is constituted by a human organism. An organism is essentially biological, but not essentially first-personal; a person is essentially first-personal, but not essentially biological. (With advances in nanotechnology, you or I could come to be constituted by a body that is largely if not totally bionic.) When I say that a person is essentially first-personal, I mean that a person essentially has a first-person perspective—either rudimentary or robust. A robust first-person perspective is the ability to conceive of oneself in the first-person, without any name or description or other third-personal referring device.

I suspect that the development of a robust first-person perspective goes hand-in-hand with learning a natural language. If natural languages—with their subjunctive moods and pluperfect tenses—could be a product of natural selection, so could the ability to support robust first-person perspectives. And, on the Constitution View, with the ability to support first-person perspectives brought into being a new kind of entity—persons. A person has a first-person perspective nonderivatively; an organism that constitutes a persons has (the same) first-person perspective derivatively. To have a property derivatively is to have it in virtue of constituting or being constituted by something that has the property nonderivatively. I have spelled out this Constitution View of persons in great detail in *persons and Bodies* (2000) and in *The Metaphysics of Everyday Life* (2007).

The reason that I think that this view of persons is a contribution is that—unlike substance dualism on the one hand and animalism on the other—the Constitution View satisfies two desiderata for a metaphysical view of persons. persons are (1) wholly part of the natural world, and yet (2) ontologically unique. If substance dualism is correct, it is difficult to see how persons could be wholly part of the natural order; if animalism is correct, persons are not ontologically unique. Moreover, the Constitution View of persons is not ad hoc. It fits neatly into the more general metaphysical account of all material objects—water molecules, tigers, computers, space shuttles, sculptures and so on.

This picture of constitution allows for ontological novelty. Genuinely new kinds of things can come about by natural selection or by intentional effort. A world with organisms is ontologically different from a world without organisms, and a world with devices like iphones is ontologically different from a world without them. So, another feature of my view that is outside mainstream metaphysics is that on this constitution view we human beings make an ontological contribution to reality by inventing new kinds of things. (Why shouldn't we? We're part of the natural world, after all.) So, although we can know something about ontology as of now and at times in the past, there will not be a complete ontology until the end of time.

The Constitution View is an example of what I call 'Practical realism': *Practical* because I believe that the everyday world—that part of reality that includes us, our languages, and the things we interact with—is no less ontologically significant than microphysical parts of reality; *Realist* because I endorse everyday objects as belonging to basic ontology, and in addition, I believe that there may exist objects and properties beyond our ability to recognize them.

Let me mention one last feature that will seem to many a dubious contribution: quasi-Naturalism. Practical realism, and in particular the Constitution View of persons, is compatible with theism without entailing it. When I say that persons are wholly part of the natural world, I mean to endorse a kind of quasi-Naturalism. The natural world is a spatiotemporal order that has its own integrity and autonomy. The sciences are sovereign in their domains, and they are silent about matters outside their domains. Regularities and processes in the natural world have naturalistic explanations—that is, explanations that make no appeal to any supernatural beings.

Nevertheless, quasi-Naturalism falls short of full-blown Naturalism in two respects—one epistemological and the other metaphysical. First, quasi-Naturalism does not claim that the sciences are the only source of knowledge; rather it allows that there are kinds of knowledge—e.g., ordinary empirical experience, humanistic studies of history—that are invisible to the sciences. A second way that quasi-Naturalism falls short of full-blown Naturalism is that quasi-Naturalism is not a metaphysical thesis at all. It does not claim that the natural world is all there is to reality; it remains neutral about whether or not the natural world exhausts reality. If the natural world is all there is, then microparticles make up every concrete object that exists. Quasi-Naturalism does not settle this question.

I must admit that this picture that I have promoted has not found universal acceptance, to say the least. What I can say for it is only this: The picture is one that I can take seriously as a picture of the ways things really are. I venture to say that it fits our experience of what we encounter and interact with. We do not have to leave it behind when we exit the seminar room.

What do you think is the proper role of metaphysics in relation to other areas of philosophy and other academic disciplines, including the natural sciences?

I am admittedly old-fashioned. With respect to other areas of philosophy, I confess that I take metaphysics to be fundamental. Ethics, epistemology, and philosophy of language raise questions in metaphysics; the most interesting (to me) questions in philosophy of religion, philosophy of science, philosophy of mind, action theory, and philosophy of art are metaphysical.

With respect to the sciences, metaphysics is neither an extension of the sciences nor is it an a priori foundation of the sciences. Although metaphysicians should respect the established results of the sciences (e.g., Darwinism), they should not be constrained by philosophical interpretations that scientists put on their work—such as making theological claims exclusively on the basis of natural selection.

While respecting the knowledge yielded by the social and natural sciences, I repudiate 'scientism'. Scientism can take many forms. Ontologically, it is view that the only genuine entities are those needed for scientific explanation; methodologically, it is the view that all genuine knowledge is validated by the methods of science; semantically, it is the view that the only respectable concepts are those used in the sciences. I think that to yield to scientism—ontologically, methodologically or semantically—would issue in a narrowing and a coarsening of human inquiry.

Metaphysics has a place along side of science. For example, physics has no need of (or place for) an ongoing 'now', but a moving present is at the heart of human experience; indeed, a moving present is constitutive of self-conscious awareness. What should we say? We should not simply ignore physics or require a convoluted route to physics from an A-theory of time that postulates an ongoing present; nor should we ignore common experience by endorsing an exclusively B-theory of time that denies the reality of a moving 'now'. Rather, we should show how we human persons contribute the ongoing 'now' to reality; the ongoing 'now' emerges along with us. Metaphysics generally should furnish accounts that are adequate both to the sciences and to human experience.

In the end, I take a moderate view: science has been a powerful engine of knowledge, but not the only source of knowledge: narrative history, the arts, ordinary experience, and even metaphysics are also valuable sources of knowledge.

The ideal metaphysician would be a well-educated intellectual, knowledgeable about the social and natural sciences, history, literature and art. But metaphysics is different from these other disciplines; it asks different sorts of questions (e.g., about the nature of causation rather than what causes what) and uses different sorts of methods (e.g., extravagant thought experiments that challenge the limits of the imagination). Although the questions that metaphysics asks are not empirical questions, the answers should be informed by empirical results of the natural and social sciences and of common experience. So, in my opinion, metaphysics can be done from an armchair with internet access.

What do you consider the proper method for metaphysics?

Metaphysics, along with philosophy generally, proceeds by argument. It begins with a description of the ways that things seem to be and gives reasons for (or grounds of or causes of) their seeming as they do. The ways things seem are explananda, and metaphysics as an account of the way things really are furnishes explanans. Metaphysics rarely replaces explananda, but typically shows why they have the features that they have. Or this, I believe, is traditionally how metaphysics has proceeded from Aristotle (and to some extent Plato) on.

If this Aristotelian picture is at all on the right track, then much contemporary analytic metaphysics is off course. First, analytic metaphysicians do not use metaphysics to understand the ways things seem; rather they try to reveal an underlying reality with which to replace appearances. Second, to the extent that metaphysicians treat what everyone takes for granted at all, it is only to explain how we can say true (or almost true!) things about, say, refrigerators or birth certificates—in light of the presumption that a complete inventory of everything that exists does not mention such manifest objects.

I prefer the Aristotelian approach to the metaphysical procedures prevalent today. However, the Aristotelian approach is somewhat bare as a method. I do not believe that, in a more finegrained way, there is a single proper method for metaphysics. I think that we have to be eclectic. It may be useful to recall the old positivist distinction between discovery and justification.

For discovery, we begin with (relatively) pre-theoretical data gleaned from common experience, the sciences, our interactions with each other and the manifest objects around us, our successful cognitive practices. We reflect on those data using whatever methods come to hand: a priori reasoning, thought-experiments, reflection on empirical results of the sciences, reflection on ordinary experience, even questionnaires (gulp!), whatever. Beginning with the way things seem and with the ways that we interact with them, we can fashion the premises for a metaphysical conclusion out of any of these. Along the way, we may winnow out or reconstruct some of the data as we reach for reflective equilibrium. But the goal is to shed light on the (relatively) pre-theoretical data.

Justification proceeds from the goal of metaphysics: to give comprehensive accounts of basic features of reality that make our experience intelligible. If a task of metaphysics is to explain our experience and to ground the rationality of our practices and attitudes towards things, we can assess a metaphysical view by how well it accomplishes this task.

Our experience importantly includes our practices and attitudes toward the manifest objects that we interact with. For example, suppose that I buy a new sofa, but I find that it is too large. So, I return it. To get a refund, I must return *it*—the very same sofa. The sofa that I bought persisted through, e.g., loss of some of its atoms in transit. Our practices of buying and returning (and much else—think of property rights and tort law) require us to re-identify manifest objects over time. If the manifest objects were not stable over time, our practices would be unintelligible. The metaphysical point is that the manifest objects that we re-identify really are the very same objects over time (unlike underlying sums of particles that may make them up over time). Holding that manifest objects are really just successive sums of particles puts our everyday attitudes and practices concerning them at risk of irrationality.

So, I propose a kind of reversal of the priorities of contemporary metaphysics. Rather than beginning with a priori deliverances of reason, and assessing the extent to which common beliefs measure up, I advise beginning with the world as we encounter it and judge metaphysical systems by the extent to which they illuminate it. Even those who, like David Lewis and Roderick Chisholm, take ordinary beliefs as data for ontology depict reality as something unrecognizable to the sciences and to common sense (and unrecognizable to me).

In contrast to the assumptions of the Cartesian project, all philosophizing, I believe, has substantive presuppositions. For example, I am an externalist about meaning: our knowledge of meanings cannot be distilled from our knowledge of the world. To have a language is to have many beliefs about the world. The world is linguistically infected, and language is world-infected: we cannot peel language off the world and consider either in isolation from the other. We have no choice but to begin in the middle of things—with everyday observations, which have proved to be quite reliable.

What is distinctive about metaphysics is not a method but a goal: to give comprehensive accounts of basic features of reality. And the basic features of reality, I have argued, include manifest objects. So, I think that philosophy is a tool, not a body of doctrine to which we owe allegiance. The view that I have labeled 'Practical realism' is a way to practice a metaphysics that answers to questions that reflective people might have outside the seminar room.

What do you consider to be the most neglected topics in contemporary metaphysics, and what direction would you like metaphysics to take in the future?

A glaring neglect is how to assess metaphysical theories. On what basis should one be preferred over another? Metaphysicians (I'm guilty here too) are too oracular. Aside from its internal features like coherence and elegance, a metaphysical theory is tested by its consequences. (I take this to be a Peircean idea.) To what extent does the metaphysical view provide comprehensive illumination of the world that we interact with? How well does it sehd light on matters that people can care about outside the seminar room? Reality as we interact with it is strange enough; metaphysics should not increase its strangeness.

I would like to see metaphysics turn from fantasized reality ("Suppose we had a complete psychological theory T,...") to reality that we actually know about and live in. Metaphysics should show how things that everyone cares about—objects like your house keys or Michelangelo's *David*, and states of affairs like having loving relationships or being employed—fit into basic reality.

If metaphysicians made a turn toward understanding things that matter, they might be more likely to be nonreductivists about ordinary objects. They might see relational and intentional properties (about which we know a great deal) as being as significant as microphysical properties (about which we know next to nothing).

And finally, they might come to see the emptiness of the distinction between what is mind-independent and what is mind-dependent. The sun contributes to reality (mind-independently) by bringing plants into existence. We human beings likewise contribute to reality by bring artifacts into existence. What we bring into existence partly by means of our intentions is just as real as what the sun brings into existence partly by means of its streams of photons.

In contrast to the brilliant metaphysicians, I do not think that what really matters should be relegated to a matter of semantics: It is not enough to have sentences turn out true when paraphrased in unfamiliar ways. Nor is it helpful to appeal to the distribution of microscopic qualities over spacetime: We know much less about the distribution of microscopic qualities over spacetime than we do about tables and chairs and dinner parties.

Metaphysicians would do well to respect what they knew before starting philosophy. As Peirce put it, "Let us not pretend to doubt in philosophy what we do not doubt in our hearts."

2
Helen Beebee

Professor of Philosophy
University of Birmingham, UK

Why were you initially drawn to metaphysics (and what keeps you interested)?

I was exposed to very high doses of Quine when I was an undergraduate. I think this cultivated a preference for the aesthetic of the desert landscape over the baroque: the sparser the ontology, the better, as far as I'm concerned. There's something incredibly attractive to me in the idea that the extraordinary richness of the world comes from really pretty meagre resources. I don't know how many kinds of elementary particle there are – not many. But put them together in the right way and you get water, dinosaurs, planets, computers ... That's just amazing, but it's just the start of it. You also get persons, minds, football clubs, Beethoven symphonies, moral responsibility, ..., and that's truly a cause for wonder.

Of course, perhaps we just need more than just the resources explicitly uncovered by physics. Perhaps we need laws, causation, universals, essences, and so on as additional items in our ontology. Perhaps we also need to add minds, ghosts, omnipotent beings and suchlike to our list. In both cases, I hope not – though I'm considerably more confident about not needing minds, ghosts and omnipotent beings than I am about not needing things like laws, causation and essences, which I suppose is why I'm more interested in the latter than the former.

Of course, coming up with a plausible story about how these things can be characterised in a way that doesn't amount to adding to our fundamental ontology is really hard – and that's part of what keeps me interested. Another part is the fact that philosophy progresses – sometimes quite quickly – throwing up new and unexpected views, arguments and challenges that need to be faced along the way. Essentialism, for example, is a philosophical position I'd never considered even thinking about; but it's suddenly become very popular in just the last five or ten years, and so the battle now has to be fought (to put it rather confrontationally) on new and unexpected fronts.

What do you consider to be your most important contributions to metaphysics?

My role, largely, has been to contribute to the campaign to Keep Our ontology Sparse, and in particular to its Humean faction, whose members' basic creed is 'no necessity in nature'. Membership of this campaign group has been dwindling since I was an undergraduate in the 1980's, when virtually everyone was signed up (it's a bit like the trade unions in this regard). But it represents – as it always has – an important and viable broad metaphysical position that deserves to be taken seriously by its opponents. Maybe some of them might even be persuaded to change sides.

I've principally banged the Humean drum in work on causation, laws of nature and free will. The connection between Humeanism and free will isn't obvious, but my basic thought is that a lot of incompatibilists about free will are implicitly motivated, at least in part, by a prior commitment to a necessitarian view of laws – hence the thought that if determinism is true we are at the mercy of the laws of nature in a way that robs us of any control over what we do.

I'm also interested in the history of metaphysics – in particular in Hume's views on causation – and I think attention to the history of metaphysical positions should sometimes prompt us to think again about commitments that we tend to take for granted. For example, Hume's authority is often appealed to when it comes to motivating the view that causation cannot be experienced, or that the concept of causation is pretty much expendable. I have argued that Hume denies both of these claims; so appeal to his authority – a dubious philosophical manoeuvre in any case – is completely worthless.

What do you think is the proper role of metaphysics in relation to other areas of philosophy and other academic disciplines, including the natural sciences?

Well, I'll say a bit more about this below, but I do think that it would be healthy if metaphysicians talked more to other academics in the arts and humanities; in particular when it comes to postmodernism, a position that, it seems to me, has had an influence in other disciplines that is out of all proportion to the extent to which it is philosophically justified.

The question of the relationship between metaphysics and the natural sciences is a difficult one; it's not something I've ever felt the need to have an explicit view about, and I don't think it has a single, neat answer. Philosophers of physics who are trying to make philosophical sense of Quantum Mechanics are doing something very different to, say, scientific essentialists, or metaphysicians discussing the implications of neuroscientific results for the existence and nature of free will.

Clearly in some areas of metaphysics, one ought to be sensitive to scientific discoveries and results. On the other hand, there are certainly some areas of metaphysics that really don't need to pay much attention to what scientists are up to. Evolutionary theory aside, I doubt science is going to come up with much that has a bearing on the existence of God or universals.

I suppose I might feel inclined to sign up to the slogan, 'metaphysics is continuous with science', except that I don't have a very good grasp of what it means. Is it a discipline that, in its entirety, should be solely conducted from the armchair and pay no attention to any science at all? Clearly not. Does metaphysics share a method with the natural sciences? Mostly not. Does metaphysics, in its entirety, examine the same questions, or perhaps more general versions of the same questions, as the natural sciences do? Again, clearly not. Is metaphysics interested in the nature of reality? Well, yes. So I suppose if what 'metaphysics is continuous with science' means is that our collective aim is to construct coherent, plausible theories about the nature of reality, and that science and metaphysics both play an indispensable role in that project, and that the appropriate division of labour between metaphysicians and scientists is not always clear-cut, then I do subscribe to the slogan.

What do you consider to be the proper method for metaphysics?

Metaphysics has come a long way since the days when virtually everyone accepted that 'metaphysics' was simply a matter of conceptual analysis: the articulation of the necessary and sufficient conditions for the application of some concept ('... causes ...', '... acts freely', '... is disposed to ...', and so on). In a sense, I sometimes think it has come too far. Respectable metaphysicians will say things like, 'I'm interested in the nature of the world, and not the meanings of words', as though the two questions were obviously completely separate. But they are not completely separate; minimally, a theory is only a theory of freedom, or causation, or whatever, if what it describes is the kind of thing we might be inclined to call 'freedom' or 'causation', or whatever.

A similar issue emerges when metaphysicians make claims about the necessity or contingency of their theories. We might be told that a theory of X is only supposed to hold contingently – but then we need a story about why the kind of thing identified as being X *counts* as an X, given that there might have been various other, apparently quite different things, that we would also have counted as X's. Similarly, we might be told that a theory of X is true as a matter of metaphysical necessity – but then we need a story about why we should think that the theory is true as a matter of metaphysical necessity, when our concept of X *appears* to be rich enough to encompass various other kinds of thing that, according to the theory, are not only not X's, but could not possibly have been.

On the other hand, progress has certainly been made. Metaphysicians are now allowed to be more revisionary than the narrow confines of straightforward conceptual analysis used to permit: we are allowed to say things that jar with common sense, so long as we can explain why the common sense view should be thought to be mistaken or incoherent, or how we might have come to have it even though it is false. And the theoretical options are correspondingly broader. For example, in the causation literature, the available options are no longer exhausted by reductionism and primitivism. (Can we provide univocal necessary and sufficient conditions for the application of the concept 'cause'? If yes, then reductionism is true; if no, then causation is a primitive feature of the world.) We have supervenience, pluralism, and so on.

One element of recent progress that I like – though with some reservations – is the rise of 'experimental philosophy'. Philosophy in general – and metaphysics in particular – should not, of course, simply be seen as a matter of articulating ordinary people's intuitions about its subject matter. On the other hand, philosophers do – and metaphysicians in particular do, quite a lot – appeal to intuitions in their theorizing. A lot of the time our intuitions about what to say in certain kinds of situation are the data on the basis of which metaphysical theories are constructed or criticized. But if we are going to appeal to our ordinary intuitions, we had better be right about what they are. And a philosopher, immersed in, and often convinced of the truth of, a particular philosophical position is hardly going to be the best judge of ordinary intuitions. It might seem to an agent-causalist, say, that her freely-made decisions are caused by *her*, and not merely by her beliefs and desires; but perhaps it seems that way because she is so convinced that that is how things really are.

Perhaps a good example of failure to pay attention to ordinary – as opposed to philosophers' – intuitions is the case of Kripkean semantics for natural kind terms. The Kripkean story has had a huge influence on contemporary metaphysics. But that story is motivated by an assumption about what ordinary language-users would say in various hypothetical situations; for example, Kripke tells us that *we* would not call a sample of some substance that didn't have atomic number 79 'gold', no matter how similar it is in its behaviour to the stuff we are actually confronted with that we call 'gold'. Well, wouldn't we? That's an empirical claim about ordinary intuitions, and as such it is subject to empirical investigation. When Kripke is taught to undergraduates, typically there are a few students who simply don't have the intuitions they are 'supposed' to have; they should be (but I suspect often are not) regarded as potential counter-examples to Kripke's claim, rather than students who simply don't 'get it'.

On the other hand, we need to be careful with 'folk' intuitions, for at least three reasons. First, the intuitions of the man on the Clapham omnibus provide metaphysicians with some data, but metaphysics would be very boring if they were counted as the final arbiter of metaphysical theories. That would, in effect, mark a return to a particularly dull kind of conceptual analysis, where all we're really doing is articulating and perhaps systematising our commonsense beliefs. Second, it's unclear how deeply ordinary intuitions cut into the nature of reality. If we ask people to choose between whether free will requires agent causalism or genuine indeterminacy right up to the moment of choice or only something much more mundane (sensitivity of choices to beliefs and desires, say), we may well be asking them a question that goes beyond even any implicit theory they might hold. Perhaps they just make up their answers on the hoof, in which case it's not clear what we should infer from their answers. And third, there's a worry about the tyranny of the majority. Experimental philosophers often talk as though the fact that 83% of respondents gave such-and-such an answer decisively establishes what 'the' folk theory is, or what 'the' folk intuition is. But what about the other 17% - why is it OK to ignore what they think? Don't the results show us that there are in fact two, competing 'folk theories' and not one? In which case, why should we assume that philosophical importance attaches to the fact that one of them happens to be a lot more popular than the other?

What do you consider to be the most neglected topics in contemporary metaphysics, and what direction would you like metaphysics to take in the future?

The area I'd most like to see more people in mainstream metaphysics working on is realism vs. anti-realism, understood as a very general issue about the relationship between the mind and language on the one hand, and the world on the other. Philosophy is an increasingly specialized discipline, so that it's possible to spend one's whole career excavating some small corner: in metaphysics, this might be thinking about universals, or persistence, or laws of nature, or whatever. That's not a bad thing in itself; if we all had to keep our eye on the whole game all the time, we'd make very little progress. But – and I think this *is* a bad thing, at least in some respects – metaphysics itself is mostly taken by its practitioners to be a pretty tightly-constrained subdiscipline, in particular in relation to the philosophy of language.

I already expressed some scepticism about the view that we can completely separate questions about the nature of reality from questions about meaning; but I think the thought that they are completely separable has led not only to a conception of metaphysics that misses out some important questions when it comes to thinking about universals or causation or whatever, but it also misses out a much bigger question about the foundations of metaphysics, as currently practised by the majority of metaphysicians.

The much bigger question, as I said, is the question about the relationship between mind and language on the one hand, and the world on the other. And I think this question gets ignored, for the most part, in the sense that metaphysicians mostly simply take it to be axiomatic that the realm of facts in whatever area they're interested in (causation, free will, and so on) is a realm of facts that are utterly mind-independent – or, to put it in Thomas Nagel's terms, they are facts that crop up in the 'view from nowhere'. So, for example, in the free will debate, most people seem to take it for granted that freedom of the will is visible from the view from nowhere – or would be if it existed. (Some philosophers think that the conditions that would be required for free will to exist are impossible to satisfy, at least for beings remotely like us.) But why should we accept that assumption? It's just not clear to me that freedom of the will isn't one of those features of the world – like colours, perhaps – that are a product of our own, distinctive perspective. This is a possibility that the vast bulk of the free will debate, as it is currently conducted, simply fails to engage with.

More seriously, engagement with the bigger question seems to me to be important because vast swathes of the broader academic culture which we inhabit have adopted a worldview that is the antithesis of that taken for granted by contemporary metaphysicians, namely postmodernism. Postmodernism is grounded in a philosophical thesis, and whether or not it is a plausible thesis is – I would guess – one that most of those who take it for granted have not considered in any depth. (This is not to single out those under the sway of postmodernism for special criticism; analytic metaphysicians, by and large, simply make the contrary assumption.) Metaphysicians are uniquely well-placed to take on – and attempt to argue against – the postmodern point of view. But, by and large, we do not; we bemoan its influence on our students, and on our colleagues in other arts and humanities disciplines, as though they were under the sway of some sort of cult, and therefore immune to rational discussion of the underlying issues. I am sure there are larger cultural reasons why this has happened; but at least one reason, perhaps, is that truth is now largely seen as a topic in the philosophy of language rather than metaphysics.

A recent exception to this has been the recently highly popular topic of 'truthmaking', and discussion of various 'truthmaker principles', the standard such principle being: for every true proposition P (or perhaps every true proposition within some limited domain), there is some entity that makes it true. Some philosophers have claimed that such a principle somehow wards off the threat of various forms of anti-realism: pragmatism, for example, or phenomenalism. This seems to me to be naïve: the view that the world is composed of – and our language is about – entities whose existence or nature does not depend in any way on what human beings think or say or have evidence for or find useful is a view that could not possibly be established simply by commitment to such a principle. If philosophy were that easy, it would be a lot less interesting.

3

Thomas Hofweber

Associate Professor of Philosophy
University of North Carolina at Chapel Hill, USA

Why were you initially drawn to metaphysics (and what keeps you interested)?

Like so many others, I got into philosophy by accident, but once infected I was drawn to metaphysics with purpose. Metaphysics held the promise to find out what reality is *really* like. Although it seems beyond question that science tells us many important things about what reality is like, metaphysics promised to go further. Metaphysics promised to be able to accept the description of reality science, and possibly a good part of common sense, provides and to augment it with an even more revealing description of reality, one that says what the world is *really* like. Metaphysics seemed to be the ultimate and final step of inquiry. It could accept everything from the rest of inquiry, that there are electrons, people, stars, and still have the question left open for itself whether in the end everything is mental, or whether in the end there are no objects at all, or whether in the end there are no minds at all. I was curious to find out what, in the end, reality was really like.

I now think that all this is completely mistaken, but I didn't know that then, when I got interested in metaphysics as a student. It is thus most fair to follow up with what keeps me interested. First, even though metaphysics doesn't give us the ultimate and most revealing description of reality, it still has some real and important questions to answer. And these questions are very interesting, although maybe not as grand as I originally thought. I do think that some important questions about reality are properly addressed in metaphysics, although it is a substantial and difficult problem to say which questions these are. I will outline below my reasons for thinking that some questions in ontology are in the domain of metaphysics, and what I think the answer to these questions is. There are many questions that are traditionally thought to be metaphysical ones that are incredibly interesting, even though there is a real issue whether these questions are in the domain of philosophy. And that issue, which questions about reality are in the domain of metaphysics and philosophy, is also terribly fascinating. Why these questions are interesting is a bit hard to justify to those who don't share this sentiment. Some questions just stick to some people, others to other people.

Besides the interesting questions that metaphysics hopes to address, metaphysics, and many other parts of philosophy as well, are also simply fascinating as a collective enterprise: it is not clear if the problems we deal with are incredibly important, totally irrelevant, or just outright confused. This can have the comforting effect that the most damage one can do with ones work is to confuse others, but it gives rise to the threat that the most good one can do with ones work is to confuse oneself. But besides the status of the problems, it is also not clear when someone has made progress on a problem. The profession is full of people, myself and most others included, who think they know the answer to one or more important problems, while hardly anyone else finds much to like about their answer, if they even listen to it. And the profession is full of people who think that the most distinguished people in the field are completely confused in their philosophy. It is hardly the case that the work that is considered the best by many people in the field is also considered to be correct by these same people. And with all this one would think that metaphysicians couldn't stand each other, but just the opposite is true.

And metaphysics is fascinating as a personal project. All of us spending our life's work writing for a couple of people that we know fully well won't actually be persuaded by what we have to say, while we also know that who is right probably doesn't make much difference outside of philosophy, and all the while we think that this is the greatest way to spend ones professional life. And it probably is, or at least its a close second.

What do you consider to be your most important contributions to metaphysics?

Some of the central problems in philosophy, and especially metaphysics, are closely related to problems in ontology. These include classic metaphysical problems like the problem of universals, and questions about the objectivity in a certain domain, for example the question whether the objectivity of mathematics is tied to the

existence of mathematical entities. However, ontology as a philosophical project is puzzling all by itself. On the one hand it aims to answer deep questions about what the world is made from. And it tries to do this by trying to answer questions like
(1) Are there numbers?
or
(2) Are there properties?
But, on the other hand, it seems that questions like these have trivial answers. It is trivial to conclude that there are properties, being a cat is one, and being a dog is another. And it is trivial to conclude that there are numbers, for example it follows form the mathematical theorem that there are infinitely many prime numbers. And there are other trivial ways to conclude this as well, discussed below. But how come the apparently deep metaphysical questions whether or not reality contains properties, which we hoped to express with (2), can be answered so easily?

I have proposed a solution to this general puzzle about ontology which is based on facts about natural language. I have argued that quantifiers in natural language are polysemous, that is they have a number of different but related readings, which in turn is to say that they can make one of several different contributions to the truth conditions of a sentence in which they occur. So, sentences like
(3) Everything exists.
have at least two readings. On one it is true, and on the other it is false. On the true one one is saying that all the objects in the domain of quantification exist. On the false one it is required that a certain inferential role obtains. That is, (3) on that reading is true only if all instances of
(4) t exists.
are true, where "t" can be any term in our language. However, this is false, since
(5) Santa exists.
is false, and thus (3) does not have the proper inferential role on that reading. It can be seen quite easily, but I won't get into this, that neither reading is a restriction of the other reading. Why we have these different readings in natural language, and what they are more precisely is spelled out in Hofweber (2000), Hofweber (2005b), and Hofweber (2009b).

The polysemy of quantifiers implies a new way to think about the relationship between the truth of quantified statements and ontological questions. And it implies something about how ontological questions should be stated. The question can really simply be stated as (1) or (2). However, these sentences have two different readings, and only one of them expresses an ontological question. One of these readings does capture what we aim to ask when we ask the questions we put together in the discipline of ontology. But the other reading asks a question which is trivially answered in the affirmative.

This view of the function of quantifiers gives rise to a non-Carnapian version of Carnap's internal-external distinction. Carnap wanted to distinguish internal from external questions about what there is, and he argued that the internal ones are trivially answered in the affirmative (at least when they are of the general kind like (1) and (2)), while the external ones are meaningless, or at best construed not as factual, but as pragmatic. The external ones are the ones metaphysics aims to answer, but since they have to have a meaningful content the metaphysical project of ontology is misconceived, or so says Carnap in Carnap (1956). I agree with Carnap that we need to distinguish two kinds of questions that we can ask when we ask what there is. But contrary to Carnap I think both are equally meaningful and factual. And contrary to Carnap I argue that the difference can be understood simply as arising from different needs we have for quantifiers in ordinary everyday communication. And still contrary to Carnap I hold that this distinction does not lead to a rejection of metaphysics, but is a crucial part of showing that metaphysics at least sometimes is a legitimate discipline that can go side by side with the sciences (I will say more about this below).

These issues so far relate to ontological questions in general. But how does it help us with ontological questions in particular, questions like the problem of universals, or the ontological questions about numbers? My work on these problems has also focused on ordinary, everyday features of our talk about numbers and properties, and how it helps us shed light on the metaphysical problems. There are certain puzzles that arise from our ordinary talk about numbers and properties that are the key to understanding the metaphysical puzzles that numbers and properties are famous for.

Talk about properties and numbers is quite puzzling, in a number of different ways. First, number words in natural languages have a curious feature that they appear to be of two quite different syntactic categories: on the one hand they appear to be singular terms, or even names, as in

(6) The number of moons of Jupiter is four.
and on the other hand they appear to be like adjectives, as in
(7) Jupiter has four moons.
On top of all that (6) and (7) seem to be quite obviously equivalent. This is a puzzle about natural language only so far, just about what these numbers are doing in sentences like this, and that can be. In fact, there are several examples of the occurrence of number words in natural languages besides the above two, which were first pointed out by Frege in Frege (1884), that give rise to this puzzle. And some of these examples are very closely related to the occurrence of number words in arithmetic. I have argued in Hofweber (2005a) and Hofweber (2007) that number words are not referring expressions even when they occur as singular terms, as in (6), nor when they occur in their symbolic form in arithmetical equations. The reason why the occur as singular terms explains why the sentences seem so obviously equivalent. And the resulting view of what the content of arithmetical equations is gives rise to a largely logicist view in the philosophy of arithmetic. Arithmetical statements are true no matter what exists, nor how many things exist. I can't spell out here why that is so, but it is spelled out in detail in Hofweber (2005a). The resulting view of arithmetic has arithmetic occupying a special place among all disciplines in mathematics. Even though it appears to be the case that arithmetical statements contain referring expressions, number words in fact are not referential expressions, even when they occur in arithmetical equations. And even though it seems that the literal truth of arithmetic requires the existence of numbers, it in fact requires the existence of no particular objects, nor of a particular number of objects. It is true no matter what, or how many, things exist.

I have looked at talk about properties and propositions, and argued that property nominalzations like "the property of being a dog" and that-clauses like "that Fido is a dog" are not referring expressions either. They do not have have function to pick out entities in natural language. In addition, quantification over properties and propositions in ordinary uses is based on the internal, inferential role, reading of the quantifiers. This gives rise to a view about the function of talk about properties and propositions that has numerous consequences for various large scale philosophical debates. It guarantees that we are capable to say, in our present language, everything there is to say about the world, and it explains how apparent differences in expressive power in different languages are to be understood. The details of all this are spelled out in my Hofweber (2006). This solves the problem of universals, or so I claim. It is true that

(8) There are many things we have in common, i.e. being human, etc.

But (8) is only true on the internal reading of the quantifier. The external reading of (8) is false. And thus even though there are many things we have in common, there is no further legitimate question what these things are, where they are located, whether they are fully present in every object that has them, and so. The latter project assumes that (8) is true on the external reading. But it is a consequence of the semantics of property nominalizations that (8) on the external reading is guaranteed to be false. Nothing is or could be the property of being a dog given that the phrase "the property of being a dog" does not even aim to refer to an object. Again, the arguments are spelled out in Hofweber (2006) and also Hofweber (2009a).

Besides the issues touched on above I have also done work in other traditional areas of metaphysics. I have argued in Hofweber (2009c) that the problem of change should play no role in the metaphysics of time and material objects, since there is no metaphysical problem about change. I have argued in Hofweber (2005c) that object dependent properties are not physical properties, since physics doesn't care which object is involved in a process, only what kind of object. I have concluded from this that object dependent properties do not supervene on physical properties and thus direct reference is incompatible with physicalism. I have also worked in the philosophy of mathematics, on the semantic paradoxes, the philosophy of logic, and on some other things that are not directly related to metaphysics.

What do you think is the proper role of metaphysics in relation to other areas of philosophy and other academic disciplines, including the natural sciences?

Metaphysics has often been under attack as a confused, illegitimate and misguided part of inquiry. Usually these attacks try to show that metaphysics tries to answer meaningless questions, or that metaphysics could not lead to knowledge. While I do not think there is all that much to these concerns, I do think that there is a serious worry about metaphysics along a different line: many traditional metaphysical questions can be seen as having been answered by other, more authoritative parts of inquiry, in particular the natural sciences, including mathematics. To consider the latter case, take the question whether there are numbers. It is intended by the philosopher who asks it to be a question about mathematics from the outside. If the answer is 'yes' then arithmetic is about a domain of objects that makes it true and objective. If the answer is 'no' then arithmetical truth and objectivity must have quite a different source. But this question doesn't seem to be what it is intended to be, i.e. a question asked about arithmetic form the outside. Instead it seems that it is answered within arithmetic itself. After all, arithmetic has shown that there are infinitely many prime numbers, and thus there are infinitely many numbers. So the question whether there are any numbers either can't be a metaphysical question at all, or at least it would seem that metaphysics is considering questions that are already answered in mathematics. Metaphysics can't hope to be more authoritative than mathematics about questions that mathematics addresses. Metaphysics has to find its place somewhere among all the other disciplines of inquiry. I think metaphysics has to meet two general constraints: first it has to be modest in that it can not hope to have the authority to override the answers given to certain questions in the sciences. Metaphysicians, as individuals, can join and contribute to the other parts of inquiry, but metaphysics can't claim to have greater authority than the sciences in areas where they overlap. Second, metaphysics has to be ambitious. That is it has to have some questions that are properly addressed by it. One way to be modest is just to hold that all questions are to be addressed by the sciences. But this would be unambitious, it would leave nothing for metaphysics to do. To be ambitious metaphysics has to hold that there are questions that are properly addressed by it. How metaphysics can be ambitious, yet modest, is the crucial question. I am not sure how much of metaphysics can be ambitious, yet modest, but I do not think that all metaphysics as it is carried out today can be ambitious, yet modest. I do think, however, that some parts of metaphysics can be ambitious, yet modest, in particular ontology.

One mistaken way to defend that metaphysics can be ambitious, yet modest, is to take it not to be concerned with questions as I have put them just now, but instead with questions like the ones discussed at the very beginning of my answers. This approach could go as follows: Metaphysics is not concerned with the question whether there are numbers. That is in the domain of mathematics. Metaphysics is rather concerned with the question whether there are *really* numbers. And more generally, this proposal goes, metaphysics is concerned with what is *really* the case. But what is the difference being there being numbers, and there *really* being numbers? In the past some philosophers have tried to make sense of such a distinction, trying to spell out what the differences comes down to, but these attempts either relied on some unexplained terms comparable to 'really', or just failed outright. Some contemporary philosophers have taken the failures to spell this difference out in understandable terms to heart, but instead of giving up on the distinction they instead propose to accept is as primitive, in particular as a metaphysical primitive. One version of this is Kit Fine's, for example, in his Fine (2000). Fine wants to distinguish what is true from what is true IN REALITY. Of course, here the difference is not intended to be between what is true in fiction and what is true in reality. What is true in the ordinary sense is generally what is true in reality, not just in fiction. Rather, the difference between what is true and what is true IN REALITY uses a primitive, distinctly metaphysical sense of reality, capitalized as REALITY. This notion is to be taken as a primitive of metaphysics, not necessarily to be spelled out in any other terms. And given such a notion metaphysics easily has a domain of questions that it aims to settle. Whereas the sciences might find out what is true, metaphysics tries to find out what is true IN REALITY. There are slightly different versions of this way to carve out a domain of metaphysics presented by various philosophers, using various metaphysical notions like PRIORITY, FUNDAMENTAL, METAPHYSICAL STRUCTURE, and, of course, *REALLY*.

But all this is a big mistake. The crucial mistake is that although it is perfectly fine to use primitive metaphysical terms in ones metaphysical theorizing, it is not fine to use primitive metaphysical terms in the questions that define the domain of metaphysics. To properly introduce primitive terms one first has to state a well defined question, stated in already accessible terms, and then propose an answer to that question, possibly in the form of a theory that contains primitive theoretical terms. But when the terms occur in the question itself then metaphysics turns into an esoteric discipline: one must understand primitive metaphysical terms in order to know what questions metaphysics is trying to answer. You have to be an insider to get in the door. (For more on this see Hofweber (2009a) and Hofweber (2009b)). Metaphysics, if it is a legitimate discipline at all, must find questions for itself that are accessible to all, and that can be expressed in ordinary terms. And at the same time these questions must not be in the domain of the sciences. The questions of metaphysics must have sufficient independence from other parts of inquiry, and they must be expressed in ordinary natural language. Whether and how this is to can be done for many traditional metaphysical problems is itself a major problem. This is much more serious than many metaphysicians like to think.

On the view outlined above, and defended in the papers cited, one gets the result that some ontological questions, in particular the ones about numbers, properties and propositions, indeed simply can be asked with the question "are there numbers, etc.?". And this question, on its intended reading, is not answered in the sciences, and thus left for metaphysics to address. This gives ontology a distinct domain of questions it can address, in harmony with the questions that the sciences address. And it meets the requirement for ontology to be ambitious, yet modest, metaphysics. But not all ontological questions fall in the domain of metaphysics. I think that the question whether there are any material objects, for example, does not fall in the domain of metaphysics. It is for the sciences to settle. Which questions fall in the domain of metaphysics and which ones fall in the domain of the sciences is a substantial and difficult question, and for most cases I have no answer to it.

Among other philosophical disciplines metaphysics has a special relationship to the philosophy of language and to the philosophy of science. The latter because it discusses what we should take science to have established, and what still is left to be done even on the questions that science clearly addresses. The former since issues about language are often crucial in getting clear what the metaphysical questions are, and what does and doesn't answer them. The work of mine outlined above is closely tied to issues about language, but not because metaphysical questions are about language, but because the study of language helps us get clearer what these questions are, and how we might hope to answer them.

What do you consider to be the proper method for metaphysics?

I do not think metaphysics has a distinct method. Metaphysics is a field that covers a number of different issues that are different in nature and often unrelated. The problem of freedom of the will and of the existence of mathematical objects are completely different problems, although both are grouped together as metaphysics. For each part of metaphysics one has to work out how to best address the problems, and one shouldn't think that different parts of metaphysics are more closely related than simply being put together for some reasons or for no reason in the same subfield of philosophy.

Some problems traditionally thought to be part of metaphysics are solved by the sciences, with empirical methods. I think this is true, for example, for the refutation of nihilism. We have sufficient reason to believe both that material objects exist at all and that they have parts on empirical grounds. These problems are not distinctly philosophical. Some traditional metaphysical issues can be resolved with empirical means. Some metaphysical problems can be resolved by reflecting on our concepts, others are largely a priori, but don't deal with conceptual truths. Some are partly empirical and partly not. Its a real mixed bag.

In metaphysics, just like everywhere else, one should start with what one already believes, and one should feel some entitlement to that. Then one should see if this is enough, coherent, explanatory, and so on, and revise it as the need arises. If one discovers that one could have started out some totally different way and would have been just as well off that way then one should take this seriously, but not panic. It is still OK to believe what one started out with, but maybe one should feel a little less confident in it. In general one should hold on to what one has unless one needs to give it up. Metaphysical reflection is, among other things, a way to see if one has to give good parts of ones prior beliefs up.

One way in which metaphysics deserves special attention is in the formulation of the questions it aims to answer. Here there is something distinct in the activity of metaphysics, although related issues arise in other parts of inquiry. Metaphysical questions are often driven by an intuition that there are two coherent ways the world might be in a certain respect. For example, time might either be just a further dimension, just an add on to space, or something completely different. Here there seem to many to be two coherent alternatives to think about time that is given different labels in the debate (3D vs. 4D, presentism vs. eternalism), and it is then debated which one of them is true. But so far we do not have two coherent alternatives. For there to be two coherent alternatives there should be a question formulated in ordinary English such that those who hold onto one side of this debate say "yes", and the others say "no". However, it is incredibly hard to say what this question is, as is well known in this debate. But this issue affects many, if not most, metaphysical debates as well, and it has gotten a lot less attention there than in the philosophy of time.[1] To be clear on the question that we are trying to ask when we have an intuition that there are different ways the world might be in a metaphysical way is one thing that applies to metaphysics more than to other disciplines. For some debates I believe the differences are merely verbal, for some there are no two coherent alternatives, although we feel that there are, and for some the question can be stated in just a few words. Figuring out which debates fall into which group is the hard part.

What do you consider to be the most neglected topics in contemporary metaphysics, and what direction would you like metaphysics to take in the future?

Metaphysical theorizing is often concerned with arguing for or against a certain picture of what reality is like. But much theorizing is driven by pictures, metaphors, and suggestive suggestions. Sometimes these different pictures can't be cashed out: there are no two coherent positions that correspond to the metaphors. (I think this is true in the contemporary debate between endurance and perdurance understood as one about temporal parts, for example, see Hofweber and Velleman (2010).) Sometimes the different positions can be clearly articulated. That is to say, sometimes there is a question expressed in ordinary English so that those motivated by one metaphor or intuition answer it in the affirmative, and those who are drawn to a different picture answer it in the negative. For a whole range of philosophical problems it is not clear whether the different positions can be clearly articulated. This is widely accepted for the debate in the philosophy of time. But it is also true for many other problems. This is one issue that metaphysics must make progress on. I find this maybe more urgent than others since I think that some of the classic problems in metaphysics disappear once you try to be more clear what the problem is supposed to be. The problem of change is one example of this. (See Hofweber (2009c).) But I do not think this is true for metaphysics in general. I suspect that some prob-

---

[1] One nice illustration of this general problem is due to Jonathan Bennett in Bennett (1963). He points out that since Descartes is a dualist and Spinoza a monist there should be a question such that Descartes answer it with "two" and Spinoza with "one". It turns out to be harder to do this than one might think.

lems are driven by different metaphors that in fact are not based on competing pictures of reality. Here the debate is misguided since the apparent conflict is really just one about which of two different but compatible metaphors should be seen as characterizing reality. But maybe more importantly, I suspect that some intuitions of a coherent position are correct, even though there is no coherent statement of that position. I suspect that this is true for idealism, in particular of a Kantian variety. I don't know of a coherent version of transcendental idealism, and I don't have one to offer. But I suspect that it is a coherent view that can be articulated. And once it is articulated it can be properly assessed. Stating the alternatives, and the questions, in ordinary terms is surprisingly neglected.

Some philosophers have been motivated by problems just like these to turn to esoteric metaphysics: metaphysics that is defined by questions that contain primitive, unexplained metaphysical terms. Fine, in Fine (2000), does just that with the problem of articulating realism. But this way to state the problem is no way to move metaphysics forward. Esoteric metaphysics is just as appealing as what we could call *absurd metaphysics*. Absurd metaphysics tries to find out what is metaphysically the case. Here being metaphysically the case is a primitive metaphysical term that can't be explained in any other way. Furthermore, what is metaphysically the case and what is the case are independent of each other: neither implies the other. Metaphysics so construed has its own questions, but it is an absurd, and irrelevant, project. It can give its own description of metaphysical reality, i.e. of what is metaphysically the case, and this description is independent of the description of reality, i.e. what is the case. But there is no reason to think that the metaphysical description is more revealing than the other description, nor is there any reason to think that the metaphysical description is a description of anything. We have no reason to pursue this project. Some metaphysicians are attracted to versions of absurd metaphysics, and it is understandable why. It gives metaphysics its own questions, it gives the metaphysicians freedom from the rest of inquiry, it allows for lots of projects within metaphysics, and so on. But it nonetheless is an absurd project. There is the false promise of quickly and easily building a coherent metaphysical project on primitive metaphysical notions that appear in the questions that define the discipline. This promise has to be resisted. We need to spend the time and effort on trying to articulate the questions we hope to answer in ordinary terms, and to make sure that these questions aren't answered in other, more authoritative parts of inquiry. Once we have the questions, and we know that they are our questions, we have our project of metaphysics. This is the project we should hope for.

References

Bennett, Jonathan (1963) A Note on Descartes and Spinoza, *The Philosophical Review* vol 74, Pages. 379f.

Carnap, Rudolf (1956) Empiricism, semantics, and ontology. Appendix to *Meaning and Necessity*. 2nd Edition. University of Chicago Press.

Fine, Kit (2000) The question of realism *Philosophers' Imprint* vol. 1, www.philosphersimprint.org/001001/

Frege, Gottlob (1884) Die Grundlagen der Arithmetik: eine logischmathematische Untersuchung über den Begriff der Zahl. Breslau.

Hofweber, Thomas

- (2000) Quantification and non-existent objects. In Everett and Hofweber (eds.) *Empty Names, Fiction, and the Puzzles of Nonexistence*. CSLI Press. Pages 249 - 73.

- (2005a) Number determiners, numbers, and arithmetic. *The Philosophical Review* vol 114.2. Pages 179 - 225.

- (2005b) A puzzle about ontology. *Nous* vol 39.2. Pages 256 - 83.

- (2005c) Supervenience and object-dependent properties. *Journal of Philosophy* vol CII. no 1. Pages 5 - 32.

- (2007) Innocent statements and their metaphysically loaded counterparts. *Philosophers' Imprint* vol 7. no 1., www.philosphersimprint.org/007001/

- (2009a) Ambitious, yet modest, metaphysics. in *Metametaphysics*. Chalmers, Manley, and Waasserman (eds.) Oxford University Press. Pages 260 - 289.

- (2009b) *ontology and the Ambitions of Metaphysics* in preparation

- (2009c) The meta-problem of change. *Nous* vol 43.2. Pages 286 - 314.

3. Thomas Hofweber

Hofweber, Thomas and J. David Velleman (2010) How to endure. *The Philosophical Quarterly.*

4

Hugh Mellor

Emeritus Professor of Philosophy
University of Cambridge, UK

Why were you initially drawn to metaphysics (and what keeps you interested)?

I wrote a Ph.D. thesis on the philosophy of chance (i.e. of physical as opposed to epistemic or subjective probability) in the History and Philosophy of Science Department of Cambridge University in the 1960s. The metaphysics of science was not taken seriously there then: the *methodology* of science was (supposed to be) what all the philosophers there did and debated. It was only when I'd completed my thesis (*The Matter of Chance*) that I realised I'd been doing metaphysics all along – rather as Monsieur Jourdain in Molière's *Le Bourgeois Gentilhomme* realises he's been speaking prose for forty years without knowing it. I've been doing metaphysics ever since, because it's the branch of philosophy that interests me most and – partly as a result – that I do best. It also seems obvious to me that the methodology of science in particular, and epistemology in general, needs an accompanying metaphysics: it's not enough to know whether, when and how you know something if you've no idea what that something is.

What do you consider to be your most important contributions to metaphysics?

The theory of chance in *The Matter of Chance* (1971), of causation in *The Facts of Causation* (1995) and of time in *Real time* (1981) and *Real time II* (1998) – and especially the way in which these works link causation both to chance and to time.

What do you think is the proper role of metaphysics in relation to other areas of philosophy and other academic disciplines, including the natural sciences?

That rather depends on how broad the scope of metaphysics is taken to be: for example, ethics will depend on it far more if it includes meta-ethics than if it doesn't. This is not just a trivial matter of terminology, since it involves substantive questions about the nature and existence of values, and how these are related on the one hand to ethical discourse and on the other to the metaphysics of the mind and of the external world. Similarly with epistemology, whose relation to the metaphysics of cognition and perception is itself a substantial issue within epistemology.

However much or little epistemology and meta-ethics depend on an independent metaphysics, the latter certainly offers an indispensable foundation for several other central areas of philosophy, notably the philosophy of mind and the philosophy of language. Less so with other areas of philosophy: for example, the philosophy of logic, understood as a philosophy of inference, is relatively independent of metaphysics, as are aesthetics and political philosophy.

In all this I've assumed that most metaphysics is not reducible to science, logic, epistemology or the philosophy of language. That assumption is not based on abstract meta-metaphysical arguments – most of which seem to me worthless – but on the substantive and clearly irreducible metaphysical work that many philosophers have been and are still doing. Why others, who cannot do it, should be so keen to disparage it, is a mystery to me. One of them, who once compared Karl Popper on induction to a competitor in a race who jumps up and down on the starting line shouting 'I've won! I've won!', is himself, on metaphysics, like an unfit competitor who lies down on the starting line murmuring, as he drifts off into a dogmatic slumber, 'Race? What race?'. I am no more impressed by such stares of incomprehension than David Lewis, the master metaphysician of our age, was by the incredulous stares that greeted many of his own doctrines, e.g. his modal realism.

What do you consider to be the proper method for metaphysics?

Great artists – painters, writers, performers – rarely have anything unobvious or profound to say about how they get their results, any more than historians, biologists or mathematicians do. (Bertrand Russell is reported to have declined a request to write a 'Teach Yourself Logic' book by saying that he had nothing to say about how he did logic.) Similarly with philosophers in general and metaphysicians in particular. The best way to learn how to do metaphysics is not by reading about how to do it but by reading *it*, while starting to do it under the supervision of people who are doing it already; in short, by becoming an apprentice.

What do you consider to be the most neglected topics in contemporary metaphysics, and what direction would you like metaphysics to take in the future?

I cannot think of any important metaphysical topic that is being seriously neglected. The range and vigour of work on the subject, well illustrated in the recent *Routledge Companion to Metaphysics*, edited by Robin Le Poidevin and others, amply justifies the claim by Peter Simons, another of that volume's editors, that 'at the beginning of the twenty-first century, metaphysics appears to be enjoying an astonishing golden age'.

5

Peter Menzies

Professor of Philosophy
Macquarie University, Australia

Why were you initially drawn to metaphysics (and what keeps you interested)?

In high school I was drawn to the study of English literature as the discussion of literary texts was often an opportunity to explore ideas. But I knew I had across the real thing when I took my first philosophy course as an undergraduate at the Australian National University. I was hooked straightaway. I loved the way philosophy discussed 'the big questions' in a rigorous fashion. I was impressed by the fact that philosophy, in contrast to the study of English literature, seemed to lend itself to analytic methods: one had to give rationally compelling arguments for one's conclusions rather rely on aesthetic or value judgements that seemed to be based ultimately on one's subjective preference.

At university, I studied Latin and Greek along with philosophy. During my undergraduate studies, I was fortunate to work with two scholars with a deep knowledge and love of the classical texts of Plato and Aristotle: Evan Burge in the Classics Department and Kimon Lycos in the Philosophy Department. I have very happy memories of classes with Burge in which we read many of Plato's Socratic dialogues in the original Greek and of classes with Lycos in which we wrestled for many hours interpreting passages in Plato's *Theatetus* and *Parmenides* and Aristotle's *Metaphysics*. Lycos' practice of close textual analysis left a deep impression on me: we would spend hours discussing a paragraph in one of the Platonic or Aristotelian texts, sometimes never progressing past a few pages in a whole semester's study. As my undergraduate studies progressed, my interest in logic and the formal areas of philosophy developed. I had shown some proficiency in mathematics at high school and I enjoyed the rigour of formal logic.

5. Peter Menzies

In my final honours year at the Australian National University, I wrote a long thesis on medieval theories of conditionals under the supervision of Paul Thom. Reading many of the important texts in the original Latin, I applied my burgeoning knowledge of modal logic to formalize the different conceptions of modality and conditionality employed by the medieval logicians. This was my first taste of real independent research and I relished it. Wanting to advance my knowledge of logic, I went to St Andrews University in Scotland to work with Stephen Read, initially with the thought of continuing my work on medieval logic. However, in the end I wrote a Master's thesis on Michael Dummett's arguments against realism. While some of the thesis was taken up with issues about intuitionist logic, most of it was devoted to traditional metaphysical themes about the nature of a realist, correspondence conception of truth. This was my first real engagement with a metaphysical theme and I developed a taste for it.

After St Andrews, I pursued study for a PhD at Stanford University, where my interests gravitated to the philosophy of science and I joined an informal group of students working with Ian Hacking and Nancy Cartwright. My budding interest in metaphysics was not especially encouraged at Stanford. The tendency in the philosophy of science group was to engage with a close study of science and to work on examining some specific question arising within one of the sciences. If anything, my fellow graduate students frowned on the kind of abstract, formal metaphysics to which I was naturally drawn. My PhD thesis started as an overly ambitious discussion of causation but eventually it was narrowed down under the guidance of my supervisor, Nancy Cartwright, to the manageable topic of formulating a causal decision theory adequate to treating Newcomb decision problems. But the central question that occupied me was the question of what causation is. This question still preoccupies me. Even after twenty years of thinking about the subject, I am animated by a strong desire to understand how the concept of causation works in all its different guises.

More generally, what keeps me interested in metaphysics is still the fact that metaphysics asks 'the big questions' and that it tries to answer them in ways that are rigorous and precise. The questions that absorb me most now are questions about whether it is possible to reconcile our commonsense conception of ourselves and our world (Sellars so-called manifest image) with the conception that is being progressively revealed by science (Sellars scientific image). I am still gripped by questions such as whether our conception of ourselves as conscious, free agents is consistent with discoveries in cognitive psychology, genetics, and neuroscience. I regard these questions as some of the deepest and most perplexing in all philosophy.

By aptitude and predilection, I am drawn to the kind of metaphysics done in the Australian tradition of scientific realism, exemplified by David Armstrong, Frank Jackson, and Jack Smart. (I would also include as members of this tradition the 'honorary Australians' David Lewis and Hugh Mellor.) In other words, I am drawn to the kind of metaphysics that attempts to tell a big picture story about the nature of the world, that sets special store by the authority of science and that has deep-seated sympathies with most forms of realism. The person in this tradition who has influenced me the most is David Lewis. Even though I disagree with many of his views, I am deeply impressed by the elegance of his metaphysical framework and the clarity and precision of his way of doing philosophy.

What do you consider to be your most important contributions to metaphysics?

Much of my work in metaphysics has focused on causation. Starting with my Stanford PhD thesis, I have been concerned to understand all the different kinds of causal relations there are, though I've been chiefly pre-occupied with token causation. Guiding my work on this subject has been the conviction that causation is linked to difference-making: a cause is something that makes a difference to its effects. This idea underlies the probabilistic approach to causation, which requires a cause to increase the probability of its effect. It also underlies the counterfactual approach, which requires a cause to be something without which the effect would not have occurred, or would have had a much lower probability of occurring. One of the biggest obstacles for the difference-making approaches to causation is the treatment of examples of pre-emption (in which one of two potential causes asymmetrically causes an effect.) Both probabilistic and counterfactual approaches tend to go awry with this kind of example, typically failing to discriminate between the actual and the potential cause because both fail to make a difference to the effect. In an early publication (Menzies 1989) I discussed a kind of pre-emption problem facing probabilistic theories of causation that hadn't been discussed previously. Much of the literature had focused on examples in which an actual cause doesn't raise the probability of its effect. In the examples I described one event raises the probability of another event even though there is no causal relation between them.

I had suggested a solution to this problem within the probabilistic approach: a cause must be connected to its effect, I claimed, by an unbroken chain of probability increases. However, a growing sense of dissatisfaction with this solution led me to revisit the problem in a later article (Menzies 1996). In this article I applied what has come to be called the Canberra Plan to causation. Based on the Ramsey-Lewis treatment of theoretical terms, the plan involves defining causation in terms of its role in a folk theory which conjoins all the platitudes about causation that are common knowledge among the folk. The article argued that causation could be theoretically defined as the intrinsic relation that typically accompanies a probability increase between two distinct events; and it suggested that in the actual world the most likely candidate for this intrinsic relation is some physical process such as energy-momentum transfer. This theory was criticized by several philosophers including Lewis (2004), who pointed out that there are kinds of causal relation involving absences, especially cases of double prevention in which one event prevents a second event from preventing a third event, in which no intrinsic relation holds between cause and effect.

As I have been forced to reconsider my views about causation, I have often come back to the discussion of causation by H.L.A Hart and Tony Honoré in their classic work *Causation in the Law* (1985). It has seemed to me that they captured the central idea behind the difference-making conception of causation in the following passage:

"The notion that a cause is essentially something which interferes with, or intervenes in the course of events which normally takes place, is central to the commonsense concept of cause. Analogies with the interference by human beings with the natural course of events in part control, even in cases where there is literally no human intervention, what is identified as the cause of some occurrence; the cause, though not a literal intervention, is a difference to the normal course which accounts for the difference in outcome." (p.29)

This passage links the difference-making conception of causation to the idea that a cause is analogous to an intervention that makes a difference to the normal course of events. Hart and Honoré adduce evidence that this idea does indeed guide many commonsense applications of the causal concept. However, it is difficult to see what this idea amounts to without some clarification of the concepts "intervention", "make a difference" and "normal course of events".

One early attempt at clarifying these concepts resulted in the joint publication with Huw Price (Menzies and Price 1993), in which we argued that the concept of causation has the structure of a secondary quality concept. In particular, we argued that a cause is something that an agent could, in principle, manipulate as a means to bringing about an effect. It is like a secondary quality in that it implicates the existence of a human subject, not as passive observer, but as active intervener or experimenter. We tried to answer the familiar objections to manipulability theories of causation: for example, that they sit uneasily with situations in which cause and effect cannot be manipulated by human agents; and that they give the concept of causation an unfortunate anthropocentric character. I have never been entirely satisfied with the answers we gave to these objections though I remain convinced that our concept of causation is intimately linked with the concept of an intervention.

Whatever its flaws, the article written with Price played a small role in the rekindling of interest among philosophers in manipulability theories of causation. This happened to coincide with a new engagement by philosophers with the causal modeling tradition, represented, for example, in the work of Judea Pearl (2000), which assigns a special theoretical role to interventions in causal inference. Following the lead of Hitchcock (2001) and Woodward (2003), I have tried in recent years to adopt the sophisticated techniques for representing systems of causal relationships in the causal modeling tradition in order to articulate a precise theory of token causation. So, for example, I have argued that applications of the concept of causation presuppose models that represent the causal relationships in terms of counterfactual dependencies among a restricted number of variables. The challenge is to see whether these ideas can be parlayed into a full-scale theory of token causation that can satisfactorily handle all the counterexamples and test cases philosophers have devised in recent years. (See Menzies 2004, 2007).

In thinking about these problems, I have become more attuned to the context-sensitivity of causal discourse, which is illustrated, for example, by the familiar distinction between causes and background conditions. Much of the context-sensitivity can be explained by the fact that causal attributions are made against the background of contrast situations, which represent what are taken in the context to be the normal courses of events. A cause, as Hart and Honoré remind us, is something that makes a difference to the normal course of events. A big challenge is to explain precisely the way in which context picks out the contrast situation for any given causal attribution. However, I think some progress can be made on this problem by describing rules for assigning 'default values' to variables in a causal model. (See Menzies 2007, 2009)

Another metaphysical topic I've worked on is that of mental causation. I have been concerned to understand whether it is possible for non-reductive physicalism to explain mental causation. As a way of focusing these concerns, I have explored Jaegwon Kim's (2005) exclusion argument that purports to show that non-reductive physicalists are forced to accept the epiphenomenal character of mental states. In some early publications on the subject (Menzies 2003) I explored a line of attack that focused on an exclusion principle that is crucial to Kim's argument. The exclusion principle states that if an event has a sufficient cause at a time, then it cannot have more than one cause at the time (except in rare cases of overdetermination.) I attempted to dispute this principle by appealing to the model-relativity of causal attributions, arguing that attribution of mental causes for some effect in one model is consistent with the attribution of neural causes in a different model. The consistency of the models, I claimed, refuted the exclusion principle since it is different from overdetermination, which is an intramodel phenomenon.

I am now very wary of appealing to the model-relativity of causal attributions in such a simplistic fashion. Indeed, there is every reason to think that it is common for scientists to describe causal models in terms of variables at many different levels. In more recent publications (Menzies 2008), I have adopted a new strategy for criticizing the exclusion principle, arguing that even if a mental state supervenes on a neural state that is causally sufficient for some effect, the mental state can nonetheless be a cause of the effect. This is a consequence of the contrastive character of causation. For example, suppose that mental state M supervenes on neural state N, which is causally sufficient for behaviour B. It may yet be true that B occurs, not because N occurs rather fails to occur, but because M occurs rather than fails to occur. In this case, a difference-making account of causation that emphasizes the contrastive account of causation will imply that the mental state is the better candidate for cause than the neural state. More recently, in collaborative work with Christian List (List and Menzies 2009; and Menzies and List 2010), I have considered the circumstances in which various exclusion principles about causation are true. We distinguish cases of upwards exclusion in which a lower-level state excludes an upper-level one from causal relevance for some effect and cases of downwards exclusion in which an upper-level state excludes a lower-level state from causal relevance. Focusing on the latter kind of case, we establish a surprising result: when a causal relation between higher-level states is realization-insensitive in the sense that it does not depend on the way in which the way in which these states are realized at a lower-level, these causal relations exclude the existence of any causal relation between lower-level states. These results have important implications, we believe, for questions about emergence and the causal autonomy in higher-level systems.

What do you think is the proper role of metaphysics in relation to other areas of philosophy and other academic disciplines, including the natural sciences?

I have reservations about some aspects of contemporary metaphysical discussions. One of these aspects is the heavy reliance contemporary metaphysicians place on their 'intuitions' about the nature of reality. What concerns me about this is the subjective character of these intuitions. When there is no widespread agreement about the intuitions, the appeal to them makes it impossible to resolve fundamental metaphysical disputes in a rational, compelling way. Disputes dissolve into a clash of intuitions. The result is that metaphysical theories are constructed on the basis of beliefs that are highly contestable.

Some examples may help to illustrate my point. I have argued (Menzies 2009) that our concept of token causation is not the concept of a natural relation – that is, the kind of relation that is empirically discoverable, non-evaluative in character, and carves nature at its joints. A close study of the concept shows that it is essentially contrastive in nature where the relevant contrasts are determined in context-sensitive ways, often on the basis of normative considerations. These features of the concept make sense in view of the role the causal concept plays in explanation and in the ascription of responsibility. But this view conflicts with the intuition of many metaphysicians that causation is a natural relation of some kind. Of course, there is a genuine issue here about whether the evidence does in fact support my claims about the concept. However, what I find counterproductive in debates with contemporary metaphysicians is their tendency to affirm their contrary intuition, which they regard as settling the issue.

Another example may help to crystallize the point. In discussions of mental causation, I have often encountered the view that causation is fundamentally a physical matter: it is a physically specifiable relation such as energy-momentum transfer. Sometimes the view goes along with the view that causation exists only at the fundamental physical level. In either case, the view is taken to be a bedrock assumption of physicalism. (Of course, this view closes off any debate about mental causation by denying there is any room for causation by mental states that are not identical with physical states.) I would dispute that scientific practice supports this view. There are countless examples of causal claims made in the natural and social sciences that posit the existence of causal relations in the absence of any physically specifiable relation such as energy-momentum transfer. The assumption that causation must ultimately be physical in character is seldom based on anything more than an intuition.

When it is pointed out that some metaphysical view is not consonant with ordinary ways of conceptualizing matters, metaphysicians often respond that they are concerned with ontological issues rather than with matters to do with semantics or epistemology. Metaphysical hypotheses about the nature and structure of reality need not be faithful, they claim, to semantic usage or epistemic practice; and indeed they may lead to dramatic revisions in our ordinary conceptions of the world. In response, I agree that there is a proper place for the kind of metaphysical theorizing that leads to radically new ways of understanding the world. However, it is important not to overstate the distinction between metaphysics, on the one hand, and semantics and epistemology, on the other. Without denying the differences between these kinds of investigations, it is also important to note the systematic links between them. A plausible metaphysical theory about some area should be able to explain why we have the semantic and epistemic practices we do, and why they are reliable and trustworthy to the extent that they are. For example, a commonplace methodological belief in the sciences is that randomized controlled experiments are the best way of testing causal hypotheses. A plausible metaphysical account of causation should be able to say whether this claim is true, and if it is true, why it is true. By requiring such explanations, we shield metaphysics from its wilder speculative excesses and anchor it in the comparative certainties of ordinary practice. The best metaphysical theories will be simple, economical and elegant, but their chief theoretical virtue will be their power to explain the relevant aspects of our accepted commonsense and scientific conceptions of the world. Such theories may ultimately lead us to revise these accepted conceptions, but only because they possess greater epistemic credibility by virtue of their superior explanatory power.

As these remarks may suggest, I find myself temperamentally disinclined to pursue large-scale, speculative system-building. The kind of metaphysics I favour takes as its starting points the intersubjectively agreed facts of commonsense or science. In this connection, I find particularly illuminating the kind of investigation that scrutinizes the fundamental assumptions of some scientific theory, testing them for coherence and plausibility or regimenting them in terms of a perspicuous formalism. This kind of work seems to me to be more likely to be useful and to lead to genuine advances in knowledge.

What do you consider to be the proper method for metaphysics?

I have suggested that metaphysics is likely to arrive at more stable knowledge and to achieve more progress by pursuing projects that build on bodies of widely accepted facts such as projects that try to unearth the underlying assumptions of commonsense or scientific theories. By this I do not mean to suggest that metaphysics should become 'naturalistic', eschewing a priori methods and mimicking the empirical methods of science. I believe that the a priori methods, especially conceptual analysis, remain an indispensable tool of metaphysics.

By the a priori methods, I mean the traditional methods that analytic philosophers employ in trying to understand some subject matter. These include articulating the logical structure of theories, formalizing such theories, distinguishing concepts, noting ambiguities, sharpening up vague concepts, and giving analyses or explications of concepts. This kind of conceptual work, especially that of giving explications of problematic concepts in terms of better understood concepts, plays an indispensable role in metaphysics, in my view. For example, in order to determine the metaphysical questions "What are mental states?", "What is causation?", and "What is free will?", one must know what one is talking about in the first place. This is where conceptual work is necessary. Without a preliminary fix on what we mean by the terms "mental state", "causation" and "free will", it is pointless trying to figure out whether there are things in the world answering to these terms. For this reason conceptual analysis seems to me to play an important first step in developing a metaphysical theory.

The traditional method of conceptual analysis accords a special role to intuitions: one tests a putative analysis of some concept against intuitions about whether the concept has been applied correctly in a range of possible situations. This may appear to conflict with my rejection of the role of intuitions in metaphysics. But there is no actual conflict here. What I oppose are appeals to unjustified intuitions that make substantive claims about the world. I am not opposed to appeals to semantic intuitions to test conceptual analyses. In this case, the intuitions concern the correct applications of concepts; and philosophers, as competent language speakers, have some reasonable authority in these matters. In contrast, philosophers have no special authority with respect to the nature and constitution of reality; and so there is no reason to give any epistemic weight to their intuitions about such matters.

It might be thought that I am advocating a reversion to ordinary language philosophy that confines itself to projects that merely describe and catalogue ordinary usage. But this is far from the case. I see conceptual analyses as forming just one part of larger normative projects –projects that evaluate the truth of large-scale theories, the coherence of conceptual schemes, and the utility of concepts. Metaphysics can serve a useful role when it addresses 'the big questions' that fall outside of any more specialized field of enquiry; and when it addresses these questions by assembling information from many different sources–from conceptual analysis, from scientific theories–and evaluating them in an attempt to form an overall picture of reality. These are evaluative projects that get their cutting edge by adverting to certain norms– the norms of good reasoning, the norms implied by the fact that a conceptual practice has certain point or function. Metaphysics under this conception need not be a conservative enterprise that leaves ordinary usage or commonplace practice undisturbed. For example, a metaphysical investigation might conclude reasonably, under this conception of its proper method, that there is nothing in the world that corresponds to our concept of a free choice. Perhaps the ordinary concept contains an ineliminable reference to agent causation –causation by an uncaused self – that is not mirrored by anything in neuroscience. Or it may be that a sustained investigation of the function of causal concepts in our commonsense and scientific practice concludes that there is no single concept that serves all the different purposes. In this case it would be pointless to look for one thing in reality to count as 'the' causal relation.

This conception of metaphysics as essentially evaluative leaves a great deal of room for individual judgement. Reasonable people might reach different conclusions without committing an error of reasoning. Metaphysics will always be more like an art than a science. But this conception of the proper method for metaphysics puts the subjectivity where it should be –in the final drawing of conclusions after all the pieces of objective information are in. Conceptual analysis will be just one source of information. Nonetheless, it will be a good place to start on any metaphysical project because by using the method of reflective equilibrium it has some chance of reaching intersubjectively agreed results. And by anchoring the enquiry in the details of ordinary practice it serves as a corrective and a counterbalance to the more speculative tendencies of metaphysics.

What do you consider to be the most neglected topics in contemporary metaphysics, and what direction would you like metaphysics to take in the future?

As I remarked above, many of the metaphysical debates that interest me concern whether it is possible to reconcile the manifest and scientific images. Often philosophers will address this issue by considering whether some commonsense feature can be located in the scientific world picture. This is fine as far as it goes. However, quite often our commonsense concepts have a perspectival character that reflects our distinctively human position in the world; and this perspectival character makes it hard to locate the corresponding items in 'the view from nowhere' that science aspires to provide. A very good example of this is the commonsense conception of colours, according to which colours are objective, intrinsic features of objects. It is not possible to identify colours, so understood, with any physical properties. For example, the existence of metamers frustrates the identification colours with spectral reflectances. It appears that the existence of colours depends crucially on brute facts about how the human visual system operates, in particular on the fact that receptor cones in the human eye have a trichomatic structure. In this case it is widely recognized that the perspectival character of our colour concepts poses problems for the attempt to locate colours with the scientific 'view from nowhere'. I think that one of the most neglected topics in metaphysics concerns whether this fact about colours holds more generally for other parts of our commonsense conception of the world.

I believe that our commonsense concept of causation is perspectival in an interesting way. As remarked above, we employ models to represent causal structures in terms of a restricted set of variables. The distinction between which variables get included in the model and which variables do not is quite central to the concept. In this connection Judea Pearl has written: "The scientist carves a piece from the universe and proclaims that piece *in*... The rest of the universe is considered *out*... This choice of ins and outs creates asymmetry in the way we look at things and it is this asymmetry that permits us to talk about 'outside intervention' and hence about causality". (2000, p.xiii) In the paradigm cases in which a human agent uses a causal model to manipulate his environment the agent leaves himself out of the model and treats his actions as interventions on the environment. In terms of such a model, the agent sees one variable as the cause of another variable just when he can intervene on the first in order to bring about a change in the second.

In my view, the connection with agency is just one of several dimensions of the perspectival character of the causal concept. But recognizing even this single dimension is enough to appreciate the difficulty of accommodating the causal concept within the scientific view of the world afforded by physics. Russell noted this when he argued that the concept of causation should be abandoned because fundamental physical theory has no use for the concept. He saw that the asymmetric causal relations between localized events that are of interest to human agents cannot be reconciled with the time-symmetric differential equations of physics that relate global time-slices of world history. The concept that holds so much utility for human agents has no echo in physical theory.

Whether Russell's argument for abandoning causation holds any force is now the subject of an interesting current debate. (See Price and Corry 2007) The important point that I wish to emphasise is that before attempting to reconcile manifest and scientific images, we need to appreciate the perspectival character of many commonsense concepts. I conjecture that a proper appreciation of the perspectival character of concepts relating to free choice and agency might help to solve some of the longstanding metaphysical debates about free will and determinism.

References

Hart, H. and Honoré, A. 1985 *Causation in the Law.* Oxford: Clarendon Press.

Hitchcock, C. 2001 "The Intransitivity of Causation Revealed in Equations and Graphs". *Journal of Philosophy* 98: 273-99.

Kim, K. 2005 *physicalism, or Something Near Enough.* Princeton: Princeton University press.

Lewis, D. 2004 "Void and Object", in J. Collins, N. Hall, and L. Paul (eds.), *Causation and Counterfactuals.* Cambridge, Mass.; MIT Press.

List. C. and Menzies 2009 "Non-Reductive physicalism and the Limits of the Exclusion Principle".*Journal of Philosophy.* 105: 475-502.

Menzies, P and List C. 2010 "The Causal Autonomy of the Special Sciences". Forthcoming in C. and G. Macdonald (eds.), *Emergence.* Oxford: Oxford University Press.

Menzies and Price, H. 1993. "Causation as a Secondary Quality". *British Journal for the Philosophy of Science.* 44: 187-203.

Menzies 1989 "Probabilistic Causation and Causal Processes: A Critique of Lewis". *Philosophy of Science*, 56: 642-64.

————— 1996 "Probabilistic Causation and the Pre-emption Problem". *Mind*, 104:85-117.

————— 2003 "The Causal Efficacy of Mental States" in . S. Walter and H. Heckmann (eds.), *physicalism and Mental Causation.* Imprint Academic. 195-223.

————— 2004 "Causal Models, Token Causation, and Processes", *Philosophy of Science*, 71 (Supplementary volume): 820-32.

————— 2007 "Causation in Context" in H. Price and R. Corry, (eds.) *Causation, Physics, and the Constitution of Reality: Russell's Republic Revisited.* Oxford: Oxford University Press. pp. 191-223

―――――― 2008 "Causal Exclusion, the Determination Relation, and Contrastive Causation", in J., Kallestrup and J. Hohwy (eds.) *Being Reduced: New Essays on Reductive Explanation and Special Science Causation.* Oxford: oxford University press. 196-217.

―――――― 2009 "Platitudes and Counterexamples" in H. Beebee, C, Hitchcock, and P. Menzies (eds.) *Oxford Handbook of Causation.* Oxford: Oxford University Press. pp. 341-67

Pearl, J. 2000 *Causality: Models, Reasoning and Inference.* Cambridge: Cambridge University Press.

Price, H. and Corry, R. 2007 *Causation, Physics, and the Constitution of Reality: Russell's Republic Revisited.* Oxford: Oxford University Press.

Woodward, J. 2003 *Making Things Happen: A Theory of Causal Explanation.* Oxford: Oxford University Press.

6
Stephen Mumford

Professor of Metaphysics

University of Nottingham, UK

Why were you initially drawn to metaphysics (and what keeps you interested)?

Metaphysics seems to me to deal with the very biggest questions of all. It investigates the fundamental nature of reality in the most abstract way possible. It tells us what the basic building blocks of the world consist in. Because it is so abstract and so speculative, it is of no obvious practical value. The world looks the same, and behaves the same, for instance, whether particulars are bundles of qualities or underlying substrata. I like the impracticality. I like the way that it has no application. I used to think this was a disadvantage. Metaphysics looks to be literally useless. And I felt a bit defensive about it, as if it was a bad thing to be useless. But then I read Bertrand Russell's essay on 'Useless Knowledge' and realized that being useless doesn't mean the same as being worthless. Some activities can have intrinsic value, and this can be the greatest value of all. Most things have very little intrinsic value and we want them, if at all, only because they get us something else that does have intrinsic value, or it gets us a further step closer to something that has intrinsic value. The most precious things are those we want just because of what they are, not because of what they get us. I think philosophy in general is like this, and perhaps metaphysics more so than any other part of philosophy. It's arguable that some parts of philosophy serve at least some purpose. We sometimes think that moral philosophy is useful, for instance, because we might be able to become better people when we understand right action. And we sometimes want to be good logicians so that we are able to reason better. But metaphysics is simply about understanding the basic nature of the world and such an understanding seems to me to have no direct spin off. It is purely for its own sake. It is not, admittedly, everybody's cup of tea, but those of us who enjoy doing it and see it as important do so entirely because of what it is, not because of anything it gets us.

I think that Plato's *Republic* offers us a good argument for the intrinsic value of philosophy, especially of metaphysical contemplation. Suppose one were a king or queen with no obligations and every material need taken care of. One didn't have to do anything one didn't want to. How, then, would one spend one's life? I like the idea suggested by the *Republic* that such a person would be a philosopher. They would never need anything other than for its intrinsic value so, it is proposed, they spend their time doing philosophy. Some people may scoff at this suggestion and say that such a king would not bother with tough metaphysics but perhaps devote their time to instead to pure hedonism. Perhaps some would, but plenty would not. I am always encouraged by how many young people want to study philosophy, even though they understand it is unlikely to bring them riches. Some students choose law, perhaps because they want to be rich, some choose medicine, perhaps because they want to help others, but plenty choose to study philosophy and I am sure it is because they see the intrinsic value of understanding difficult and abstract questions. The satisfaction metaphysics intrinsically produces is what keeps me still interested.

I like this kind of defence of metaphysics but in an answer to another question, below, I will concede that it is possible for metaphysics to have some indirect benefit, namely where it inspires, informs or shapes thinking in the empirical sciences. My views have moderated a bit on the question of how metaphysics and science relate in that I think there is a continuum of thinking between them rather than a very sharp division and thus I think that there can be some pay-off to metaphysics even though I find its intrinsic value to be more precious. I have been told, for instance, that my own work illuminates a new understanding in biology and I am very happy if it does.

What do you consider to be your most important contributions to metaphysics?

I am best known for promoting and developing an ontology of dispositions or causal powers. My book *Dispositions* (Oxford UP, 1998) sought to revive the prospects of a non-Humean metaphysics. In the powers ontology, not everything is loose and separate but, instead, having a certain property naturally disposes towards having another. When the book was written, the topic of dispositions was not really in the mainstream. There were some papers and books but I think it was regarded as a specialist side issue. At the time, for instance, it was still possible for a research student to read everything that had ever been written on the topic. A number of philosophers seemed to think I was wasting my time with the subject. Quine had solved all those problems back in the 60s, I was told. I was very keen, therefore, to explain the motivation for a closer study of dispositions and I still think the book is quite good on that. It tells us that the topic is worthwhile. I also still like the way the associated problems are set out even though I am no longer sure that all my solutions were correct. I think the book was a success, however, if for no other reason than that many philosophers are now interested in dispositions and take them seriously. I no longer think a graduate student could read all the literature on the subject within the space of their PhD studies. Perhaps my book is in part responsible for spawning such a literature, though it's possible it was just an idea for which the time was right and I was merely riding the crest of a wave rather than creating it.

To begin with, I thought I would deal swiftly with dispositions and then move on to more important things but I came to see more and more why they were important. Dispositions were not a specialist side issue at all but could be at the centre of an all-encompassing philosophy of nature. Since then I have written on various other topics to show how a dispositional ontology has a bearing on a range of traditional metaphysical problems. My *Laws in Nature* (Routledge, 2004) was in my view a much better book than *Dispositions* though it hasn't stimulated quite as much interest. I argue there that a dispositional ontology can dispense with laws of nature, which offer a very misleading metaphor for the workings of the universe. There is also an ontology offered for properties as powers, or rather clusters of powers. Each property is to be understood as being for other properties, via its dispositions, and thus properties will have a purely structural/causal essence. The world thus forms a holistic web where all the properties are interrelated. As Jonathan Schaffer has argued, this brings us back to a Hegelian monism. I have also written on powers and persistence, modality, and in my next book – *Getting Causes from Powers* (with Rani Lill Rani Lill Anjum, Oxford UP) – the aim is to show what theory of causation a dispositionalist should hold. Even though other dispositionalists have suggested that one ought to be able to get a theory of causation from a theory of powers, I don't think we have yet seen the details of what it would look like. The theory builds on the basic idea that a cause is something that disposes towards an effect and, in the case of token causal claims, succeeds in producing it. Things will become more complicated than that, however, and I think some of the findings will be a surprise even to other dispositionalists. The aim is to offer an alternative to the Lewisian paradigm that is coming to dominate contemporary work on causation and lots of other areas of metaphysics. I think the dispositional ontology is the best alternative. It offers a realism about causation that I think is also naturalistic. Other concrete worlds are not needed to get this ontology off the ground. The truthmakers for all our metaphysical truths can be found in this world.

What do you think is the proper role of metaphysics in relation to other areas of philosophy and other academic disciplines, including the natural sciences?

I am a little old fashioned in this respect. I think of metaphysics in the Aristotelian way, as First Philosophy. Everyone, including those whose pursuits appear entirely empirical, have to assume an ontology. We all have to make metaphysical assumptions in order to get started on any thinking at all. A scientist, for example, is likely to believe in mind-independent persisting objects, that stay there, pretty much as they were, even when they are unperceived. One has to make some such assumption. Even a Berkeleyan phenomenalist, who perhaps tries to claim they make no assumption about the fundamental nature of things when they are unperceived, nevertheless has some kind of ontology. They may assume, for instance, that there are things called ideas, which in some views might even be able to exist without any thinker. But these assumptions can also be challenged. Is an idea of the right kind to count as a 'thing' at all? Those who try to pursue purely an empirical line, hoping not to dirty their hands with metaphysics, are fighting a hopeless battle. It is arguable that metaphysical assumptions are a precondition of any knowledge at all. One might aim for a presuppositionless report of one's experience but how is that possible unless one accepts certain features of it to be real? That presupposition is something that only metaphysics questions and tests.

There is sometimes discussion of what has priority: metaphysics or science. Of late, it has become popular to argue that some of the traditional problems of metaphysics can be solved empirically, if only one had an adequate understanding of physics. This seems to me a mistake. It would be to assume that the physicist and metaphysician are concerned with the same questions, but they are not. Admittedly, they have the same object of investigation – the world around us – but they ask different kinds of question about it. Science, as traditionally understood, is concerned with the a posteriori facts and how best to organize them, explain them, predict them, and understand them. Metaphysics is far more general and abstract. It is general in so far as it questions everything, including whether there are any such things as facts, as the scientists traditionally understood them. It is abstract in that it moves beyond all the particular pieces of knowledge we have and looks at the bigger picture. But I would concede that there is a continuum with pure abstract thought at one terminus and pure concrete at the other. There is plenty of room for 'mixed' thinking in between.

Metaphysics is sometimes explained as being beyond physics, and I think this is largely right. In that case, its practitioners ought really to be called metaphysicists, not metaphysicians. A physician practices medicine and we are not specifically aiming to go beyond that (though we do that as well). We aim to ask more general questions about the world than the physicist does, and try to explain in the abstract how it all fits together and works. But although metaphysics and physics are different disciplines, and ought not, therefore, to tread directly on each other's toes, this is not to deny that some people may do a bit of each at different times. Theoretical physics, for instance, has at times strayed into metaphysical territory, become entirely speculative and theoretical. That is fine when it does so: I would want everyone to exercise their metaphysical muscle a bit more often. But one then perhaps ought to be honest that one has stopped doing science and started doing philosophy. Similarly, the swap can work the other way round. Philosophers can cease doing metaphysics and start engaging in the empirical details.

Why are people tempted to swap roles, from scientist to philosopher and vice versa? Although I maintain that metaphysics and physics are distinct, and answer different kinds of question, there is no harm in working on both problems, perhaps even simultaneously, and thereby aiming to achieve some kind of reflective equilibrium: an understanding that is satisfactory at both the abstract and concrete levels. Some problems are best solved by considering them both in the abstract and in the concrete to see if we can find a unified account. Despite this interaction, however, I would still maintain the distinctness of the two disciplines and that neither is in a position to dictate to the other, simply because they do not address each other's problems.

What do you consider to be the proper method for metaphysics?

Roughly, I think that truth consists in correspondence between the world and our linguistic attempts to describe it. That shouldn't mean that there is only one true description of the world nor does it exclude meaning holism in respect of the languages we use in our descriptions. There are many problems around the correspondence theory of truth but I think it is the only realistic game in town. Metaphysical truth is therefore in the same boat as truth in any other discipline, consisting in some kind of correspondence. Hence, it is true that there are universals if and only if there are universals, it is true that substances are bundles of qualities if and only if substances are bundles of qualities, and so on. Metaphysicists have been a bit too self-conscious and self-defensive of their discipline of late. Some lose their nerve and say that we are looking only for truth as coherence or truth as the best satisfier of the pragmatic virtues, as exemplified in a cost-benefit analysis, for instance. But there is no reason why truth in metaphysics shouldn't just be like any other truth.

The complication comes from difficulties around discovering and knowing that truth. The difference between philosophy and the empirical sciences is not that they deal in a different kind of truth but in how we are to come to know that truth. Empirical truths are ones where the proper method of discovery is empirical and philosophy is, as I said above, abstract and non-empirical. The question to ask, then, is what the correct non-empirical method is for discovering the truths of philosophy in general, and metaphysics in particular. This question is an epistemological one: it is asking what the correct epistemology is for metaphysical discovery.

In answer to that, we can only offer all the usual methods that philosophers utilise and techniques they deploy. We have to use reason and argument, some of it purely a priori but much of it less than deductive. We can use arguments from analogy, for instance, where they may fall well short of deductive certainly but nevertheless allow us to understand some aspect of reality. We can also rule out theories on the grounds of inconsistency, which is what we do when we find *reductio* arguments. The latter, of course, can only tell us that a theory is false, not that it is true. This may not give us everything but it is nevertheless a useful thing to be able to do. On the positive side of things, it may well be that we cannot know for sure that a metaphysical theory is true, only that it has been rationally scrutinized, has remained intact after such scrutiny, and is perhaps an explanatorily useful theory. Maybe it unites various phenomena with a single common idea and explains some long-standing problems. This is not to resort to truth in metaphysics as coherence, only to say that such factors as these are in the equation when we are trying to discover such truth. Given truth as correspondence, a theory could look the best to us on explanatory grounds, yet still be false.

One may be tempted to say that all this sounds quite bad for metaphysics because we do not have a method that can guarantee the production of truth. But these same points are, one should accept, already well established in epistemology and philosophy of science in respect of our empirical knowledge. The traditional view of science – Baconian, for instance – was that if only we found the correct method we could discover truths that were known with complete certainty. That ideal was abandoned in the Twentieth Century to be replaced by a greater modesty in our attempts at knowledge. What's good for empirical knowledge ought therefore to be good for metaphysical knowledge. It too is fallible, provisional and defeasible. But such shortcomings, if they are shortcomings at all, are of knowledge in general, not just metaphysics. I do not subscribe to the KK-principle, hence I accept that you could know that p without knowing that you knew that p. One could believe p, and have a good reason for doing so, and if p is also true, then that can count as knowledge, even though it is fallible. There may be some cases where one believes p with good reason but it is actually false, and this is not knowledge, but that doesn't stop it being knowledge in the corresponding cases where p is true.

Metaphysical knowledge, like all knowledge, can be accepted as less than certain. Acceptance of it as such is, I think, an advance over some of the rationalist metaphysicists whose ideal was to achieve complete certainty by constructing a purely deductive system where everything had logical proof. I think we need to have some more relaxed standards of evidence than that.

What do you consider to be the most neglected topics in contemporary metaphysics, and what direction would you like metaphysics to take in the future?

Since philosophy has become professionalized, I think few stones have been left unturned. Rather than subjects being neglected, I think there are more topics that have received too much attention. Most of the journals are filled with material that but a few people will ever read and which I think will not stand the test of time. The problem is that in various ways professional philosophers are obliged to publish, whether they have anything new and substantial to say or not. I would really like to see the journal editors take a lead in this respect and stop publishing papers on the negative basis of them making the fewest errors or fewest controversial claims and start publishing on the positive criterion of them having something important or interesting to say. I found a wonderful quotation from C. J. Ducasse which encapsulated my sentiments very well. It starts with some barely disguised irony:

"Were one unacquainted with the difficulties of the field, one would be tempted to accuse philosophers of having aimed much less at making definite progress possible, than – in fear of the fancied disgrace of an honest error – at playing safe by committing themselves only to the irreducible minimum. There is more merit, however, in being a good, solid corpse over which others can step and climb on, than in the safe role of heaping the obstacles over with rhetorical or other flowers." (*Causation and the Types of Necessity*, Dover, 1924: 2)

I like papers that offer bold new insights but it is all too rare that one finds them. The system of edited, peer-reviewed journals is an inherently conservative one where paradigm-challenging work is very unlikely to be accepted because it threatens the interests of the editor and referees. It saddens me, for instance, how many very bright minds seen occupied largely in David Lewis exegesis. Lewis was one of the finest philosophers of the era, certainly, but he was fine precisely because he offered a totally new insight. It is a shame that in the last few decades, one is far more likely to have a paper published if it is about Lewis's insights than if one offers a new insight of one's own.

I think contemporary philosophy has become too self-congratulatory, with an arrogant self-assurance that the work we are producing is vastly superior to that of the interested amateurs of the past. But has anyone of late produced as fine and appealing a work as Hume's *Treatise* or Locke's *Essay*? On the contrary, I fear that in future centuries, the current era will be looked upon as a philosophical dark age where very little of interest was authored.

In the spirit of developing a this-worldy alternative to Lewis, I have a few plans for future books before my career ends. I think there are some very interesting metaphysical issues around absences and nothingnesses. Causation by absence, negative properties, truthmakers of negative truths, perceptions of absences and non-existent objects are all problems where sensible analytic philosophers have been tempted to posit nothingnesses as solutions. I want to show how all these problems can be solved naturalistically in terms of what there is and what there isn't, without the posit of degrees of being. I hope to turn this into a book, provisionally entitled *A Book About Nothing*. After that, I may try to write a large book that is a critique of Humean metaphysics in general, but that may have to wait until my old age.

7
Daniel Nolan

Professor of Philosophy

University of Nottingham, UK

Why were you initially drawn to metaphysics (and what keeps you interested)?

As I recall, I started thinking a lot about metaphysics fairly late as an undergraduate at the University of Queensland, and it was largely prompted by André Gallois and Ian Hinckfuss. 'Hinck' was a staunch nominalist, and I got interested in how to argue that there really are such things as numbers, propositions, space and time, truth, and many of the other things we often say there are, but without seriously thinking about it. I think André was, if anything, an even bigger influence, though I find it more difficult to isolate particular effects of his philosophical example. My thesis project in postgraduate honours (a 1 year degree), also at the University of Queensland, was on the relation between Forms and ordinary objects in Plato's *Parmenides,* though the final thesis ended up being as much about David Armstrong's views on instantiation as it was about Plato!

By that time I think I was hooked, and I went on to do my PhD on modality and possible worlds at the Australian National University. I was excited in part by realising that so many aspects of our everyday experience and view of the world turned out to be surprising and mysterious when we stopped to think about them: how colours and shapes connect with coloured things and shaped things, for example, or what was going on when some outcomes were possible but others not. I also thought, and I still think, that metaphysical questions are vital to many other issues in philosophy. I was also of the view that we had made very little progress on metaphysical questions, especially given their importance, so it was a field that especially needed attention. I guess these days I'm more confident that metaphysics has made a lot of progress than I used to be.

I continue to be interested in metaphysics for a number of reasons. Among them are that I still think the issues in metaphysics are important, often relatively neglected, and vitally connected to many other questions, especially in philosophy. But there are other attractions as well. There is the sheer variety of issues that come up, and the range of considerations one needs to evaluate - it's a large enough field that I never need to worry about getting bored. It is also an exciting time to be engaging in metaphysics. There seems to me to have been a great re-awakening in metaphysics in the second half of the twentieth century, after a bit of a drought in the middle of the twentieth century in Anglo-American circles, and the baleful effect of Heidegger in France and Germany. Whatever the reason, metaphysics seems to be flourishing on a large scale at the moment, with lots of good people doing interesting work.

A final reason I am interested in metaphysics is that, to a large extent, it is a field where there is no generally agreed procedure for answering the questions that come up. Of course, that is frustrating at times too - at times it can feel like walking a tightrope, not only without a net, but without any assurance that there is a tightrope there either. But it does keep things interesting, and ideally it keeps us from taking our metaphysical starting points entirely for granted, particularly our methodological starting points. This widespread deep disagreement is something metaphysics has in common with most of philosophy, of course - and I suspect it is one of the things that got me into philosophy, and keeps me here!

What do you consider to be your most important contributions to metaphysics?

My earliest significant contribution was to the metaphysics of modality: that is, to the metaphysics of possibility, necessity, and related matters. My PhD thesis was a loosely connected series of chapters on the theory of possible worlds, and mainly on the metaphysics of possible worlds. Unfortunately I am still not sure what to think, exactly, about what possible worlds are. I think they exist, and are abstract objects, or at least I hold those opinions most days of the week: but my views about their nature are not much more precise than that. I also believe that possible worlds are not the key to understanding or analysing possibility and necessity, though I do not have a positive alternative to put in the place of possible-worlds-first theories yet. I have written a few things about the interaction between possible worlds and cardinality paradoxes (Nolan 1996, 2002 chapters 6 and 7, 2004), and I think that is fertile ground for future work.

As well as possible worlds, I am also a fan of impossible worlds (Nolan 1997). I think many of the philosophical applications of possible worlds "technology" have significant limitations due to their usual inability to distinguish propositions that are necessarily equivalent: for example, possible-worlds models of mental content have a tendency to treat all necessary propositions the same, even though our cognition treats many of them as very different from each other. For many of the purposes where it is convenient to wheel in possible worlds, using impossible worlds as well does the job even better. My 1997 paper was primarily about conditionals with impossible antecedents: Stalnaker-Lewis treatments of such conditionals treat them all as true, but this is too crude. Extending a Stalnaker-Lewis-style system to discriminate among impossible worlds enables us to model conditionals with impossible antecedents, and a lot of the other reasoning we do about impossibilities, without requiring radical changes in the logics we use. I am also interested in using models of the truth-conditions of conditionals in terms of worlds more generally (see e.g. Nolan 2003), and I hope in future work to have more to say about the question of *why* these accounts in terms of worlds seem to be getting at what is going on with conditionals.

A different project that I've spent a lot of time on over the last decade is work on fictionalism: the approach to theories that treats them like useful fictions. A lot of fictionalism goes on well outside of metaphysics, of course: there's fictionalism about morality, and fictionalism about areas of the natural sciences (e.g. a van Frassen-style fictionalism about unobservable physical objects). Some of the important issues in debates about fictionalism are not particularly metaphysics: philosophy of language debates about what semantic resources a fictionalist using a language like ours can avail herself of, for example. But fictionalism is closely enmeshed in metaphysics for two reasons. One is that fictionalism seems like an attractive option to many as an approach to many metaphysical commitments: possible worlds, properties and relations, sets and numbers, even ordinary macroscopic objects. The other is that some of the important debates between fictionalism and realism turn on the role of postulating the existence of objects, the role of explanation, and whether trading other metaphysical commitments in for the metaphysical commitments of fictions is worthwhile. I am afraid I am not actually fictionalist about very much myself, but I think those debates are vital for assessing the prospects for the sort of "Australian realist" metaphysics I generally favour.

What do you think is the proper role of metaphysics in relation to other areas of philosophy and other academic disciplines, including the natural sciences?

One of the best things about doing metaphysics at the end of the twentieth century and the beginning of the twenty-first is that we can pursue metaphysical questions without thinking they are ultimately questions about the meanings of our words or the structures of our concepts; or that metaphysics is downstream of epistemology, as Kant seems to have thought; or with the constant worry that the questions of metaphysics and our answers to them might be trivial, or meaningless, or whatever other terrible status the positivists and their fellow travelers wanted to pin on it. Neither are we at the stage where metaphysics is reconstrued as a minor branch of physics, or otherwise rolled into the natural sciences, as some metaphysicians may wish.

While I would resist the pressure to reinterpret metaphysics as really being a species of some other sort of philosophical or scientific inquiry, I also think it is very important to recognize that metaphysics is connected to many other areas of inquiry, in philosophy and outside of it. The questions dealt with in metaphysics often overlap with questions dealt with by other branches of inquiry, and indeed often some of the questions themselves are the common property of both disciplines.

One kind of example that I think illustrates the overlap with other disciplines well are questions about the nature of space and time. Einstein's special and general theories of relativity and elaborations of them by others, starting with Minkowski, have had a huge impact on the way educated people think about space, time, and spacetime. Some philosophers have been at the forefront of developing new perspectives on spacetime that reflect what we have learned. On the other hand, a lot of effort and ingenuity on the part of other philosophers has been devoted to the project of carrying on as if the relativistic revolution never happened, and to try to quarantine it so that it has basically very little to teach us about the fundamental nature of space and time. And while this is still a matter of controversy, I think a lot of this latter effort is misguided: we *have* learned important things about e.g. the nature of time from twentieth century physics, and we should not try to ignore that to continue constructing theories of time only out of reflections on common sense beliefs about it. I think more recent advances in physics also shed important light on the nature of space and time: I've tried to contribute to the argument about that recently in Nolan 2008a.

While the example I offered above is on the boundaries of metaphysics and physics, metaphysics asks questions that overlap with theoretical work across the range of natural and social sciences, as well as areas of inquiry outside the sciences altogether. I will say a little in my answer to question four about the links between metaphysics and the study of language, but nearly any area of inquiry has metaphysical implications. Not least, of course, metaphysics is closely tied to many other areas of philosophy, and I think it is important for metaphysicians to be interacting with philosophers of language and mind, epistemologists, metaethicists, and other specialists.

As well as connections in subject-matter, I also think that metaphysics and other areas of philosophical inquiry have important methodological connections to other areas of inquiry. I am hopeful that some kind of holistic methodology is possible, according to which fundamental methodological principles are in common across all (good) human inquiry, and the differences we see between, e.g. physics, and sociology, and looking for car-keys, can be explained in terms of the fundamental general principles. That is a view that needs to be argued for, of course, and I hope to do so in some of my future work. But if it is true, then we might expect methodological lessons learned in one area will often be useful in others. That would be especially good news for the methodology of philosophy, since we seem to be better at mathematics, natural sciences, and a range of other investigations than we are at philosophy: so learning lessons about how to answer philosophical questions by seeing how other questions get answered could be very useful. I think many philosophers are already doing this, and have been to some extent for a long time, but as usual it would be better if we could get clearer and more explicit about how to do this.

What do you consider to be the proper method for metaphysics?

I am inclined to think that there are many proper methods of doing metaphysics, and I benefit from the work of many different people who take different approaches. So rather than trying to demarcate good metaphysical method from bad, perhaps the most useful answer to this question I can offer is to discuss a number of sources of good metaphysics.

One of the things that is still a starting point for a lot of metaphysicians is conceptual analysis, whether of "free will", "same person as", "causes", "intrinsic", or some other metaphysically important term. I am very far from the view that this is the metaphysicians' *entire* job, though that view may have had some supporters at the high-water mark of analytic philosophy. But I think it deserves a role - it is often the best way to start to get clear on questions that can be asked, and to notice tensions in our ordinary understanding of the phenomena that fall under the concepts. Or at least the thing we in fact do that gets *labeled* "conceptual analysis" has this important role: I suspect that the characteristic armchair reflection that people do that they call conceptual analysis bleeds over into taking account of commonplaces and things that seem obvious but may well not be conceptual truths. For example, some will be happy to say that "numbers do not cause anything" is a conceptual truth. Even if it is not, though, it is something we are ordinarily inclined to believe, and it would be well to take note of it in coming up with a theory of numbers, or of causation for that matter. A similar project to reflecting on our "concepts", whatever exactly they are, is reflecting on our words and their meaning - this latter activity has sometimes been called "linguistic analysis" by philosophers. I think it can be useful in the same sort of way, and probably also easily steps over the line from discovering analytic truths to discovering things widely believed, and taken for granted, by competent users of the vocabulary.

Another important starting point, connected to the first one, is putting together commonplaces about our subject matter: what sorts of things typically cause what, for example, is an important thing to keep in mind when coming up with a theory of causation: and it may sound too trivial to be an important part of the project, until we keep in mind that many ambitious theories of causation have foundered by being unable to handle rather prosaic counterexamples, such as those involving prevention of various sorts. Some of the commonplaces and ordinary beliefs that we have may turn out to be analytic truths or conceptual truths, or involve an important mixture of those: but even if they do not, ordinary "common sense" has an important role to play in metaphysics. (For more of a discussion and justification, see Nolan 2009.)

A third source of evidence and insight for metaphysics is looking at the specific metaphysical commitments of other inquiries. I talked about this in my answer to the previous question, but it bears repeating on this list of sources of good metaphysical conclusions. Of course, this source is not cleanly separated from the first two I mentioned either, since inquiries other than metaphysics rely on "conceptual analysis" to some extent and on ordinary commonplaces about their subject matters, though to varying extents. (Contemporary physics might not use ordinary opinion as much of a source of evidence, but I suspect psychology and economics still do, however much that might be hidden in some of the final publications in those disciplines.)

A particular inquiry that has been throwing up a lot of interesting metaphysical evidence and problems in the last half-century or so has been the study of language, both as carried on by many philosophers of language and as carried on by linguists working on semantics. Some issues have concerned the ontology of language: the nature of propositions, of truth, of word-types, and so on. But many more have come from trying to systematically give the truth-conditions of natural language sentences. Whether it is arguments for postulating events, qua-objects, non-existent intentional entities, possible and impossible worlds, situations or many other metaphysical exotica, or just arguments about the case for accepting the existence of sets, systematic theorising about language seems to have been a rich source of metaphysical views and arguments. This source of insight from the study of language is probably connected to the "linguistic analysis" I mentioned above, though the exact connections are controversial, and one could of course think that a theory of language requires special ontological posits, for example, even if one thought that there were no analytic truths.

Metaphysicians have more to do than to take information from conceptual analysis, common sense, and other areas of organised inquiry, and then arrange that information for public consumption. I think it is a very important part of the metaphysician's task to construct good and systematic theories from the inputs provided. I think a large part of what is going on at this stage is that metaphysicians are constructing and criticising theories on the basis of theoretical virtues: they make sure the theories are internally consistent, are as simple as feasible, cohere with related theories, unify disparate phenomena, provide good explanations, and so on. A lot of this is not entirely explicit, even to the metaphysicians themselves, nor is it obvious what the best way to operate with these virtues. But as far as I can tell, at least, this is a very important part of what we do.

One part of the activity of metaphysicians I have been thinking about lately, from the point of view of seeing how it feeds into good metaphysical theories, has been metaphysicians' engagement with metaphysical traditions, both contemporary movements and traditions in the past. Engaging with contemporary and historical traditions takes up a lot of a metaphysician's time, and energy as well, though my impression is that it has not been widely discussed in the contemporary debates about good metaphysical method. I try to say something useful about it in Nolan forthcoming.

I suppose I should say something about a currently fashionable methodological topic, the status of "intuitions" in metaphysics. Where does the appeal to intuitions fit into my categories, above? Well, I suspect that different metaphysicians have quite different things in mind when they talk of their "intuitions", and some may not have anything very specific in mind at all. If operating metaphysical "intuition" is meant to be activating a *sui generis* rational faculty for direct insight into the nature of the world, then I am as sceptical of that as the next person. But there are a lot of sensible and useful things that could be going on when metaphysicians are "relying on their intuitions". They might be employing a tacit grasp of the relevant concepts to produce justified beliefs in candidate conceptual truths, for example. Or they might be relying on implicit information they have about how the world works. Or they might be making judgments about the quality of theories, or theory-fragments, or guesses about how theories that the fragments are embedded in will turn out. Or perhaps some mixture of these. I suspect relying on not-yet-articulated plausibility judgments is an important part of the practice of many investigators, inside and outside philosophy, and having a nose for a good piece of speculation is an asset. If we want to call using those capacities "relying on intuition", I'm all for it.

What do you consider to be the most neglected topics in contemporary metaphysics, and what direction would you like metaphysics to take in the future?

My initial thought is that the most neglected topics are probably topics I neglect as well! It is also hard to claim that any areas are being neglected when we keep in mind the sheer number of people writing and thinking about metaphysical topics today - probably more than in any time in history. I suspect that some of the topics that may appear "neglected" might just be being pursued in work outside the mainstream. Finally, what I would say about which topics are neglected does rather depend on whether we want to talk about which topics are getting little attention, or which topics are getting little attention but should be getting more. The metaphysics of angels is one area that receives little attention today, for example, but I think that is a topic that is justly neglected. Part of the reason I think it should be neglected is because there are no such things as angels, but I suspect that a number of metaphysicians who do believe in angels still think it is a topic that is not worth much attention - perhaps because they take themselves to not have much information that bears on the topic, or that the information they have is exhausted by religious revelations that have already been worked over.

As for topics that are unjustly neglected, I think the metaphysics of categories is one area that should receive more explicit attention. By "categories" I do not mean the mathematical objects, though they are metaphysically interesting and unjustly neglected by metaphysicians as well, but rather the study of the fundamental kinds of things that there are. (Metaphysicians recently have developed a habit of calling this study "category theory", though I wish they would leave that expression to the mathematicians.) Plenty of systematic metaphysicians have drawn up lists of the categories of things they believe in, but less attention has been paid to what these categories themselves are or, if there are no such things, what is going on when we talk as if there are categories.

Another area that deserves more attention is the integration of some studies in the history of metaphysics into contemporary metaphysical investigation. Work on some historical figures is tolerably well integrated into contemporary metaphysics: work on Hume stands out, but also work on Leibniz, Aristotle, and of course many twentieth century figures such as Russell, Wittgenstein, Reichenbach and Carnap. But work on other historical figures is much less well integrated with contemporary metaphysical work. A lot of medieval metaphysics seems to fall into this category, and I think a lot of Hellenistic metaphysics fits here too. I'm not saying that the historians of these figures are unaware of contemporary metaphysics - more and more, historians of metaphysics seem to be adequately aware of contemporary developments. The problem seems to me to be in the other direction: there's not enough of an attempt to use insights of the medievals in contemporary approaches to metaphysical problems. (I leave aside the contemporary neo-Thomist tradition: I suspect their faults are too much in the other direction, though I couldn't argue for that here.)

A final area of metaphysical inquiry that seems to be unjustly neglected, at least by metaphysicians, is the metaphysics of ethics, and of normative inquiry more generally. Partly this is because the metaphysics of ethics is treated as "metaethics" and considered a branch of ethics, so many of the people working on it see themselves as having more in common with ethicists than metaphysicians. I think my main concern is that the metaphysics of ethics, and normativity in general, is not integrated as much as I would like with mainstream metaphysical inquiry: I would be pleased if more people who see themselves as metaphysicians contributed to metaethics, and people who saw themselves as metaethicists contributed to metaphysics topics outside the metaphysics of normative matters.

As for the direction I would like to see metaphysics move in, I hope it will continue to move in lots of directions at once, with different people kicking off from different assumptions, and a continuing interest by many metaphysicians in exploring a range of theoretical options other than the ones they themselves hold. That said, there are some things I would like to see more of in the future. I would like to see metaphysicians become more self-conscious and critical about their own methods: that's not to say I want everyone to start doing methodology of metaphysics, but it would be nice if the support given for metaphysical premises was always made clearer than just reports of strongly-held idiosyncratic intuitions. I would also like it if work in metaphysics became less fragmented - I see a lot of people these days who work on very specific topics in metaphysics, without appearing to do much hard thinking about related topics. For example, metaphysicians who work on causation but who have not thought much about laws or necessity, or metaphysicians who work on numbers without thinking much about propositions. Obviously there is a place for fragmentary work, and everyone has to start somewhere, but a general move to more consideration of the influence of theories on related topics in metaphysics seems desirable to me.

Finally, I would like to see more work done on *ideological* commitments in metaphysics: not political ideology, but "ideology" in the sense that is a descendant of the one introduced by Quine into metaphysics. What I mean, roughly, is the theoretical commitments we incur with devices other than names and quantifiers: the ones we incur through using predicates, sentential operators, logical connectives, and so on. In particular, how should we go about deciding what primitive ideology we should incur - ideological commitments that are not to be analysed in terms of ontological commitments of one sort or another, or in terms of further ideological commitments? There is some general sense that we should keep these commitments to a minimum, everything else being equal, but I have not seen a lot of work on why, or when everything else is equal. (I have engaged with this issue in Nolan 2002 ch 2 and Nolan 2008b, but there is still a lot to do!)

References

Nolan, D. 1996. "Recombination Unbound". *Philosophical Studies*, 84.2-3: 239-262

Nolan, D. 1997. "Impossible Worlds: A Modest Approach". *Notre Dame Journal for Formal Logic*, 38.4: 535-572

Nolan 2002. *Topics in the Philosophy of Possible Worlds*. Routledge, New York.

Nolan, D. 2003. "Defending a Possible-Worlds Account of Indicative conditionals". *Philosophical Studies*, 116.3: 215-269

Nolan, D. 2004. "Classes, Worlds and Hypergunk". *The Monist* 87.3: 3-21

Nolan, D. 2008a. "Finite Quantities". *Proceedings of the Aristotelian Society* 108.1: 23-42

Nolan, D. 2008b. "Truthmakers and Predication". *Oxford Studies in Metaphysics* 4: 171-192

Nolan, D. 2009. "Platitudes and Metaphysics" in David Braddon-Mitchell and Robert Nola (eds) *Conceptual Analysis and Philosophical Naturalism*. MIT Press, Cambridge MA. pp 267-300

Nolan, D. forthcoming. "Metaphysicians and Their Traditions". *Philosophical Topics*.

8

Eric T. Olson

Professor of Philosophy
University of Sheffield, UK

Why were you initially drawn to metaphysics (and what keeps you interested)?

It was metaphysics that made me a philosopher. I grew up in a remote place where no philosophy ever penetrated, and went away to university wanting to become a scientist. (I had at least some inkling of what science was.) As it happened, every first-year student at Reed took a year-long "Humanities" course, and near the end of the first semester of this course we were assigned Plato's *Apology*. The *Apology* left me cool, but I skipped ahead and had a look at the *Phaedo*, where Plato argues for the immortality of the soul. Here I suddenly found myself gripped. Having had a religious upbringing, I already believed in something like the immortality of the soul. In spite of this, I found Plato's arguments completely unconvincing. But the very idea of giving a rational argument for immortality, or for that matter against it, was the most fascinating intellectual project I had ever come across.

The next item on the syllabus was the *Republic*, and here too it was the metaphysical claims that excited me. With the naive audacity of youth, I wrote an essay arguing that Plato's doctrine of the Forms couldn't possibly be right. (My teacher, as I recall, was unconvinced; but she was not a philosopher, and was unable to defend the doctrine against my objections.) The subject I had stumbled across was so much more fun than chemistry and mathematics that before the year was out I had given up the career plans I had nursed since my adolescence and changed the focus of my studies to philosophy.

Reed's metaphysician in those days was George Bealer. His lectures on Spinoza and Leibniz were spellbinding, and it was clear to everyone that we were in the presence of a great mind. I was unable to understand the subtleties of his own research, however. (I wish I could say that now, 25 years later, I have grown equal to the task. But Bealer's writing still makes me feel like an undergraduate.)

My philosophical interests later became more catholic, and I started graduate study at Syracuse without any clear idea of what sort of philosophy I wanted to go in for. It was Peter van Inwagen who reawakened my love of metaphysics. At some point I took a seminar he was teaching on a draft of *Material Beings*. The book is now a favourite of mine, and I never tire of rereading it; but on first exposure it was so unfamiliar that I didn't know what to make of it. Here was a stark landscape, set out with enormous clarity and care, but whose features and lighting were completely alien.

It was only later that I began to find van Inwagen's views attractive. At first I was simply fascinated with his style of doing philosophy. Just as a great mathematician can tell you something extraordinary about any given number, he had the ability to tell you something extraordinary about any given philosophical claim. He would take some plausible conjecture–the sort of thing that philosophers commonly appeal to as a premise–and draw out consequences from it that would make you choke on your coffee. These consequences were not always things that seemed obviously false, but they were usually far too momentous to accept casually. Students of van Inwagen's learned that metaphysics was an arena of great danger, where almost anything you wanted to rely on was certain to lead to any number of unsettling commitments. Ever since then I have wanted to do philosophy like that.

What do you consider to be your most important contributions to metaphysics?

When I started thinking about the metaphysics of personal identity in the early 1990s, most of the debate was about what sort of psychological continuity our persistence consists in: what mental properties you could lose and still exist, and how much of your psychology a future being had to inherit in order to be you. A central question was whether your persistence required only the preservation of some of your mental contents–beliefs and memories, say–or whether it was the preservation of your psychological capacities that counted, such as the capacity for thought and consciousness. Elaborate thought experiments were devised to isolate the various proposed conditions and "test our intuitions" about their role in our survival. Peter Unger's book *identity, Consciousness, and Value*, which I read at an impressionable age (in one of van Inwagen's seminars), is the most sustained and ingenious example of this project. That our identity over time had something to do with psychology, and that the way to find out what it takes for us to persist was to note our reactions to science-fiction stories, were never questioned in the mainstream literature.

At some point it became clear to me that any account of personal identity over time that had a psychological component–that is, all the accounts seriously discussed by the likes of Unger–were incompatible with our being biological organisms. It was easy to see that no sort of psychological continuity, whether of contents, capacities, or what have you, was either necessary or sufficient for a human organism to persist. I started wondering what we might be if we were *not* organisms. This line of thought convinced me that psychology was completely irrelevant to personal identity.

The total dominance of psychological-continuity accounts is now a thing of the past, and I would like to think that this is due partly to my book *The Human Animal* and related papers. The thesis of the book was that we are animals, and that our identity through time therefore had nothing to do with psychology. The main argument for this was that the human animals we see in the mirror are psychologically just like ourselves: just as conscious, just as intelligent, and so on. Those who deny that *we* are those animals have two choices. They can accept that there are in fact two beings thinking your thoughts–you and the animal–and try to explain how you can know that you are the one that isn't the animal. Or they can deny that human animals think as we do, and try to explain why not. Psychological-continuity theorists hadn't done either of these things. Although I was not the first to give this sort of argument, I think I put it more forcefully than others had.

By temperament I am a critical philosopher rather than a creative one: a troublemaker. I am better at casting doubts on philosophical claims than at thinking up new ones. (With some people it's the other way round. It's a useful division of labour.) In fact I find it hard to endorse any positive philosophical claim in more than a tentative way. Often the best one can say about a view is that the alternatives look even worse.

What do you think is the proper role of metaphysics in relation to other areas of philosophy and other academic

disciplines, including the natural sciences?

I don't think metaphysics has any privileged role, either within philosophy or more broadly. It's at best one source of knowledge among many.

I suppose there are two main questions about the role of metaphysics in relation to other areas and disciplines: What should we do when metaphysics conflicts with claims from elsewhere? And what can metaphysics and other areas or disciplines learn from each other?

Suppose our best metaphysics throws up a result that conflicts with the best thinking in some other area of philosophy. For instance, we might seem to have strong metaphysical grounds for a claim that our best epistemology says we couldn't possibly have grounds for. Then either the metaphysics is wrong or the epistemology is (or both). But I know of no general reason to think that one side or the other is more likely to be wrong, or that one discipline ought to bow down before the other. If there is a conflict, both parties ought to worry. Whether one ought to worry more than the other will depend on the particulars of the case.

What if a metaphysical claim that we fancy is inconsistent with a well-confirmed result in some stunningly successful discipline—physics or mathematics, say? It's easy to think that the metaphysicians are more likely to be wrong than the physicists or mathematicians. But real cases are rarely as simple as that. There is room for honest disagreement about what the well-confirmed results of physics or mathematics actually are—that is, what propositions the rigorous methods of those disciplines endorse. Quantum mechanics is the most notorious example of this. What the experimental data confirm is an austere formal theory expressed mostly in mathematical terms. The interpretation of this formalism is controversial, even among physicists. When the physicists try to explain what the formalism means—how it says the world is—they bring in metaphysical assumptions. (And because few physicists are trained in metaphysics, they often do this badly.) It is fiendishly difficult for anyone, especially an outsider, to tell what part of a successful science is well confirmed and what part is interpretation (even supposing that there is a definite boundary between them). So clashes between metaphysics and physics are often not so different from clashes between metaphysics and epistemology.

Still, metaphysicians ought to worry if they find themselves saying things that their colleagues in the sciences take themselves to have strong grounds for denying, just as they should if their views clash with the best epistemology. It's better not to set oneself against the considered views of large numbers of eminent authorities if one can help it. They know things that we don't.

So much for conflict. What about cooperation? Metaphysics impinges on many other areas of philosophy. Debates in practical ethics, for instance, frequently turn on premises about "the metaphysics of human persons" (to use the ugly phrase current in the literature). Those engaged in these debates often brandish metaphysical claims with the reckless abandon of small children playing with sharp knives. More often than not these claims are highly dubious, or opaque, or suffer from a combination of both defects. A bit of metaphysical competence would improve the quality of the debates to no end. And there are cases where metaphysics turns up a problem best solved not with more metaphysics, but by turning to the philosophy of language or some other area of philosophy.

Clearly the sciences tell us things of great metaphysical interest. For example, the physics of colour and the physiology of colour vision have revolutionary implications for the metaphysics of colour: Larry Hardin's book *Color for Philosophers* is a wonderful example of how philosophy can learn from science. The philosophy of time, to take another example, has suffered from metaphysicians' ignorance of special relativity. And of course quantum mechanics is an endlessly fertile source of metaphysical problems. It would be foolish to spurn the fruits of humanity's most brilliant success just because those responsible for it work in another building.

The sciences can learn from metaphysics too. Again, you can't make any sense of quantum mechanics without engaging in metaphysics: you face metaphysical questions the moment you try to interpret the equations. The more metaphysics quantum physicists know (those who worry about what the equations mean, anyway), the better they will be at their job. If it were up to me, I would require anyone getting a PhD in physics to learn some metaphysics and epistemology, and anyone getting a PhD in philosophy to learn biology and physics.

What do you consider to be the proper method for metaphysics?

I don't think metaphysics has its own special method, distinct from those of other areas of philosophy. So what is the proper method for philosophy in general? This is such a large question that I would have to think about it for twenty or thirty years, free from teaching or administrative duties, before venturing even a preliminary answer. I don't think the funding bodies would support this project, and in any case the editor of this volume needs my contribution by next week. So I will say something about how *I* try to do philosophy, and what I try to teach my students to do, without claiming that it's the right method. It is notoriously hard to describe how to do something, and what I'm about to say may be pedantic or useless or even dangerous. That's something I'll have to risk.

I suppose philosophers (qua philosophers) do three things: they ask questions; they try to understand those questions; and they try to answer them. I will say nothing about what questions philosophers ought to ask, or at least what questions they ought to start with. That amounts to asking what the proper subject matter of philosophy is, and that's too hard for me.

Let me say something about understanding philosophical questions. Students almost invariably neglect this step, and professionals sometimes do too. The temptation is almost irresistible. It is all too common to start philosophizing without first making clear what question one is talking about. The result is always disappointing: if you put muddle in, you get muddle out. Understanding a philosophical question is often more difficult than answering it (likewise, understanding a philosophical claim can be more difficult than working out whether it's true). I remember as a student reading a paper by Chisholm in which he spent many pages setting out in precise and seemingly tedious detail what a certain question meant, until suddenly, as if by magic, the answer became obvious. It made a big impression on me. I have never been able to do the trick myself, but it remains an ideal.

How do you get a clear understanding of a philosophical question or claim? Well, state it as clearly and precisely as you can. Your understanding of a question or claim is no better than your best statement of it: if you can't state it, you don't understand it, and you need to do more thinking. It's important to put it in the simplest terms possible. Avoid technical jargon as much as you can. Stating a claim in technical language has a tendency to insulate it from critical inquiry. Jargon is comforting to those familiar with it and baffling to those who aren't, making it a hazard for both. It's much easier to see what something means when it's put plainly. If you can't put it in plain language, then again you don't fully understand it. (I don't mean that philosophers should never use jargon. But jargon gets its meaning from ordinary language. It is an abbreviation, and it's important not to forget what it is an abbreviation of.) Think of how you would explain the question to someone who knew nothing about it: a child, say. I don't know whether the central question of the *Critique of Pure Reason* could be stated so plainly that a child could understand it–certainly Kant's own writing falls short of this ideal. But that's what we ought to aspire to.

Some questions resist this treatment: we can't make them clear. The reason may be that they *have* no clear content. Or it may be that we just haven't been clever or persistent enough. Either way, there is little point in trying to answer such questions.

Suppose we've got our question tolerably clear, and our best statement of it has failed to make the answer obvious. Then we need to think about what answers are available. (Think of the claim that the question has more than one answer, or no answer, as answers in themselves.) These answers should be stated with as much care as the question itself. It then remains to work out which one is true.

My best suggestion about how to work out whether a philosophical claim is true is to think about what follows from it, and from its negation. (Unless it's an empirical claim, in which case you need to get out of the armchair and look at the empirical evidence.) Think about what it would mean if it were true: think of states of affairs, the simpler and more concrete the better, that follow from it. Think likewise about what it would mean, in concrete terms, if the claim were false. Try to forget what your teachers and peers say about the claim and approach it afresh. (Much of the conventional wisdom about philosophical claims consists of muddled half-truths.) The better we understand the claim, the easier this task will be. Even if you have no idea what to make of it at first, if you think hard enough you will often find that it has implications for issues that you do know something about: something that will lead you to conclude that the claim is doubtful, if not false.

In practice, these three steps–understanding the question, listing possible answers, and working through their consequences–are interconnected. Part of understanding a question is knowing what would count as an answer to it, and what sort of thing follows from it.

Of course, philosophers notoriously disagree about whether a given implication is acceptable. Two philosophers may agree completely about the implications of a claim, and understand them perfectly; yet one may find them absurd while the other finds them tolerable or even attractive. At least that's how it seems to be. There is probably little that such philosophers can do to reach agreement. The sort of thing one finds attractive or repugnant depends on deep convictions formed early in life, often before acquiring any formal education in philosophy. (Many undergraduates have a distinctive philosophical temperament from the outset of their studies.) Because these convictions are the standard by which philosophical claims are judged, they themselves are extremely resistant to rational persuasion. Nor is this problem unique to philosophy: scientists also disagree about the foundations of their disciplines in ways that are resistant to rational persuasion.

In this case, I think, we ought to be cautious. If I find a view incredible, while others no less able than I, who have thought about it just as carefully, are untroubled, it would be epistemically irresponsible for me to be confident that I'm right and they're wrong. However powerful my convictions may be, I have to accept that they are fallible. We ought to be more confident about what follows from what than about which premises are true.

What do you consider to be the most neglected topics in contemporary metaphysics, and what direction would you like metaphysics to take in the future?

Some topics in metaphysics are neglected because there has never been anything of much interest to say about them: solipsism, for example. Then there are topics whose time has come and gone: idealism, mind-body dualism, arguments for the existence of God, free will and determinism, and many of the other topics we teach our first-year undergraduates. At one time or another, debates on these issues were among the best things going. But nowadays the positions are entrenched and the arguments on all sides are well known and there's not much happening. There may, of course, be great insights lurking within those tired old debates, just waiting for some brilliant 21st-century mind to uncover. Who knows? But it looks pretty unlikely.

Just as some topics are well neglected, others that ought to be neglected remain popular. The mere fact that there is nothing interesting to say about a topic does nothing to discourage people from writing about it. I hesitate to give examples for fear of antagonizing worthy colleagues, but property dualism in the philosophy of mind strikes me a paradigm case of an unjustly unneglected topic: the arguments for it rely on "intuitions" that we have no reason to think are reliable, and the claim itself is notoriously unclear.

(Then there are topics—some neglected and some not—that are so poorly understood that it's hard to see what's going on. I myself don't understand the questions these debates take themselves to be addressing, and I don't think it's entirely my fault. Discussions under the heading 'particulars and universals' almost invariably have this effect on me.)

I suppose what this fifth question is angling for is a list of unjustly neglected topics, areas where important work needs doing—some hot tips for up-and-coming metaphysicians casting about for a place to make their mark. Reliable information of this sort, I'm afraid, is as hard to come by as reliable information about undervalued stocks or horses. But I will venture a few vague remarks.

Physics is a treasure chest of facts and problems of metaphysical interest, with riches enough to keep philosophers going indefinitely, especially as the supply is always being replenished. It seems a safe bet that the philosophy of physics will continue to be a growth industry. Naturally, the better our grasp of physics, the more of this treasure we'll be able to get our fingers on. The unfortunate fact is, however, that few metaphysicians know much physics (I include myself here). This is not due merely to laziness: it takes huge sacrifices to become expert in two different academic disciplines, and the bureaucracy of higher education discourages it. (In Britain, our political masters like to promote interdisciplinary research, but they do nothing to make it possible for someone to acquire real interdisciplinary competence.)

Another rich and underexploited area for metaphysics, I suspect, is non-Western philosophy. Indian and Tibetan philosophy in particular have a great deal of what looks like metaphysics. There is bound to be wisdom there that we Westerners can learn from. The trouble is, it's even harder to become expert in non-Western philosophy than it is to become expert in physics. More seriously, there are vast problems of communication. When I try to read books about Asian metaphysics written by eminent authorities for Western audiences, I usually find that I can't make head nor tail of them. The impression I get is that the material is simply impossible to explain in terms that someone trained only in the Western tradition can understand. If they're talking about any of the things that we're talking about, it's hard to get even a vague notion of what they're saying about them. In order to learn non-Western philosophy, it seems, you have to travel to the relevant place and study with the local experts. But those who have done this seem unable to communicate to the rest of us what they have learned. (The same is true, to a lesser extent, of ancient Greek philosophy. If anyone alive today understands Aristotle's metaphysics, no one i able to put much of it in a way that the rest of us can grasp.) We can only hope that someday someone will break down this barrier.

9
L. A. Paul

Associate Professor of Philosophy

University of North Carolina at Chapel Hill, USA

Why were you initially drawn to metaphysics (and what keeps you interested)?

When I first entered graduate school, I couldn't see the point of doing metaphysics, much less what made it interesting. What was the point of building elaborate fairy-castles in the sky made of a priori speculation? But, as I pursued other interests, especially in the philosophy of science and the philosophy of mind, I kept bumping up against metaphysical questions. What are properties? What is the nature of the structure of the world? What is causation? Is a pain state essentially painful? What do puzzles about phenomenal properties imply about what is ontologically fundamental? It gradually became clear to me that I was not satisfied with brushing aside these ontological questions, since the answers to such questions often defined the shape of the logical space for the view I wished to explore.

My initial interests in the philosophy of science led me to explore the nature of time and temporal experience, and to investigate questions about the nature of the causal relation. In 1997, David Lewis gave a graduate seminar on a number of unsolved problems for counterfactual analyses of causation, and I became fascinated with the topic and determined to contribute to the debate. I was hooked. From that point on, I worked intensively with Lewis, who became my main advisor at Princeton. I spent many long afternoons talking with him about time, causation, and the many related topics that came up (such as properties, counterfactuals, naturalness, modality...) and developed a love for the way that metaphysics tried to address the deepest questions one could ask about the nature of the world. That love was surely fostered by the way that Lewis could see to the heart of many of the issues we discussed, even if we rarely agreed on the way to address them.

I remain interested in metaphysics for precisely these reasons; i.e., my beliefs that metaphysics is the best tool to use to investigate the parts of the fundamental structure of the world that is not investigated by natural science, and that metaphysical issues should frame philosophical discussions of topics in mind, science and even ethics. I also like the way that insights drawn from metaphysics can be fitted with epistemological questions about the way we, as situated agents in the world, can understand reality as a whole.

What do you consider to be your most important contributions to metaphysics?

I believe my most important contributions derive from my theory of objects as fusions of property instances, and the property mereology that accompanies that view. The idea of objects as fusions of property instances and my companion idea of a property mereology were first discussed in my "Logical Parts" (Paul 2002). The classical mereology of analytic philosophy takes objects, especially ordinary objects like statues and persons, to be nothing more than sums of spatiotemporal parts. But classical mereology overlooks an entire region of the mereological landscape, since objects can have property parts as well as spatiotemporal parts, and a property mereology is more fundamental than a spatiotemporal mereology.

Thinking of things in terms of property instances opens up a bunch of new avenues one can use to approach traditional topics. One place where I have used the account of objects as fusions of property instances to do a lot of work is in my account of how numerically distinct ordinary material objects coincide with and constitute one another, developed in "Coincidence as Overlap", Paul 2006a. Part of what that paper does is provide a worked-out account of how constitution is not identity. But there are three other parts to the paper. The first part shows that classical mereology violates our ordinary understanding of what objects are, since it requires that objects are reducible to hunks of matter in spacetime. The second part shows that one needs a theory of the structure of objects in order to understand the questions about grounding, modality and parthood raised by the puzzle of material constitution. And the third part develops a reductive theory of de re modality in terms of counterpart theory that supports essentialism. Paul 2006b develops this account of de re modality and essence in more detail.

What do you think is the proper role of metaphysics in relation to other areas of philosophy and other academic disciplines, including the natural sciences?

I believe that many of the questions and problems addressed by metaphysicians are related to, yet are distinct from, those addressed by scientists. (Of course, many questions are not distinct—in such cases, metaphysics needs to be informed by science. Usually here the metaphysician is interested in drawing out the consequences of contemporary scientific theories or in investigating presuppositions or themes of the scientific theory on offer.)

For example, one important discussion in metaphysics involves the question of what categories exist. Metaphysicians try to determine what categories of entities there are in the world, and what something would have to be like to be a member of a particular category. Scientists investigate instances of the categories, and also try to determine which instances of the categories exist. For example metaphysicians argue about whether there is a distinctive category of properties in the world (separate from the category of objects) and try to determine whether properties are universals, sets of tropes, sets of worlds, or some other sort of thing. Scientists try to determine which properties exist in the actual world, and, of those that exist, which ones are suitably natural, although they wouldn't use the term "natural." They also try to determine the features and behavior of the actual properties. Another discussion in metaphysics concerns whether and how objects are mereologically composed from parts. Metaphysicians try to determine what composition *is* and whether we can justifiably infer that it occurs. Scientists usually rely on pretheoretical notions of composition, instead concentrating on the discovery and investigation of new sorts of parts. These sorts of connections between metaphysics and science, where the projects are different, yet dovetail in important ways, are very common.

What do you consider to be the proper method for metaphysics?

The right method depends on what the project is. For metaphysical work on the nature of the world, as opposed to the analysis of metaphysical concepts, one uses a priori combined with a posteriori reasoning and relies on theoretical virtues such as simplicity, strength and elegance to support inferences to the best explanation of what there is. As a metaphysical realist who focuses on theories of what the world is like as opposed to theories of the proper analysis of metaphysical concepts, I prefer to avoid conceptual analysis unless it is necessary in order to refine the enquiry. In other words, sometimes some conceptual analysis is necessary in order to clarify what one is talking about and what the central issues are. But apart from that, I rely on a priori reasoning in conjunction with a posteriori knowledge drawn from ordinary experience and discoveries in science in order to reason about the nature of the world itself.

This sort of a priori reasoning is not the sort of pre-Kantian reasoning that Leibniz and other rationalists used. Rather, it is a form of model-building similar to what we see in the sciences. The theoretical methods used by ontologists are (modulo a few differences because of the change of subject) the same as the theoretical methods of science endorsed by scientific realists. Metaphysical realists should agree with scientific realists that certain theoretical virtues such as simplicity, strength, elegance and the like increase the likelihood of the truth of and the reasonableness of belief in theories. Metaphysicians constructing theories of what the world is like are building models that represent the world as being a certain way, and those models are evaluated based on how well they fit what we know a posteriori about the world along with how well the theory guiding the model maximizes theoretical virtues. I've developed this account of metaphysical modeling in detail in two places: see Paul (forthcoming*a*) and Paul (forthcoming*b*).

What do you consider to be the most neglected topics in contemporary metaphysics, and what direction would you like metaphysics to take in the future?

As your earlier questions suggest, one of the topics that needs more attention is the question of the methodology for realist, post-Kantian metaphysical theories of the world. I am not speaking here of "metametaphysical" questions involving the analysis of language or concepts, but of questions about the method used by metaphysicians who construct theories of the world based partly or largely on a priori reasoning.

A related topic that needs more attention is the role of cognitive science and experimental philosophy in connection to work in metaphysics. Metaphysicians of all sorts need to have a clearer sense of the way that conceptual analysis is (or is not) involved in their work. To the extent that our concepts and experience determine the structure of the theories we develop, experimental work on concepts and on the nature of experience may be relevant. For example, Christopher Hitchcock and Joshua Knobe (forthcoming) have done some experimental work on the way norms affect the way we (including philosophers who work on the metaphysics of causation) judge certain types of cases of causation, which ought to be taken account of by metaphysicians interested in developing an ontological account of the causal relation.

Another topic that needs more attention is the nature and structure of objects. One's theory of what objects fundamentally are is often the bedrock that supports one's larger philosophical view: for example, if one takes objects to be ontologically unstructured hunks of matter in spacetime, then it is most natural to hold that constitution is identity, that de re modality reduces to counterpart theory, that properties are sets of objects, and that classical mereology is true. Precision about one's theory of objects helps to clarify debates, map problem spaces, and identify points where technical moves are available or where further explanation needs to be given. Object theory enjoys a distinguished history but has received much less attention (with some notable exceptions) in recent years.

A topic that is important and that is starting to receive a lot of attention is the nature and direction of grounding and fundamentality. Related to this, I think more attention needs to be paid to the intersection between metaphysics and the philosophy of mind. One's metaphysical commitments to the structure of objects and states of affairs, the account of grounding, priority and supervenience, and to the nature of material constitution and modality connect very closely with a range of topics in the philosophy of mind. The ways in which these topics in philosophy of mind are affected by metaphysical positions on them have not been adequately explored.

References

Hitchcock and Knobe, forthcoming. "Cause and Norm," *Journal of Philosophy*.

Paul, 2002. "Logical Parts." Noûs 36, 578-596. Reprinted in *Metaphysics*, vol. V, edited by Michael Rea, Routledge 2008.

Paul, 2006a. "Coincidence as Overlap." Noûs 40: 623-659.

Paul, 2006b. "In Defense of Essentialism." Philosophical Perspectives (Metaphysics), edited by John Hawthorne, 333-372.

Paul, forthcoming*a*. "Psychology and the Metaphysical Method." *European Review on Philosophy and Psychology* special issue, edited by Joshua Knobe, Tania Lombrozo and Edouard Machery.

Paul, forthcoming*b*. "The Handmaiden's Tale: Ontological Methodology." Collection on Metaphysics and Methodology, edited by James Ladyman. Oxford: Oxford University Press.

10
Lorenz B. Puntel

Professor of Philosophy

University of Munich, Germany

Why were you initially drawn to metaphysics (and what keeps you interested)?

Initially I was not drawn to metaphysics. I was drawn to philosophy. I therefore simply began studying philosophy in general and that meant to me philosophy as a universal theoretical enterprise with a long and very rich tradition. Within this tradition I encountered great philosophers whose thinking was called "metaphysical" (in some sense). I became interested in the thinking of some of those philosophers, including among others Plato, Aristotle, Thomas Aquinas, Descartes, Leibniz, Kant, Hegel, Heidegger, and Whitehead. Later, I became acquainted with analytic philosophy and investigated its highly significant trajectory from nonmetaphysical and in some cases explicitly antimetaphysical positions to one of accepting and developing what analytical philosophers today call "metaphysics". But I have never primarily termed my own thinking "metaphysical," although I do not entirely reject this designation. The reason is that the term "metaphysics" has a long and very complicated—not to say chaotic—history that renders its usage extremely ambiguous unless it is preceded by careful explanation. I most especially disagree with the usage current analytical philosophers make of the term "metaphysics," because what they understand this term to designate covers only a small sector of the huge range of contents and topics included within the scope of what the Western philosophical tradition terms "metaphysical." I therefore prefer the term "comprehensive systematics," which I use to designate an essential part of the kind of systematic philosophy I take to be central to the philosophical enterprise. The architectonic of the specific systematic philosophy I presented in 2006 in *Struktur und Sein* (Tübingen: Mohr Siebeck) and in its English version, *Structure and Being* (University Park, PA: Penn State UP, 2008, translated by and in collaboration with Alan White, who has been working with me on this systematic philosophy since 2003, and who aided me in formulating this essay in English) consists of the following parts: global systematics, systematics of theoreticity, systematics of structure, world-systematics, comprehensive systematics, and metasystematics.

The answer to the question what keeps me interested in "metaphysics" ensues from what has been explained and is twofold. First, since philosophy in my understanding must be systematically oriented, I cannot neglect those essential parts of it that I call the systematics of structure, world-systematics, and comprehensive systematics, which relate in ways indicated below to what has been called "metaphysics" in the history of philosophy. Second, my special interest in so-understood "metaphysics" derives from the fact that I consider its neglect to be the most deficient and regrettable aspect of analytic philosophy. In my opinion the development of a metaphysical conception that does not reduce metaphysics to quite few questions, as do many contemporary books, handbooks, lexica etc., is one of the most important and urgent tasks in contemporary philosophy.

What do you consider to be your most important contributions to metaphysics?

At the beginning of my philosophical career I set out to outline the idea of a systematic philosophy (I never planned to develop a "philosophical system" of the sort envisaged by the German idealistic philosophers). Because I wanted to take into account, as far as possible, the entire richness of ideas propounded by the most important philosophers, it was a long time before I got to the point where I could try to present my own conception of systematic philosophy. My most important historico-critical studies in the history of philosophy, written and published during this long period of time, have been reprinted in a volume published in 2007 (*Auf der Suche nach dem Gegenstand und dem Theoriestatus der Philosophie – Philosophiegeschichtlich-kritische Studien.* Tübingen: Mohr Siebeck Verlag). As indicated above, I presented my own conception of systematic philosophy—the *structural-systematic philosophy*—in *Struktur und Sein* (and *Structure and Being*). This philosophy arose from three insights, which can be formulated as three theses, resulting from a long and intensive occupation with the fundamental philosophical conceptions from history and of the present. The first thesis is that throughout most of its long history, philosophy has attributed to itself a comprehensive character, even if that character has taken various distinct forms. The second thesis is that contemporary philosophy – and quite particularly so-called analytic philosophy – does scarcely any justice to this universal character of philosophy, in that it exhibits, virtually exclusively, a fragmentary character. The third thesis is that analytic philosophy has developed powerful methodical and formal tools enabling philosophical thinking to attain high degrees of clarity and rigor.

Central to the structural-systematic philosophy is the concept of the *theoretical framework*, which it presents in connection with and as a modification of the concept, introduced by Rudolf Carnap, of the linguistic framework. The account proceeds from the fundamental insight that every theoretical questioning, every theoretical sentence, argument, every theory, etc., is intelligible and evaluable only if understood as situated within a sufficiently determinate or determinable theoretical framework. If this presupposition is not made, then everything remains underdetermined: the meaning of any given sentence, its assessment, etc. To every theoretical framework belong a language (with its syntax and its semantics), a logic, and a conceptuality, along with all of the other components that constitute a theoretical apparatus. Failure to attend to the dependence of theories on frameworks – or, as is most common, failure even to recognize it – is the source of countless catastrophic mistakes from which philosophy has suffered throughout its history and into the present. It should be added that as a matter of fact there is a plurality of theoretical frameworks that are or have been relied on and an immensely larger plurality of them that are possible.

The other central concept of the structural-systematic philosophy is *structure*, a concept taken from mathematics and applied in a suitable way to all philosophical topics. This philosophy develops three kinds of fundamental structures relevant to philosophy: the formal (logical and mathematical), the semantical, and the ontological fundamental structures. Opposing the currently dominant "compositional" semantics based on the principle of compositionality, the structural-systematic philosophy develops an alternative semantics that is based on a strong version of the Fregean context principle: "Only in the context of a sentence do words have meanings." One of its central theses is that sentences of the subject-predicate form are not acceptable for any philosophical language equipped with an appropriate semantics; what make them unacceptable are their ontological consequences. (If, as can hardly be avoided, sentences with the subject-predicate syntactic form are nevertheless used, they must be semantically interpreted and understood as convenient abbreviations of sentences without subjects and predicates.) The ontology that corresponds to subject-predicate sentences is so-called "substance ontology;" *Structure and Being* demonstrates that this ontology is unintelligible and therefore unacceptable.

Sentences without subjects and predicates, like "It's raining," are termed "primary sentences;" they express "primary propositions" that are more precisely interpreted as "primary semantic structures." The qualifier "primary" is not a counterpart to anything like "secondary," and is not to be understood as synonymous with "simple" (or "atomistic," as in "atomistic sentence"). The term "primary" designates sentences that do not have the subject-predicate form. It is therefore wholly consequent to speak of "simple primary sentences and propositions" and of "complex primary sentences and propositions" (i.e., sentences or propositions that consist of more than one and indeed often of a great many simple primary sentences or propositions).

The ontological structures emerge directly from the semantic ones in that semantics and ontology are two sides of the same coin. The only ontological "category" (according to traditional terminology) is the "primary fact," which *Structure and Being* interprets as and calls "primary ontological structure." According to the theory of truth the book elaborates, primary sentences express primary propositions, which, when true, are identical with primary facts (in the world). All "things" (in more appropriate philosophical terms: all beings or entities) are configurations of primary facts (of primary ontological structures). The term "fact" is taken in a comprehensive sense, corresponding to the way this term is often used at present (e.g., "semantic fact", "logical fact," etc.). The concept of the configuration of primary facts or of complex primary facts (thus also, correspondingly, of configurations of primary sentences/propositions or complex primary sentences/propositions) emerges as one that is central within the structural-systematic philosophy.

On this basis, the structural-systematic philosophy is, according to its "quasi-definition," a theory of the most general or universal structures of the unrestricted universe of discourse. The structural-systematic program investigates the unrestricted universe of discourse by presenting it as the comprehensive configuration of these fundamental structures or, in other words, it discovers and articulates the structures of the universe of discourse. In the book's terminology, structures are connections or configurations and all entities, simple and complex, are such configurations. The unrestricted universe of discourse is the totality of all structures/configurations.

Comprehensive systematics emerges when the question is asked as to whether the various simple and complex configurations/connections, including the entire theoretical dimension, i. e. the theorizing subjects, the ideal theoretical world, all the formal structures etc., constitute or presuppose an all-encompassing configuration/ connection, such that the entire unrestricted universe of discourse, as the comprehensive primary fact, is itself subjected to theorization. The structural-systematic philosophy upholds an affirmative response and calls this all-encompassing dimension the *primordial dimension of being*. In a certain sense, then, the structural-systematic philosophy is inspired by Heidegger's epoch-making step of renewing the question of being. To be sure, I consider the manner in which Heidegger addressed the question completely unacceptable. His strange misconception and rejection of logic, of conceptual and especially of rigorous thinking and his increasing inclination to use a poetical language cannot be considered a valuable way of doing serious philosophy. My own way of developing a comprehensive systematics (in Chapter 5 of *Structure and Being*) consists in taking absolutely seriously the grand question concerning the connection of all elements or all configurations of the unrestricted universe of discourse and in treating this question by means of the theoretical tools elaborated in the long tradition of logically oriented philosopohy and most especially in analytic philosophy.

In using the expression "(the primordial dimension of) being" I don't presuppose any special meaning of "being". I introduce this expression in order to designate the all-encompassing dimension just indicated. So, "being" is not what in general is called "existence," neither in the traditional sense (i.e., to designate what characterizes the dimension "outside" our thinking) nor in various other senses, for instance, in Quine's sense ("existence is what existential quantification expresses").

It should be noted that I don't simply identify "metaphysics" with the comprehensive systematics just explained. "Metaphysics" in *this* sense has been present in some respects (albeit almost always implicitly) in the works of some great thinkers, especially in those of Thomas Aquinas, who wrote important things about *Being* (*esse*) as well as about *beings* (*entia*). As is well known, Heidegger criticized what he called "(Western) metaphysics," without distinguishing among its often highly diverse forms, for having forgotten "Being (*Sein*)" ("forgetfulness of Being," *Seinsvergessenheit*). He is right only in part, as I have shown in several writings and will show in a forthcoming book. Until about the 18th-century the term "metaphysics" was used in many senses, which is not surprising given its controversial origin in the wake of Aristotle. But in general and to a certain extent the term designated a general or universal discipline in conjunction with special or particular disciplines. Christian Wolff (1676-1754) and his disciple Alexander Baumgarten (1714-1762) "systematized" (in a certain sense) this widespread traditional sense of metaphysics by defining it as a conjunction of four disciplines: ontology, general cosmology, rational and empirical psychology, and natural theology. Wolff termed the four disciplines "the complete work of metaphysics (*integrum metaphysicae opus*)" (*Theologia Naturalis* (1737), *Praef.*). A fundamental distinction was then made between ontology—also called First Philosophy (Wolff) or Universal Metaphysics (Baumgarten, Metaphysica § 4)— and three particular or special disciplines. This distinction has come to be known as that between *general metaphysics* and *special metaphysics*. General metaphysics as ontology deals with the general properties of all beings (*entia, Seiende*), whereas special metaphysics treats three specific (kinds of) beings (*entia, Seiende*) within its three subdisciplines: cosmology considers the world and its nonhuman beings, psychology, the human mind or soul, and natural theology, the supreme being, i.e., God. This concept of metaphysics exerted a powerful influence on many philosophers, including, perhaps most importantly, Kant and Heidegger.

What *Structure and Being* calls "comprehensive systematics" cannot be identified with any of the disciplines identified by Wolff and Baumgarten, because their division has no place for theories of *Being* (*Sein, esse*) *as such and as whole*. Their "general (or universal) metaphysics" explicitly concerns only *beings* (*Seiende, entia*). Furthermore, according to *comprehensive systematics* "God" is not a topic belonging to special metaphysics, because God is not conceived of as "a being (*Seiendes, ens*)," not even the First or Highest or Supreme Being. Instead, *Structure and Being* shows that God should be thought as (Absolute, Necessary) *Being* (in the sense of *"Sein, esse"*), not in the sense of "a being, (*Seiendes, ens*)". If the term "metaphysics" is used in the sense just explained of comprehensive systematics, then an additional qualifier is required; one appropriate candidate is "grand."

Within the structural-systematic philosophy, the distinction between "general" and "special" metaphysics can be retained, but only on the condition that they are *not* understood in the traditional and currently prevailing senses. According to the *new* sense, *"general metaphysics"* would be identified with most of the *Systematics of Structure: the Fundamental Structures* (Chapter 3 of *Structure and Being*) and with some topics dealt with in the *Comprehensive Systematics* (thus, in Chapter 5); one could introduce an additional qualifier, yielding "general-structural metaphysics". The term *"special metaphysics,"* according to the *new* sense envisaged here, would cover only and quite exactly what in *Structure and Being* is called *"World-systematics"* (the topic of Chapter 4).

In sum: within the framework of *Structure and Being* the term "metaphysics" is intelligible and illuminating if and only if the threefold distinction just introduced is made: grand metaphysics—general(-structural) metaphysics—special metaphysics. Worth noting is that *Structure and Being* uses the term "metaphysics" only in the sense of *grand metaphysics,* although it does not specify that this is the case.

What do you think is the proper role of metaphysics in relation to other areas of philosophy and other academic disciplines, including the natural sciences?

The question of the proper role of metaphysics (in the three senses just explained) in relation to other areas of philosophy is in my view one of the most important and urgent questions in contemporary philosophy. The fact that this question is wholly ignored or neglected constitutes one of the most serious weaknesses of analytic philosophy. Analytic philosophy remains extremely fragmentary. In general it treats single questions in complete isolation. To be sure, there are certain – and important – features all analytic philosophers more or less share, but they are virtually exclusively methodological and instrumental ones: conceptual clarity, argumentative strength, use of logical-mathematical tools, and the like. But those features are by no means sufficient to establish what could be called a coherence among the treatments of questions belonging to different philosophical areas as regards their theoretical content.

Perhaps the most significant example of this failure is analytic philosophy of mind. It purports to develop an ontological conception of the human mind. In doing so, it must rely – and in fact it relies – on fundamental ontological assumptions. But what kind of ontology is presupposed by philosophers of mind? As a matter of fact this question remains almost always completely unexamined. One presupposes the "normal" analytic ontology of "objects" that have "properties" and stand in "relations" with each other. It is simply the direct continuation of Aristotelian ontology as generally understood. That instead of "substance" the term "object" is used obscures the real status of and the issue posed by this ontology. It is an ontology, in one appropriate phrase, of *middle-sized dry goods*. But what is a dry good—what is an *object*? The usage of first-order predicate logic to formalize the ontological commitments masks the real problem. In saying that a property is predicated of or attributed to an *object*, one takes the *object* to be the presupposed X of which the property is predicated (or to which it is attributed). What is this X *as such*? If all properties are thought away, what remains? A "bare particular"? This putative entity called "object" (traditionally: "substance") is a pseudo-entity, because it cannot be made intelligible. Some analytic philosophers have pointed to this serious problem, but the discussions of it have not significantly changed the theoretical scene, most especially in the philosophy of mind. Many philosophers of mind distinguish, for example, between mental and physical properties and attribute both to an "object" (called "mind" or "human being" or the like) they consider to be a physical entity. But what can this "object" be? Given the unanswerability of this question, the central questions in the various distinct philosophical areas, but most especially in the philosophy of mind, require radical rethinking of the ontology accepted or presupposed.

To correctly answer the question regarding the proper role of "metaphysics" in relation to other areas of philosophy the threefold sense of *metaphysics* introduced and explained above must be taken into account: *special* metaphysics, *general(-structural)* metaphysics, *and grand* metaphysics. Today's analytic metaphysics is almost completely restricted to special metaphysics and to certain topics from general(-structural) metaphysics, namely, to the treatment of single domains, single questions, and some central concepts, as the many books and articles devoted to analytic metaphysics clearly show. The interconnections among those domains are largely neglected, although there are significant efforts aiming to clarify some conceptual topics including the (metaphysically understood) modalities, essentialism, and the like, that are suitable tools for articulating at least some fundamental aspects of those interconnections.

Grand metaphysics, as I understand and explain it in the sense of comprehensive systematics, is not a theory about beings or domains of beings; it is instead a theory about being itself, being as such and as a whole. In my view, grand metaphysics is absolutely indispensable for a philosophy that endeavors to be critical and thoroughly rational. The reason is that every philosophical theoretician presupposes (albeit usually implicitly) some kind of grand-metaphysical view as the most fundamental background or basis for his theoretical work. A striking example can be found in analytic philosophy. As is well known, the vast majority of analytic philosophers hold (most frequently implicitly) a purely materialistic and/or physicalistic view of the "world," taking "world" as synonymous with "being." But such a view is rarely considered explicitly and even more rarely explicitly treated and justified. It cannot be denied, however, that this view plays a tremendous, indeed a decisive role in the framing and delimiting *a limine* the kinds of solutions those philosophers offer for specific problems. The importance of developing an explicit, rational, and well-argued grand metaphysics could not be exaggerated.

As for the proper role of special, general, and grand metaphysics in relation to other academic disciplines, including the natural sciences, the answer can be very short. Two aspects should be addressed. First, what was said about the role of metaphysics in relation to the other areas of philosophy should be analogously applied to its relation to non-philosophical areas, especially the natural sciences. Of particular importance is the development of metaphysics in order to inhibit unfounded extrapolations and inappropriate uses of natural-scientific results by many philosophers, and even by scientists and other authors of books presenting those results to the general public. Second, special metaphysics should be extremely careful to avoid entering the proper spheres of other academic disciplines, most especially the natural sciences. This is a point of highest importance, because it is all too evident that very often there have been and still are conflicts between metaphysical and natural-scientific views.

What do you consider to be the proper method for meta-

physics?

The structural-systematic philosophy does not recognize or develop a special method for metaphysics, i.e., for the systematics of structure, world-systematics, and comprehensive systematics. Instead, it develops a *philosophical method* on the basis of the concept of theoretical framework. The method consists in working out and putting to work all the pieces or elements that constitute the suitable theoretical framework and in applying it to a determinate area. This determinate area is the subject matter of the philosophical theory envisaged. It presents itself initially as a collection of area-related *data*. The concept *datum/data* is not taken in the sense of sense data or the like; instead, it has the technical meaning of "given information" already linguistically articulated. In other words, data are sentences that express propositions in such a way that they appear initially as being not foundationally understood truths, but only *truth candidates*. Philosophical theorizing consists in reinterpreting those data as (fundamental) structures, by which process the data reinterpreted as structures are sufficiently determinate to be classifiable as truths and falsehoods.

Philosophical data can mostly clearly and understandably be presented in conjunction with questions. Because every question presupposes (or includes) a declarative sentence, the datum is what this sentence expresses. Examples for so understood philosophical questions (and, consequently, data) are: What is an individual (in the "robust" sense, for instance, of a living being, a human person)? What is a domain of individual beings? What are the differences between and connections among different domains of beings? What is the connection among all domains of beings, i. e. the world? Such questions call for (or presuppose) the data for world-systematics or special metaphysics. But a further grand question—what is being itself or as such and as a whole?—calls for (or presupposes) the grand datum, i.e., the datum that is the subject matter of comprehensive systematics or grand metaphysics.

Questions and declarative sentences presuppose theoretical frameworks, which contain among other things the concepts they rely upon. The ensuing task for metaphysics (in all three senses) is to articulate the right questions, assemble the relevant data, and theorize about them in the indicated manner. The method for doing that, the philosophical method, is a complex one, consisting of four stages. Starting with single theories about single and restricted domains of data, the guiding idea behind the four-stage method is simple and can be described as follows. With respect to the *data* – be they individual phenomena or events, entire domains, or even the comprehensive datum, i.e., the unrestricted universe of discourse as a whole – the task of theorization is the following: first, the theoretician must seek structures for the data (and thus structures of the data), thereby both acquiring the material for theorization and formulating initial or informal theories. Next, these informal or elementary theories must be put into the strictly theoretical form; that is, theories in the genuine or strict sense are to be formulated. Third, the thus-presented individual theories must be brought into systematic form, which requires the development of a network of theories. Fourth and finally, it must be determined whether the individual theories and the theoretical network within which they are integrated, thus the comprehensive theory, are theoretically adequate, i.e., whether they satisfy the criteria for theoreticity, which include, most importantly, that of truth.

In normal philosophical practice, these steps are scarcely ever even recognized, much less taken in this order. The second and third steps or stages are usually wholly ignored. Typically, only incidental aspects of the first and fourth stages are applied, and the fourth stage is usually taken to involve "justification" of an only vaguely determinate sort. More ambitious philosophical presentations ignore only the second step. In such cases, the informal or minimal theories that result from the application of the first stage of the method are directly integrated into a network-theory that is itself only informally articulated. (Worth noting is that the philosophical four-stage method just delineated is an *idealized method*; it can be conceived of as a kind of "regulative method", in analogy to Kant's "regulative idea.")

What do you consider to be the most neglected topics in contemporary metaphysics, and what direction would you like metaphysics to take in the future?

The answer to this question is already contained in the answers to the preceding four questions, so here only three points need be summarily reiterated. First, among the most neglected topics today is that raised by the question whether traditional analytic semantics and ontology and the formal tools hitherto used to clarify them require profound revision. I have tried to show that this question must be answered in the affirmative. Second, even more radically neglected has been and still is to a vast extent the need for philosophical theorization of the unrestricted universe of discourse—or, differently stated, for a philosophical *theory of everything*, not only in the sense of a theory of all beings (Seiende, *entia*), but also—-and most importantly—-in that of a theory of being as such and as a whole, which can be called grand metaphysics. Third, given the neglect of these two topics, the direction I would like metaphysics (in all three senses, but especially in the sense of grand metaphysics) to pursue in the future is to take seriously the fact that these topics have been neglected and to find ways to fruitfully address them.

11

Gonzalo Rodriguez-Pereyra

Professor of Metaphysics
University of Oxford, UK

Why were you initially drawn to metaphysics (and what keeps you interested)?

Metaphysics is perhaps my oldest intellectual interest. Indeed at a very young age – perhaps when I was eleven or twelve years old – I became for a while fixated on the question whether there could be two "identical" stones. This is, of course, the question whether the Principle of identity of Indiscernibles is true – a metaphysical question *par excellence* – and, as I formulated it then, I was bound to fall into confusion about it.

But what drew me into it? I believe it is the unique combination of fundamentality, simplicity and difficulty peculiar to Philosophy: its questions, although fundamental, can be formulated in a very simple and clear way, but are nevertheless extremely difficult to answer. Metaphysics, in my view, is the study of the most general nature and basic structure of reality. In a sense, then, Metaphysics is the most fundamental theoretical discipline, and so it is the field in which that unique combination of factors common to all fields of Philosophy becomes most attractive. Whether or not that is what initially drew me into Metaphysics, it is certainly what keeps me interested in it.

What do you consider to be your most important contributions to metaphysics?

It would be more interesting to know what others consider to be my most important contributions to Metaphysics. But, anyway, I am going to answer this question. I list what I think are my most important contributions in what I think is their order of importance.

(1) The full development of a version of Resemblance nominalism that can avoid the Imperfect Community and Companionship difficulties, as well as other difficulties, using a dyadic non-contrastive resemblance predicate. The main place where I effected this contribution is in my book *Resemblance Nominalism* (Oxford University Press, 2002).

(2) The development of arguments for the existence of truthmakers for a large class of synthetic propositions that includes negative existentials. These arguments are presented in my article "Why Truthmakers" (in Beebee and Dodd (eds.) *Truthmakers: the contemporary debate*, Oxford University Press, 2005, pp. 17–31).

(3) Showing that the Bundle Theory neither entails nor is otherwise committed to the Principle of identity of Indiscernibles and, furthermore, that the Bundle Theory can be developed in such a way that it is committed to the falsity of the Principle of identity of Indiscernibles. This is done in my article "The Bundle Theory is compatible with distinct but indiscernible particulars" (*Analysis*, 64 (1), pp. 72–81, 2004).

(4) A philosophically illuminating specification of the properties that, when quantified over, render the Principle of identity of Indiscernibles trivial. This is done in my "How not to trivialize the identity of indiscernibles" (P. F. Strawson and A. Chakrabarti (eds.) *Concepts, properties and Qualities*, Ashgate, 2006, pp. 205–223).

(5) Showing that Modal Realism and Metaphysical Nihilism are compatible with each other. This is done in my article "Modal Realism and Metaphysical Nihilism" (*Mind* 113 (452), pp. 683-704).

(6) Providing a refutation of the so-called Entailment Principle, according to which a truthmaker for a proposition is a truthmaker for any proposition entailed by the proposition in question. This is done in my "Truthmaking, entailment, and the conjunction thesis" (*Mind*, 115 (460), pp. 957-982).

What do you think is the proper role of metaphysics in relation to other areas of philosophy and other academic disciplines, including the natural sciences?

As I said above, being the study of the most general nature and basic structure of reality, Metaphysics is the most fundamental theoretical discipline. The concepts of metaphysics, concepts like time, space, identity, resemblance, substance, property, fact, event, composition, possibility, etc., are the most fundamental concepts. This does not mean that Metaphysics is about concepts; Metaphysics is about reality, but those concepts are supposed to apply to the most basic features of reality – and although Metaphysics is about reality the elucidation of those and other concepts is useful to Metaphysics and it is one of the tasks of the metaphysician. In one way or another all other disciplines (whether philosophical or not) employ these concepts and/or others derived from them and so Metaphysics contains the conceptual foundations of the rest of knowledge. The role of Metaphysics in relation to other disciplines, whether philosophical or not and including the natural sciences, is thus a foundational role. Lack of clarity in the concepts of Metaphysics implies lack of clarity in other disciplines (both theoretical and practical) employing those concepts or employing concepts that depend on those of Metaphysics.

In the Preface to the French edition of the *Principles* Descartes compared Philosophy to a tree whose roots are Metaphysics, its trunk is physics, and its branches are all the other sciences, which he thought reducible to three principal ones: medicine, mechanics and morals. Although I would not classify physics, medicine, mechanics and morals as part of Philosophy, I share the Cartesian idea that the totality of knowledge forms a tree whose roots are Metaphysics.

What do you consider to be the proper method for metaphysics?

The question of the method of Metaphysics can be taken in two ways. In one sense it refers to the method by which one arrives to metaphysical truths. I cannot say much more about this than the following triviality: the best method to follow is to be sufficiently informed about the matter at issue and to think clearly and hard about it. Being informed about a metaphysical matter *might* require knowing not only what other metaphysicians have thought about it, but also what other philosophers and scientists have thought about that matter and related ones, and what the pre-philosophical and pre-scientific intuitions about the matter are. What counts as being sufficiently informed will depend, to some extent, on the metaphysical matter at issue.

There is thus a kind of influence of non-Metaphysics on Metaphysics (and I think in many cases there should be a similar kind of influence of Metaphysics on non-Metaphysics), but this does not go against what was said in the previous answer, namely that Metaphysics has a foundational role with respect to the other disciplines at the conceptual level.

In another sense the question refers to the way in which we are supposed to decide between competing metaphysical theories. Here I think the task is to develop a set of criteria or parameters by which to judge metaphysical theories, and to assign such parameters different relative weights. In my book *Resemblance Nominalism* I proposed to evaluate solutions to the problem of universals with respect to six such criteria: (a) coherence (understood in a broad way that goes beyond merely logical coherence and that counts explanatory circularity, among other philosophical vices, as incoherence); (b) preservation of intuitions and received opinions; (c) ideological economy; (d) quantitative ontological economy; (e) qualitative ontological economy; and (f) avoidance of *ad hoc* ontology. These parameters differ in their relative importance. And of course different parameters might be relevant in different metaphysical areas or with respect to different metaphysical problems. And the same parameters might receive different relative weights in different metaphysical areas or with respect to different metaphysical problems.

Since the opinions (or even the intuitions) referred to in (b) need not be *metaphysical* opinions (or intuitions), there is a sense in which metaphysical theses can depend for their justification on extra-metaphysical thought. Again, this does not go against what was said in the previous answer, where the point was merely that the concepts of Metaphysics are prior to those of other disciplines.

What do you consider to be the most neglected topics in contemporary metaphysics, and what direction would you like metaphysics to take in the future?

I am happy with the level of productivity and creativity shown in Metaphysics in the last 30 years or so. And I believe that it is likely that this trend will continue for a while. But, in general, I would like Metaphysics to become more conscious of its own history. Not that there are not enough books or articles on the history of Metaphysics. But by being more conscious of its own past contemporary metaphysicians might come to discover neglected topics and problems, and might involve metaphysicians of the past in their contemporary discussion. The idea is to make the past participate of the contemporary discussion to a greater extent than is now done.[1]

---

[1] I thank Ezequiel Zerbudis for a conversation in which we discussed some of the issues touched on in this questionnaire.

12

Gideon Rosen

Stuart Professor of Philosophy
Princeton University, USA

Why were you initially drawn to metaphysics (and what keeps you interested)?

I drifted into philosophy from literary theory, so the first courses that caught my interest were classes in the philosophy of art. At the time — the early 1980s — aesthetics was preoccupied by a range of problems in ontology. Two in particular were of special interest. The first (and probably the more important for aesthetics) concerned the philosophical significance of Duchamp's readymades and Warhol's Brillo Boxes: items that were in all relevant intrinsic respects indiscernible from ordinary things, but which had somehow been endowed with aesthetic significance when they were placed in a gallery by an artist (Danto 1981). The metaphysical lesson of these examples seems banal in retrospect, viz., that the aesthetically relevant properties of a thing often include extrinsic properties. But for someone who had been raised to think of the paradigmatic encounter with a work of art as a matter of gazing intently at the thing itself and soaking in whatever aesthetic significance it might possess, the idea that historical or contextual features may be relevant, not just to the evaluation of a work of art but to its status *as* a work of art, came as a revelation.

The other important problem concerned the ontological status of works of art like novels and plays, but also films and prints, which cannot be identified with concrete physical objects (Wollheim 1980). Hitchcock's movie *The Lady Vanishes* is not identical with any of the concrete prints or discs from which the film may be projected, nor is it identical with the any of the datable showings of the film. So it's an abstract object of some sort, but unlike the platonic abstract objects that arise in mathematics, it seems to inherit at least some of the properties of its concrete 'tokens'; one can see it, for example; it might be beautiful, or 97 minutes long. More importantly, it clearly owes its existence to human activity, so it's not eternal. So far as I know, contemporary metaphysics does not have a worked out view of these hermaphroditic entities that seem to partake both of the abstract and the concrete: no account of the conditions under which such things exist, and the conditions under which (and the sense in which) they may share features with their concrete embodiments.[1] But anyone who comes to metaphysics from aesthetics will see this as a project worth pursuing. More importantly from my point of view, anyone who comes to metaphysics from aesthetics will find nominalism — the blanket rejection of abstract objects —fundamentally implausible.

When I came to Princeton for graduate school in 1984, whatever I knew about metaphysics I had gleaned from this sort of work in aesthetics. The focus at Princeton was rather different. David Lewis was working on *Plurality of Worlds* (Lewis 1986), which argues for the reality of concrete alternative universes on the grounds that it is "useful" to suppose that such things exist, and John Burgess had just published "Why I am not a Nominalist" (Burgess 1983), which contains the first version of his distinctive case for "antinominalism" about mathematical objects — an argument that has obsessed me ever since. What these otherwise very different views have in common is the thought that philosophy can supply us with (or remind us of) positive reasons for believing in things we cannot see, and things that are in no way constituted by or grounded in things we can see, and all within a framework of a broadly naturalistic epistemology that does without extra sensory perception. That struck me then, and strikes me now, as an astounding idea. On the other side (so to speak), Paul Benacerraf was giving seminars that made the perils of platonism acutely vivid, and Bas van Frassen had just published *The Scientific Image* (van Frassen 1980) — a manifesto for an alternative picture that sharply separates science and ontology.

For me, the issue that divided Lewis and Burgess on the one hand from Benacerraf and van Frassen on the other came down to this. Our best theories in the sciences, mathematics and in other areas (including aesthetics and literary criticism) appear to posit *transcendent* things — objects that are not parts of nature.

---

[1] For valuable discussion, see (Wolterstorff 1980).

Some of these theories are clearly *acceptable* by the standards of these disciplines, which in the case of science and mathematics amount to the most exacting standards that human beings have ever brought to bear for intellectual purposes. The question is whether we have reason to believe in transcendent things for this reason. Benacerraf says, "maybe not", on the ground that while these theories may be (as it were) locally defensible, when we try to integrate them with our best theories in other areas (including the theory of content and the theory of knowledge), a global incoherence emerges which may undermine the credibility of these theories when taken at face value (Benacerraf 1965, 1973). van Frassen says, "not at all", though for a different reason. His idea is that since a theory may be *ideally* acceptable for every important scientific purpose without being true (or close to true) in its claims about transcendent things, the fact that our most acceptable theories posit transcendent things gives no reason whatsoever (by itself) for believing in them.[2]

This set up one of the problems that has gripped me ever since. It's not really a problem in metaphysics so much as a problem in the methodology or epistemology of metaphysics. What counts as a reasonable standard for fixing belief about transcendent things, and about metaphysical questions more generally, and to what extent are those standards *compelling* (in the sense that one is rationally required to believe what those standards deem acceptable) and not just merely permissive? I have some tentative views about this, about which more below.

What do you consider to be your most important contributions to metaphysics?

My contributions, such as they are, exhibit what I like to think of as a fruitful tension, but which may in fact be a kind of incoherence. I've intervened in three main areas: The debate over nominalism in the philosophy of mathematics, the debate over modal realism, and the debate over realism in general philosophy, and in each case my views are in one sense consistently conservative. In the philosophy of mathematics, I have followed John Burgess in offering a defense of a weak form of platonism — or as we prefer to call it, antinominalism (Burgess and Rosen 1997, Rosen and

---

[2] Van Fraassen's focus was the status of unobservable physical objects and structures. For discussion of the implications of his view for the debate over nominalism, see Rosen 1994.

Burgess 2005). Taken at face value, ordinary mathematics affirms the existence of numbers, functions, and other distinctively mathematical objects. The claims of standard mathematics are clearly credible by mathematical and scientific standards. No mathematician seriously doubts the infinity of the primes, or the existence of solutions to Einstein's field equations for general relativity. So *we* are justified in believing in these things unless there is some good reason to doubt the claims of standard mathematics. But there are no good reasons of this sort. So we are justified in believing that mathematical objects exist.

This argument presupposes an epistemological view that takes its inspiration from Quine's rejection of 'first philosophy' — an extra-scientific standpoint from which it makes sense to say that a claim may be perfectly acceptable by scientific standards and yet incredible all things considered.[3] The special twist here is to insist, as Quine did not, that mathematics is a perfectly respectable science in its own right. This is to reject the main presupposition of the 20th century debate over nominalism, viz., that the existence claims of mathematics are credible only insofar as they are somehow indispensable for the *natural* sciences (Putnam 1971, Field 1980). Burgess and I have also defended Platonism against arguments that *accept* this presupposition. As Field, Burgess and others have shown, there is a sense in which it *is* possible to rewrite certain standard physical theories in such a way as to purge all reference to mathematical objects. But of course no working scientist would dream of *using* these nominalistic alternatives in her work: they are clunky, fragile, imperspicuous and in general hard to work with. The nominalist maintains that these theories are nonetheless *better* (more acceptable) than standard theories by scientific standards, and that we should therefore reject the standard theories in favor of these nominalistic alternatives. But in what sense are these novel theories better? They are clearly

---

[3] My favorite statement of this view is due to Putnam:

"The very factors that make it rational to accept a theory 'for scientific purposes' also make it rational to believe it, at least in the sense in which one ever believes a scientific theory — as an approximation to the truth that can probably be bettered, and not as the final truth ... [I]t is silly to agree that a reason for believing that p warrants accepting p in all scientific circumstances, and the to add 'but even so it is not *good enough*'. Such a judgment could only be made if one accepted a trans-scientific method as superior to the scientific method; but this philosopher, at least, has no interest in doing *that*." (Putnam 1971: 356)

worse for "practical" purposes. But they are also clearly worse for the various theoretical purposes to which a real theoretical physicist might put them, as is shown by the fact even the most high-minded mathematical physicist, concerned to present (say) Maxwell's Electrodynamics in its purest, most elegant form for the purposes of analyzing its relation to quantum electrodynamics, would never dream of employing a nominalistic version of Maxwell's theory.

Philosophers who regard these nominalistic versions of standard theories as superior to their platonistic parents are importing a principle for grading theories that has no clear role in real science or mathematics. We have a name for this principle: Ockham's razor. It is supposed to favor theories that posit fewer basic categories of object. Over the years I have become sensitive to invocations of the Razor in metaphysics. The background mythology seems to be that this principle gains its authority from its role in science. But as this example shows, that is almost certainly a mistake. Scientists do care about various kinds of simplicity: they may prefer theories with relatively few 'degrees of freedom', theories with relatively few independent parameters that need to be filled in 'by hand', theories with relatively few basic laws, etc. But there is no evidence anywhere in real science of a general concern for *ontological parsimony* — a concern to reduce the number of entities or kinds of entity posited by one's theories, where this would include *mathematical* entities. If the philosopher wishes to appeal to such a principle as part of his motivation for nominalism, he should admit that the principle has no support from science and that he has left epistemological Naturalism well behind. To criticize a bit of science or mathematics on the ground that it flouts this sort of principle is to appeal to an invented, extrascientific standard for evaluating such theories.[4]

This is a preliminary defensive case for antinominalism. If it is sound, then we are justified in believing in abstract objects. But there are two ways to take this. The claim might be that a commitment to abstract objects is *rationally permissible* for us given our evidence; alternatively, the claim might be that a commitment to abstract objects is rationally *required* — that it would be unreasonable to *doubt* the existence of abstract objects given our

---

[4] See Maddy 1997 for a compelling case that certain parts of mathematics seem to incorporate an anti-Ockhamist impulse to *maximize* the number of objects and structures posited by the theory.

evidence. In Rosen 2001 I distinguish these ideas and argue that while antinominalism is clearly permissible, it is not required. The key argument involves a fictional tribe — the Bedrockers — who are raised from infancy to treat mathematics as a useful fiction, and so to suppose that the credible content of any well established physical theory T that involves mathematics is roughly this: The concrete part of the actual world is in all intrinsic respects as T says it is. The Bedrockers may be sophisticated scientists and mathematicians, but they do not believe the existential claims of the mathematics they employ: they rather regard such claims as consequences of the best 'nominalistically adequate' theories available to them. The key claim about the example is that the Bedrockers are not unreasonable in declining to believe in mathematical objects. In a notional dispute between one of us and one of them, there is nothing that either can say that ought rationally to change the other's mind. If that is so, the case for abstract mathematical objects sketched above justifies a belief in such things only in the weak sense: it shows that such a belief is rationally permissible, but not that it is rationally required.

The Bedrocker's attitude towards mathematics is a form of fictionalism. I have not defended fictionalism about mathematical objects myself (except to say that it may be rationally permissible), but I have defended fictionalism in other areas.[5] In the metaphysics of modality, I have argued that insofar as it is useful for philosophical purposes to indulge in the picturesque idiom of possible worlds and individuals, we might understand this as a form of pretense (Rosen 1990, 1993, 1995). When we say that there are possible worlds in which Aristotle's geocentric physics i true, we might take ourselves to mean: According to the fiction of many worlds — the metaphysical theory of the modal realist — there are worlds of this specific sort. I still endorse this view when it comes to casual, unsystematic uses of possible worlds idiom. It is less clear to me that the fictionalist can make good sense of the serious analytic employment of the idiom — e.g., the identification of properties with sets of possible individuals — that figure centrally in Lewis's work. I haven't pursued this question, though it strikes me as worth pursuing.[6]

---

[5] In addition to the papers mentioned below, see Rosen and Dorr 2002 for a defense of fictionalism about composite entities.

[6] For criticism of the view, see especially the work of John Divers and Daniel Nolan. For an authoritative account of the state of the art, see Nolan 2008.

The debates over nominalism and over modal realism are debates about *realism* in one straightforward sense of the word. The antinominalist asserts that *there are abstract objects*, and in one sense of the word, this is enough to make him a *realist* about abstract objects. But many philosophers believe that even after we have agreed that numbers exist — or, to change the subject, even after we have agreed that it is morally wrong to kick your dog for fun — there is a further question of mathematical or moral *Realism* that remains unaddressed. In my view, philosophers have been so eager to take sides in these subtle 'second-order' debates over realism that they have failed to formulate a clear question to which 'realism' would be the answer. This inclines me to *quietism* on these issues: the view that once we have accepted the ordinary first-order claims in an area, and certain commonsensical claims about them — e.g., the claim that it would have been wrong to kick your dog even if we had been all raised to believe otherwise— then there is no further question about the *reality* of the underlying domain that needs an answer (Rosen 1994, 1998).[7]

What do you think is the proper role of metaphysics in relation to other areas of philosophy and other academic disciplines, including the natural sciences?

Locke was roughly half right in thinking that the main role for philosophy in general, and metaphysics in particular, is to serve as an "Under-Labourer" employed in "clearing Ground a little, and removing some of the Rubbish, that lies in the way to Knowledge" (Locke 1975: 10). He was certainly right that metaphysics should not pretend to place a priori constraints on the development of science. Hardly anything worth saying in metaphysics is a priori in *that* sense (which is not to say that the claims of metaphysics are all empirical). One of the most important tasks for metaphysics is to isolate the metaphysical content of the various candidate theories that emerge in the sciences — to say as clearly and explicitly as possible what the world would be like if that theory were true; or better, since there will often be no single correct answer to this question, to identify the various versions of the world that are consistent with the theory. This is the metaphysical side of the philosophy of science, and only a philosopher with a deep mastery of the relevant science (not *me*) is in a position

---

[7] I have had second thoughts about this. See Rosen, forthcoming. For a potent antidote to quietism, see Fine 2001.

to do this properly. Another useful task for metaphysics, especially in relation to the humanities and the social sciences, is to resist the bad metaphysics that tends to insinuate itself into these disciplines. The sophomoric antirealism that was once the official metaphysics of Comparative Literature departments is less virulent now than it was even 10 years ago. But anyone who spends his time in serious interdisciplinary discussion with colleagues in the humanities is familiar with the tendency of such discussions to degenerate into unsatisfying discussions of the objective reality of the external world or the possibility of objective knowledge. Apparently it is still important to fly the flag for a certain naïve realism according to which there are real things that exist independently of us in every important sense, about which we can know a great deal when all goes well.

This task is of more than academic importance when it comes to the metaphysics of ethics. In a famous exchange with Ronald Dworkin, Justice Antonin Scalia of the United States Supreme Court contrasts two ways of understanding the word "cruel" as it figures in the 8th Amendment to the United States Constitution, which prohibits "cruel and unusual punishment" (Scalia 1997). As Scalia understands it, the word "cruel" here can either be taken to refer to those forms of punishment deemed cruel by the authors and ratifiers of the Constitution in 1789, in which case it is preposterous to suppose that the 8th amendment prohibits capital punishment; or it may be taken to refer to whatever some crew of unelected judges *now* deems cruel, in which case the provision will lack democratic authority. Scalia never even considers the possibility that the 8th amendment might prohibit punishment that *is in fact cruel,* and that 18th century (or 20th century) views about the cruelty of judicial homicide might have been straightforwardly *mistaken.* Dworkin may not be the first person who comes to mind when one pictures the modern analytic metaphysician; but in his effort to get Scalia to see a real option that is simply invisible to him given the bad metaphysics he has somehow imbibed, Dworkin is fighting the good fight.

What do you consider to be the proper method for metaphysics?

If a "method" is meant to be something like a recipe for solving problems of the sort Descartes imagined in his *Discourse on the Method*, then *pace* Descartes, there is no method in metaphysics or anywhere else in philosophy. The closest we come is the vague quest for 'reflective equilibrium', in which we begin where we are, with our confident opinions drawn from science and mathematics and common sense, and then seek a systematic picture of reality that irons out the kinks in this hodgepodge of received ideas, reconciling tensions, deepening the account so that unanswered questions receive answers, and rendering the underlying picture as plain and explicit as it can be made. Just to take one example, hardly anyone denies that things have properties and stand in various relations to one another, and hence that there are properties and relations. But our presystematic thinking about properties and relations leaves a thousand fundamental questions open. Are properties located in things? Are they pure abstract objects on a par with numbers? Under what conditions does a predicate or an abstract noun express or denote a property? Can a particular and a property share a property, or are properties 'typed', etc. The first step (to revert the image of a recipe) is to bang out a theory that answers these open questions — or better, a collection of theories that answer these questions in different ways. The next step is to assess theories. But how? David Lewis invited us to think in terms of costs and benefits. This theory vindicates a large swath of ordinary discourse about properties, but at the cost of a profligate ontology; that theory brands much of what we ordinarily think literally false, but gets by with a more economical catalog of things, etc. But I have never had much confidence in this way of proceeding. It's obviously important to identify the consequences of the theories under consideration. But when it comes to attaching weights to these consequences — to identifying some as significant costs and others as compensating benefits — the whole business strikes me as soft and arbitrary. (Lewis takes it for granted that certain roughly *quantitative* principles govern theory choice in metaphysics: ontological parsimony; ideological economy, etc. If I believed *that* I might be less pessimistic; but in fact I think these forms of economy count for very little.) The truth is that every worked out theory in metaphysics has counterintuitive consequences: bits that clash with some other aspect of our evolving view. To accept any theory for serious purposes is to bite a bullet, and for the most part I have no idea how to have a rational discussion about which bullets are worth biting. This is the point at which we have no method worth the name.

I would find this horribly depressing if I thought the aim of metaphysics was to settle disputed questions at this basic level — to arrive a theory of these things that we can ultimately *believe;*

a theory that might ideally amount to knowledge. But in many parts of metaphysics, I think we can abandon this aim. In ontology generally, there is plenty of work to be done at the first stage, the stage at which various possibilities are elaborated. It would be excellent to know the truth about properties and relations — or about the nature of modality, or about the existence conditions for abstract objects, or about the true principles of composition. But it would also be excellent (and quite enough for me) to have a worked out menu of possible answers to these questions — answers that were internally coherent, and sufficiently coherent with what we think we know in other areas to be worth discussing. What we do not have, and what we may not need, is any method for choosing among the options that survive this filter.

What do you consider to be the most neglected topics in contemporary metaphysics, and what direction would you like metaphysics to take in the future?

The most important development in recent metaphysics is the renewed interest in fine-grained, 'hyperintensional' notions. The modal revival of the '60s and '70s made it possible to talk about essence and accident again by reinstating a notion of metaphysical necessity and then defining essence in terms of it. The essential properties of a thing, we were told, are the properties it could not have failed to have: the properties it has in any possible world, or in any world in which it exists. This is a coarse grained notion. It allows us to say, perhaps, that I am essentially an animal. But it forces us to say, in the same sense, that I am essentially an element of the set {GR, π, 25.6}. As Kit Fine (1994) has stressed, we seem to understand a more discriminating notion, according to which the essential features of a thing are the features that *make it the thing that it is*, or (to employ a somewhat different gloss), the features it possesses simply in virtue of *its* nature. Intuitively, you might know everything there is to know about my essential nature — about what makes me the thing that I am — without knowing the first thing about sets, or about pi, and so without knowing that I am an element of {GR, π, 25.6}. By contrast, it does lie the nature of this set that I am an element of it. Fine's idea is to take this notion as basic and to define metaphysical necessity in terms of it. A proposition p is a metaphysical necessity on this view just in case it lies in the nature of some thing or things that p should hold.

This fine-grained notion of an essential truth belongs to a family of metaphysical notions which also includes

real definition — For a thing to be the number 2 *just is* for it to be the item that is the number of Fs iff there are 2 Fs; for a thing to be *steam* just is for it to be constituted by a quantity of water molecules in the gaseous state;

metaphysical reduction — For it to be the case that p *just is* for it to be the case that q; p's being the case consists in q's being the case; e.g., the fact that the number of Fs = the number of Gs simply consists in (reduces to) the fact that the Fs and the Gs are in one-one correspondence;

and also, in a somewhat different key, a certain notion of

metaphysical grounding — The fact that p obtains *in virtue of* the fact that q; the fact that q *makes it the case that* p; e.g., this flower is red in virtue of being crimson.

It seems quite likely to me that all of these notions make good sense, that none of them can be defined in terms of the vocabulary of ordinary modal metaphysics, and that much is to be learned by trying to understand their relations to one another. In a recent paper I make a preliminary case for this, but there is much more to be said. Kit Fine has done an extraordinary thing in his papers on these topics — exploding the idea that the vocabulary of modal metaphysics with its notions of necessity and possibility and the various forms of supervenience that can be defined given the possible worlds machinery suffice to express the most important forms of grounding and dependence among things and facts. One important job for the next decade is to nail down the fundamental notions in this family, to develop explicit principles in which they figure, and then to put them to work in shedding light on other topics. I've tried to do a bit of this already (Rosen 2010, Rosen and Yablo forthcoming), but I think it is likely that these new resources will transform the subject by making it possible to raise new questions and to entertain new answers to old ones. Whether we will ever find ourselves with grounds for *endorsing* these new answers is of course another matter.

References

Benacerraf, P. "What Numbers Could Not Be", *Philosophical Review* 74 (1965), pp. 47-73

Benacerraf, P. "Mathematical Truth", *J. Phil.* 70 (1973) pp. 661-79

Burgess, J. "Why I am not a Nominalist", *Notre Dame J. Formal Logic* 24:1 (1983), pp. 93-105.

Burgess, J. and G. Rosen, A Subject with no Object: Strategies for Nominalist Interpretation of Mathematics. (Oxford University Press, 1997)

Danto, A. The Transfiguration of the Commonplace. (Harvard University Press, 1981).

Field, H. Science Without Numbers. (Princeton University Press, 1980)

Fine, K. "Essence and modality", *Phil. Perspectives* 8 (1994), pp, 1-18.

Fine, K. "The Question of Realism", *Phil. Imprint* 1:2 (2001), pp. 1-20.

Lewis, D. On the Plurality of Worlds. (B. Blackwell, 1986)

Locke, J. Essay Concerning Human Understanding.P. Nidditch, ed. (Oxford University Press, 1975).

Maddy, P. Naturalism in Mathematics. (Oxford University Press, 1997).

Nolan, D. "Modal fictionalism", *The Stanford Encyclopedia of Philosophy (Fall 2008 Edition)*, Edward N. Zalta (ed.), URL = <http://Plato.stanford.edu/archives/fall2008/entries/fictionalism-modal/>.

Putnam, H. Philosophy of Logic (1971), reprinted in Putnam, Mathematics, Matter and Method: Philosophical Papers, v. i. 2nd ed. (Cambridge University Press, 1979).

Rosen, G. "Modal fictionalism", Mind 99, pp. 328-54

Rosen, G. "A Problem for fictionalism about Possible Worlds" Analysis 53 (1993), pp. 71-81

Rosen, G. "What is Constructive Empiricism?", *Phil. Studies* 74:2 (1994), pp.143-78.

Rosen, G. "Objectivity and Modern Idealism: What is the Question" in M. Michael and J. O'Leary-Hawthorne, Eds. Philosophy in Mind. (Kluwer, 1994)

Rosen G. "Modal fictionalism Fixed" Analysis 55 (1995), 67-73.

Rosen G. "Critical Study of Blackburn's Essays in Quasi-Realism", Nous 32:3 (1998), pp. 386-405

Rosen, G. "Nominalism, Naturalism, Epistemic Relativism", *Phil. Perspectives* 15 (2001), pp, 69-91.

Rosen, G. "The Reality of Mathematical Objects", forthcoming in a volume edited by J. Polkinghorne.

Rosen, G. "Metaphysical Dependence: Grounding and reduction" in B. Hale and A. Hoffman, Eds. modality: Metaphysics, Logic and Epistemology, (Oxford University Press, 2010)

Rosen, G. and J.Burgess. "Nominalism Reconsidered", in S. Shapiro, ed., Oxford Handbook of Philosophy of Mathematics and Logic, (Oxford University Press, 2005).

Rosen, G. and C. Dorr. "Composition as a Fiction", in R. Gale, ed., Blackwell Guide to Metaphysics. (B. Blackwell, 2002)

Rosen, G. and S. Yablo. "Solving Caesar — with Metaphysics", forthcoming in a festschrift for Crispin Wright ed. Alexander Miller.

Scalia, A. A Matter of Interpretation. (Princeton University Press, 1997)

van Frassen, B. The Scientific Image. (Oxford University Press, 1980)

Wollheim, R. Art and Its Objects, 2nd ed. (Cambridge University Press, 1980)

Wolterstorff, N. Works and Worlds of Art. (Oxford University Press, 1980)

13
Jonathan Schaffer

Professor of Philosophy
Australian National University, Australia, and Arché, St. Andrews, UK

"We are what we pretend to be, so we must be careful about what we pretend to be."
(Kurt Vonnegut, *Mother Night*)

Why were you initially drawn to metaphysics (and what keeps you interested)?

I blame my mom. She promised herself to never say that I should do something just because she told me to do it, and so she always gave me reasons—and soon discovered, to her dismay, that I would argue back. I also blame my dad. His highest praise for a man was that he was a scholar and a gentleman, and so I have at least tried to be one of the two. My sister Talia deserves some blame as well. She was the studious intellectual older sister (now she is an English professor), and of course I had to compete with her!

When I consider why I was initially drawn to philosophy generally and metaphysics in particular, I find that I can construct a story of an intellectual journey. It would be the story of an unreflective child, who grew to become an argumentative teen, and has now become a somewhat mature adult with a penchant for metaphysical thought. It could even be a story—triumphant yet somehow inevitable—of how the deepest questions eventually seeped in to a shallow mind, allowing me the deepest contentment of the life *sub specie aeternitatis*. Yet I feel that, at least in my own case, such a story would not be the whole truth. It would leave out the minor personal details and accidents of circumstance that on some deeper level formed me. I think my life could easily have gone in any of many other directions had I encountered slightly different people at slightly different moments under slightly different conditions.

After all, my first choice was not to be a metaphysician. My first choice was to be a fireman. As I grew up my plans evolved, from fireman to astronaut, then to soccer player, computer programmer, lawyer, and poet. And then I entered college. I needed to fill out my course schedule, and I added philosophy because it met in the afternoon. (Aristotle says that philosophy begins in wonder—in my case, it might be said that philosophy begins in the afternoon.)

My first philosophy professor—Cyrus Banning, at Kenyon College—seemed to take his sole delight in confounding his students with a minimum of words. I remember an early lecture in which he pointed at the table and said: "This is a dog." We spent the rest of the class failing to move him from this position. Perhaps this was supposed to teach us about the conventionality of language. I was never quite sure. But in any case I was intrigued. We spent much of the rest of the year engaged in close readings of Plato's *Republic*, Descartes's *Meditations*, and Mill's *Utilitarianism*, and soon I was completely hooked.

In my second year of college I took a course—from Barbara Krasner—on post-Kantian continental philosophy. Our first assignment of the semester was to read a few sections of the preface to Hegel's *Phenomenology*. Reading so few pages seemed like a joke. But I spent many hours not understanding a thing. This must have occasioned in me the belief that the content was especially subtle and deep. For I became an enthusiastic Hegelian. I remember being especially moved by the brief summary of Hegel that Russell gave in his *The Problems of Philosophy*: "[E]verything short of the Whole is obviously fragmentary, and obviously incapable of existing without the complement supplied by the rest of the world." (Indeed, this is an idea that has remained with me, and which I have since returned to in my "The Internal Relatedness of All Things".)

As college went on I lost some of my enthusiasm for Hegel and developed an interested in logic, which I learned from Beth Cohen. She generously allowed me to pursue a couple of independent studies, including one on Boolos and Jeffrey's *Computability and Logic*. But I retained a strong interest in metaphysical questions. In my third year I took a metaphysics seminar—again from Cyrus Banning—and got engaged in questions of metaphysical realism, and especially in Putnam's arguments against realism from *Reason, Truth, and History*. I was also fascinated by Nagel's *The View from Nowhere*, which we read in an honors seminar taught by Ron McLaren. I tried to bring some of these ideas together in a paper on the connections between metaphysical realism and skepticism, which became my writing sample for graduate school.

At that point I was fortunate enough to be admitted to Rutgers for my graduate work. In my first two years at Rutgers, I took a couple of logic courses with Vann McGee, and also some courses in metaphysics and philosophy of science with Barry Loewer, Tim Maudlin, and Brian McLaughlin. These captivated me. I found my main interests tilting away from logic and more towards metaphysics. I became especially interested in David Lewis's thesis of Humean Supervenience, and the metaphysical basis for laws of nature and causation.

Perhaps the biggest event for me in graduate school was attending David Lewis's seminar on causation (at Princeton). He kindly allowed me not just to sit in, but also to give one of the seminar presentations. He was very supportive and encouraging of my presentation, suggesting I try to publish the material. Months passed while I tried to write something even close to being worthy. Then I learned that he had been giving talks in Australia discussing one of the issues I had raised in my presentation (trumping preemption), and was considering changing his own view on causation in response. This astonished me. Suddenly my foolish ideas were being taken seriously, and being taken seriously by no less than David Lewis. To this day I still cherish—as a source of pride and inspiration—the memory of a phone call from Laurie Paul in which I first learned of this.

Buoyed by this experience, I went on to write a dissertation on the metaphysics of causation, with Brian McLaughlin as the supervisor, Barry Loewer and Tim Maudlin as committee members, and David Lewis as outside reader. And so my career as a metaphysician—with interests in both causation and in monism—was well underway.

So I was initially drawn to metaphysics in part because—much to the dismay of my poor family—I grew up as an argumentative and competitive brat. And I was drawn in part because I met E. Robert Bunten—my high school debate coach—when I was an alienated and introverted fourteen year old, and he gave me the chance to excel at something. It was in part because Cyrus

Banning shook me of my sophistical confidence, because Barbara Krasner and Beth Cohen had the patience to put up with an arrogant, precocious, and lazy sophomore, because Barry Loewer, Tim Maudlin, and Brian McLaughlin made metaphysics seem vital, and because David Lewis taught me that I actually could contribute something. And I went with it because it was all very interesting, but because my friends thought it was cool, and I thought it might impress certain women (alas!), and the courses were never ever scheduled in the morning.

My answer to the question of what keeps me interested could also be a continuing story of an intellectual journey. It could even be a story—beautiful yet tragic—of how the deepest questions remained of abiding interest to me long after I had despaired of knowing the answers, and of how I came to accept the journey itself as its own reward, through a landscape I knew I could only barely begin to explore. But you probably already know how that story goes. So I will offer a more personal answer here as well, if only in the hope that it might be more entertaining.

These days I wake up fairly early in the morning, drink some coffee, and spend an hour or two answering emails. Then I'll play with a paper, and perhaps read something relevant to what I am writing, or just read something that someone has sent me for comments. At various points I might chat with my partner Susanna Schellenberg—also a philosopher—or chat with another colleague, or a student. And this is what I do with my day (not counting running, cooking, carousing, reading novels, and other necessities). And then one looks up ten years later and notices that from such days one has built a life. Mostly I have found it pleasant and engaging, and occasionally I have found it fascinating. But at any rate I have gone with it.

So what keeps me interested in metaphysics is that the emails, writing, and reading I engage in every day tend to concern metaphysics. Many of my friends and correspondents have become my friends and correspondents in part through shared interests. So in answering my emails and reading papers that get sent to me, I wind up reading a lot of metaphysics paper, and that keeps me interested in and connected to the field. When I write I often build on my earlier work, or draw on ideas that have come from conversations with others. And so metaphysical themes recur in my own work. All too often I am scrambling to finish an invited contribution not too long after the deadline, and these invitations tend to be in metaphysics. And finally many of my students have come to me to do work in metaphysics, and this too keeps me interested. In short, what mainly keeps me interested in metaphysics is a happy inertia. I would need to make a radical change in my daily life to escape metaphysics.

One thing that definitely keeps me going is the ongoing feeling of play. What I do seldom feels like *work*. Newton famously wrote that "to myself I seem to have been only like a boy playing on the sea-shore, and diverting myself in now and then finding a smoother pebble or a prettier shell than ordinary." While I would never compare myself with Newton, and am not sure I have even found a single pebble, I share the feeling of play. To myself I seem to be like a boy gaping dumbly at a handful of sand, hoping for a glimpse of the world.

What do you consider to be your most important contributions to metaphysics?

As to what I consider to be my most important contributions to metaphysics, I subscribe to the motto "the author is usually the last to know." Metaphysics to me is a continuing conversation, and a large part of what makes a contribution important to a conversation is the role it plays in shaping the discussion that follows. So—if I make any important contributions to metaphysics at all—this will be determined by other participants in the conversation, in due time.

That said, I can speculate. And I can play a role in encouraging others to pick up certain ideas found in my work (and to pay less attention to other ideas that I now consider confused). So—as much by way of encouragement as speculation—I would mention three sorts of ideas. First, in my early work on the metaphysics of causation I think I managed to describe several scenarios—including trumping preemption and overlappings, which are difficult and interesting scenarios that just might help shed some light on the nature of causation. I also think I managed to make a decent case for the causal status of absences (in my work on causation by disconnection), which raises a range of metaphysical puzzles. This led me to a positive account of causation (causes as probability-raisers of processes) that I now consider hopeless. But I think the problem cases may still be interesting, and I think they remain unresolved.

Second, in my subsequent work on knowledge and causation I have helped develop contrastive views (drawing *inter alia* on work by Fred Dretske on knowledge, and Chris Hitchcock on causation).

I suspect that the positive accounts, on which knowledge is a three place relation (s knows that p rather than q), and on which causation is a four place relation (c rather than $c*$ causes e rather than $e*$), may well be wrong. Certainly they are *prima facie* implausible. But I think that the arguments are interesting and point to a single sort of phenomenon that we might not as of yet have an adequate way to account for. So I would encourage others to consider the sorts of arguments that have led to the contrastive views, if only to consider how to accommodate these considerations in a better way.

Third and finally, in my most recent work I have tried to revive the classical monistic picture. This has involved drawing a distinction between the thesis that only one thing *exists* (which is the crazy thesis that most contemporary metaphysicians had saddled the classical monists with), and the thesis that only one thing is *fundamental*, and it is the whole (which is the natural interpretation of the idea that the whole is prior to its parts). I hope that this work will prove to be interesting, in three main respects. First, I hope it will be useful for historians of metaphysics, in providing an alternative (and arguably more charitable) way to read the texts. Second, I hope it will be useful in meta-metaphysics, in encouraging a move away from questions about what exists, towards questions about what is fundamental. Third and finally—whether the parts or the whole be judged to be fundamental—I hope it will stimulate discussion of the proper means to judge what is fundamental. So if nothing else, I hope my work on monism will help inspire us to articulate clear and plausible standards for being fundamental. For only then can we metaphysicians have any hope of articulating the fundamental structure of reality, in a reflective and defensible manner.

What do you think is the proper role of metaphysics in relation to other areas of philosophy and other academic disciplines, including the natural sciences?

This is an extremely hard question. I am doubtful that there should be one clearly right answer. Indeed, I do not think I even understand what metaphysics is as a unified discipline, or what other academic disciplines are. So—in classical philosophical style—I will answer by raising some doubts about the terms of the question.

Overall, when it comes to intellectual pursuits, it seems to me that there are lots of interesting questions we can ask, and some of these questions tend to cluster together in interesting ways. For instance, some of these questions might be about the same portion of reality, and some might be addressed by similar methods, and some might be generalizations of others. I believe in the reality of questions and in various respects of similarity between these questions.

But I do not believe that the space of questions comes naturally partitioned into *academic natural kinds*. Rather I consider disciplinary groupings to be fairly arbitrary ways of dividing questions, imposed by deans for administrative reasons, helpful insofar as those clumped together can usefully communicate, and harmful insofar as those pulled apart could have usefully communicated. So I consider myself a *moderate conventionalist* about academic reality. I do think there is a structure to academic reality given by questions and the respects of similarity between them, but I think the further structure of sharp hierarchical disciplinary divisions involves an overlay of convention.

As a moderate conventionalist about academic reality, I think that different traditional metaphysical questions may be similar to questions traditionally assigned to different disciplines in various respects. For instance, consider traditional metaphysical questions about the nature of time. This is an area where metaphysical questions and physical questions have a common subject matter, and where physicists seem to have achieved a lot of knowledge. So the metaphysician should draw on this knowledge. This is simply an instance of the following general rule: when trying to answer a question, draw on all relevant knowledge. And in many cases the sciences will have achieved some knowledge of the world that the metaphysician can and should draw on.

But I also think that there are some traditional metaphysical questions that have little to do with physics or the sciences, at least in any direct way. For instance, consider traditional metaphysical questions about the existence and nature of free will. There might be some very general physical claims that are relevant, such as whether or not the physics is deterministic. But as is well known, there are problems for the existence of free will given both determinism and indeterminism. So the metaphysician can perfectly well discuss the compatibility of free will with both determinism and its absence, without needing to draw on any physics at all. Instead she might draw on relevant knowledge about human psychology or about moral responsibility. This is also an instance of simply drawing on all relevant knowledge.

So overall my perspective is one that says, *ask a question, and draw on all relevant knowledge in order to try to find the answer*. I don't see any need to postulate a distinctive class of metaphysical questions. The field is unified as much by analogy and historical contingencies as by any unified subject matter or methodology. And I don't see any need to delimit a special area of relevant knowledge that metaphysicians should always dip into, or any need to postulate a distinctive sort of methodology for metaphysical inquiry.

What do you consider to be the proper method for metaphysics?

This too is an extremely hard question. When it comes to methodology I find it hard to go beyond vacuous injunctions (*work hard!*). If I had a substantive answer to this question that would immediately become my most important contribution to metaphysics, by far.

As mentioned in my answer to the previous question, I don't think that metaphysics constitutes an academic natural kind. Rather I think that there are many different sorts of traditional metaphysical questions, united as much by analogy and historical contingency as by subject matter or methodology. Accordingly I think that different metaphysical questions may call for different methods. I thus hold a *pluralist* view on metaphysical methodology.

But pluralism does not in any way answer the methodological question. Indeed it only postpones and complicates the answer. For now it seems that I owe a plurality of answers, corresponding to the various proper methods for the plurality of metaphysical questions. Moreover, given that disciplines united in part by analogy and historical contingency are somewhat open-ended in the sorts of questions they can potentially take in, no fixed list of methods can be enough. That said, I will focus on two sorts of central metaphysical questions where I happen to have some specific and perhaps distinctive views about methods. There will be no pretense of characterizing "the" proper method for metaphysics, or even all the proper methods.

So first, there is a cluster of metaphysical questions about what exists, which have been the focus of much post-Quinean metaphysics. For instance, there is the question of whether numbers exist. With respect to this cluster of existence questions, my general recommendation is to be *permissive*. That is, I think that in many of these cases there are truisms that entail the existence of the entities in question. For instance, it is a truism that there are prime numbers. And this directly entails that there are numbers.

In general there seem to me to be two main reasons why people have opted for less permissive views of what there is. One is that people have felt methodologically compelled not to multiply entities without necessity (Occam), or have professed a taste for desert landscapes (Quine). But I think this arises from a failure to distinguish fundamental entities from derivative entities. Fundamental entities should indeed not be multiplied without necessity. But derivative entities come for free given their fundamental grounds. An analogy with conceptual economy might be useful here. We measure the conceptual economy of a theory not by the total number of concepts it employs, but by the total number of *primitive* concepts it employs. A theory with a single primitive concept and a thousand defined concepts is not uneconomical for having a thousand-and-one concepts. Rather such a theory is highly economical for having a single primitive concept, and moreover is seriously powerful for being able to define a thousand further concepts on this basis. This is a highly virtuous theory, methodologically speaking. Likewise a theory with a single fundamental entity and a thousand derivative entities is not uneconomical for having a thousand-and-one entities. Rather such a theory is highly economical for having a single fundamental entity, and moreover is seriously powerful for being able to derive a thousand further entities on these grounds.

A second reason why people have opted for less permissive views about what exists is that they have felt that there are causal and/or epistemic principles that reveal that the disputed entities would have to be causally inert and/or epistemically inaccessible. I must say I have never found these principles overly compelling (they are certainly less compelling than existence-entailing truisms like "there are prime numbers"). But at any rate I think that distinguishing between fundamental and derivative entities tends to solve the problem. For as long as the fundamental entities are causally ert and epistemically accessible, then there can be no objection along causal or epistemic lines to the grounds. And given that derivative entities come for free given their fundamental grounds, there is no problem in recognizing the derivative entities either.

Alongside the cluster of metaphysical questions about what exists (towards which I have just recommended a permissive stance), there is a cluster of metaphysical questions about what is fundamental, which I would trace back to Aristotle's conception of metaphysics a concerning the substances. For instance, there is the question of whether numbers (given that they exist) are fundamental abstract entities, grounded in the concrete realm, or perhaps dependent on our minds. I regard these fundamentality questions as the most important and interesting questions in metaphysics. Indeed, my permissive stance on questions about what exists was defended in part by taking an *impermissive* (or *sparse*) stance on questions about what is fundamental.

One of the crucial methodological questions that then arises is the question of *diagnostics for fundamentality*. In other words, by what means do we determine whether a given entity is a fundamental entity? I would suggest three sorts of diagnostics for certain entities being fundamental. (Strictly speaking these are diagnostics for whether a plurality of entities comprises the fundamental entities. Whether a given entity is fundamental then just reduces to the question of whether it is part of the elite plurality.)

As a first diagnostic for fundamentality, I take it that the fundamental entities should be *minimally complete* in characterizing reality without redundancy. A plurality of entities is *complete* for a given world w if and only if that plurality serves as a supervenience base for w (there can be no difference in w without a difference in that plurality). This is the idea of a full characterization of reality. A plurality of entities is then *minimally* complete if and only if it is complete, but it has no complete sub-plurality. This is the idea that the characterization is non-redundant. One can't delete any of the fundamental entities and still retain a full characterization of reality.

As a second diagnostic for fundamentality, I take it that the fundamental entities should be *empirically specified*, in that one should expect that they will turn up in fundamental science (if nature is kind). This is a point where metaphysical questions about what is fundamental should be informed by physics.

As a third diagnostic for fundamentality, I take it that the fundamental entities should be *metaphysically general*, in that they should be the sort of entities that can characterize any metaphysically possible scenario. In other words, I take it that there is a sphere of possibilities—the metaphysical possibilities—which hold fixed what sort of entities are fundamental, and hold fixed how derivative entities are grounded in the fundamental.

I should clarify that I have not tried to argue for these three diagnostics, and I have not tried to claim that there are no further diagnostics. I have only tried to list three diagnostics that strike me as plausible. So this is merely a tentative starting point on a methodology for answering one sort of metaphysical question.

What do you consider to be the most neglected topics in contemporary metaphysics, and what direction would you like metaphysics to take in the future?

To my mind the most neglected topics in contemporary metaphysics—and the topics I would most hope to see addressed by future changes in the direction of metaphysics—cluster around the notion of fundamentality and allied notions such as ontological dependence. Metaphysicians often speak of "the fundamental structure of reality" in unreflective ways. Likewise metaphysicians often speak of "ontological dependence" but characterize it merely in terms of modal notions like supervenience.

So I hope to see further discussion of the notions of fundamentality and dependence and their ilk. My current view is that dependence is best taken as a primitive (with fundamentality characterized in terms of lack of dependence), but there are many other possible views. I hope to see the range of options get more fully explored. In this way the conceptual framework for thinking about issues of fundamentality would be clarified.

And I hope to see further discussion of the underlying question of what is fundamental. This question might be usefully subdivided into two questions. The first subquestion would concern the ontological category(s) of the fundamental entities. For instance, should one think of things as fundamental, and derive properties via how things resemble? Or should one think of properties as fundamental, and derive things from how properties bundle? The second subquestion would concern the census of fundamental entities within the fundamental category(s). For instance, if one holds that things are fundamental, there is still room to debate *which things* are fundamental. For instance, should one think of the ultimate parts as fundamental, and derive wholes from their parts? Or should one think of the one ultimate whole as fundamental, and derives parts from the One?

A second and related cluster of neglected topics—which I would also hope to see addressed by future changes in the direction of metaphysics—center around the idea of ontological categories. It is not obvious what categories are, how many of them there are, what structure they have, and what connections they bear to each other. Metaphysicians often speak of "objects" and "properties" and other categories of entity in unreflective ways. I hope that future work in metaphysics will help clarify this core issue.

14
Peter Simons

Professor of Philosophy
Trinity College Dublin, Ireland

Why were you initially drawn to metaphysics (and what keeps you interested)?

Metaphysics crept up on me. Initially I was interested in the philosophy of logic and language, phenomenology and philosophy of mind, philosophy of science, and just a bit in ontology. (Never epistemology: tedious debates about sense-data and scepticism immunized me against that.) It slowly dawned on me that the philosophers from whose work I derived most stimulation were all interested in objects for themselves. They were Aristotle, Ockham, Leibniz, Brentano, Meinong, early Husserl, early Wittgenstein, Quine, Strawson. Two important events stand out in my memory as pushing me decisively towards metaphysics. The first was when Barry Smith, my fellow-student at Manchester, discovered the Polish realist phenomenologist Roman Ingarden. His work showed you didn't have to be a transcendental idealist to be a phenomenologist. Ingarden defended the primacy of ontology against Husserl, who thought you could bracket off ontological questions and examine phenomenological evidence first. That always struck me as somehow self-defeating, but Ingarden's staunch realism gave us courage to be realists while not rejecting descriptive phenomenology. Ingarden was actually very traditional and Aristotelian, but then in important respects so was the early, pre-transcendental Husserl. The other event was hearing a talk on nominalism given by David Armstrong. Armstrong rejected arguments from meaning for the existence of universals, and preferred to grapple with the realism/nominalism issue directly. To hear that done was very liberating. Even Quine, whom I heard around the same time and whom I admired in many ways, was too wrapped up in language for me to be wholly comfortable with his indirect, arm's-length approach to ontology. In the end I thought his views tended back to a modified version of the Viennese phenomenalism that Armstrong and other Australians had worked hard to overcome in the 1950s.

It's much easier to say what keeps me interested. Metaphysics is the most important and for me the most enjoyable part of philosophy. In any philosophical debate I always ask myself what ontology we should deploy to give an adequate account of the phenomena in question. Actually this is not so far removed from Quine's concern about ontological commitment, but freed from its more idiosyncratic concern with first-order quantification. The more general question (which also goes back to Aristotle) is: What has to exist for certain things to be true and others false? Quine's ontological commitment is a particular take on that question. A related question is: Given one's general metaphysical position, which entities suffice to make certain things true (and others false)? One is a matter of ontological commitment, the other of truthmaking: they are two sides of the same issue.

What do you consider to be your most important contributions to metaphysics?

I am not a radical innovator: nothing of what I've done in metaphysics is completely new. Metaphysics has been around for so long that it's hard to invent anything at all new, but one can move discussion on by stressing topics and concepts that have been unjustly neglected or downplayed or have been out of fashion. My most important single contribution to metaphysics has been in drawing attention to the importance of mereology (part–whole theory) as a central conceptual area and toolbox of metaphysics. When I first looked at mereology in 1972 there was very little mention of it in philosophy at all. It was widely assumed you did metaphysics by doing semantics of this or that logical language, mainly predicate calculus with set theory. I preferred to try and deal with the ontology of things directly because it struck me the approach via language was much too indirect and uncertain. In mereology I was intrigued by the differences between Husserl's essentialist approach and the different extensional approaches of Lesniewski and Whitehead, and wanted to pull the scattered discussion together. In doing so I found that earlier formal mereology had been motivated not by purely ontological concerns but by agendas in the philosophy of mathematics. I found that mereological concerns pervaded many ontological disputes such as the question whether ordinary continuants can persist though change in the way Aristotle thought, or whether they have temporal parts, like processes. Having spent fifteen years working on mereology and publishing the results I assumed I would be able to leave it behind, but I have been forced to come back to it from time to time. While I consider my book *Parts* still basically right on most things mereological, I now think the ontology explored there is relatively superficial and descriptive rather than fundamental and revisionary.

Other areas in which I have made contributions include the use of tropes in the theory of truthmaking. Again that was something relatively underexplored at the time we (Kevin Mulligan, Barry Smith and myself) wrote our joint essay "Truth-Makers" in 1984. Nowadays both tropes and truthmakers are part of many a modern metaphysician's stock in trade. I later exploited some ideas of Husserl to give a two-layered trope bundle theory of substantial individuals (1994). I have also come up with a new and idiosyncratic abstractionist position in the endurantism/perdurantism debate. I have tackled the ontology of pluralities and their role in giving a decent account of the semantics and ontology of number. I strongly deplore the excessive encroachment of set theory into ontology. Set theory is a very late mathematical invention by Cantor and it is back to front to try and use it as a framework for ontology. Rather we need a good ontological account of sets, which in my view are (like all abstract entities) not genuine existents, but rather cognitive projections, driven by a range of pragmatically useful cognitive operations such as singularization, abstraction, proposition, complexification and others. I am currently working on the metaphysics of quantities (things that can be measured). At any one time I am always looking at a variety of metaphysical issues, trying to nudge things forward in different places.

What do you think is the proper role of metaphysics in relation to other areas of philosophy and other academic disciplines, including the natural sciences?

Metaphysics is the queen of all disciplines. It is, and has been since first so identified by Aristotle, the science of everything, at the most general level. Physicists talk about a "theory of everything" but that is a misnomer: they are after a unified theory integrating all the basic physical forces and interactions. They do not aspire to say anything about life, love, music, history, art, politics, medicine, sport. Nor of course does metaphysics try to deal with *everything* about everything: it is not about the nitty-gritty details, but about the general principles and basic categories. It *covers* everything—and would still do even if physicalism were false and there were abstract entities, immaterial minds and deities (though in fact I think physicalism is right and none of those things does exist). That metaphysics covers absolutely everything is as true now as it was when Aristotle first realised it. The general question of what there is, what exists, is a primary one in every area of life, in every discipline, and in every part of philosophy. Initially like many others I was guided by Quine's criterion of ontological commitment, but then rejected it, firstly because I do not agree with Quine's interpretation of the quantifiers, preferring that of Arthur Prior, and secondly because the more important role of individuals and other entities in contributing to truth is not in being there to be quantified over, but in making truths true. Any entity can make something true, if only a truth to the effect that it exists. In any case, the truthmaking role is incidental to entities: an entity about which no one ever formulates a statement whose truth it secures never functions as a truthmaker, but it is just as good an entity as one which does. Obviously in saying this I cannot accept that the truthbearers are abstract propositions, since that would run counter to physicalism.

One of the problems about being a philosopher is that you cannot shove the hard unanswered questions off onto someone else. Other sciences can leave a hard question aside, saying "That's a problem for philosophers, not for us." The buck stops with us. Within the philosophy family though, ultimately everything comes back to metaphysics. No matter how good your account of mind, or language, or knowledge, it unfolds within a set of assumptions about what entities are at your disposal to make this account work. Throughout much of the twentieth century, even where it was admitted that metaphysics is meaningful and legitimate, it was assumed that metaphysics could only be pursued through the linguistic turn, by examining issues of language and meaning. I have always thought the boot was on the other foot. Give me your ontology, and I will see whether it can serve to frame a decent theory of meaning and truth. It is gratifying to see that what Gustav Bergmann called the ontological turn is steadily gaining ground in philosophy generally. In this regard, it's back to Aristotle.

How metaphysics should stand to the other sciences is a question requiring a delicate answer. The positive sciences, formal and natural, inspire the envy of philosophers for their global progress. It bodes ill for a metaphysics that flies too obviously in the face of established scientific opinion. For example a metaphysician who clings to essentialism about biological kinds is refuted by the evidence in favour of evolution; a dualist who rejects the neurophysiological evidence for the physical basis of mind is living in the past. But all the sciences raise issues which land them in metaphysical territory. Are viruses alive? Can spacetime exist independently of its occupants? Are fundamental particles endurants? Can historians ignore counterfactual scenarios? Do social wholes have emergent properties? What are functions in artefacts? Are mathematical objects discovered? In all these cases metaphysics can provide or at least adjudicate among alternative answers, which requires metaphysics to be more than the most general parts of the sciences. Similarly with common sense. Not everything the bloke in the pub believes is true, but enough of it is to provide a heavy constraint on metaphysical theorizing. Parmenidean monism, Leibnizian panpsychism, solipsism, or the denial of mereological composites may not be logically false metaphysical doctrines, but they are presumptively false because in contradiction to massively entrenched opinions with tentacles throughout our system of knowledge.

Metaphysics can, should and must be applied to other disciplines. Pure metaphysics is necessary and can be exciting, but it risks remaining just a glass-bead game if metaphysicians don't get out and see how their work relates to other disciplines and domains. It simply follows from the total coverage of metaphysics that there has to be a connection to all the special sciences. That conviction stems in good part from consulting work I did for many years for a software firm in California: we applied ontology not just within software design but also to manufacturing engineering and enterprise design, and I have since made excursions into the ontology of physical geography, music, and the thorny question of the emergence of mental intentionality. I take the injunction to apply metaphysics seriously: for example I talk to geographers, business managers and engineers when I get the opportunity, and have occasionally published joint papers with non-philosophers. Most of my fellow-philosophers tend to treat my extra-mural excursions with amusement at best and contempt at worst, but I think they are the ones who are wrong to ignore the outside world. In any case I always get a fair reception from people in other disciplines.

Philosophy does not fit happily into the standard classifications of the sciences. It is obviously not a natural science like physics or a formal science like mathematics. For reasons going back to the curricula of medieval Europe it is traditionally grouped with the arts and humanities. Sometimes in universities, for local administrative and organisational reasons, it is put with classics or theology or politics or social science, or even gets pushed together with unlikely subjects like journalism. In fact it belongs properly with none of these: by virtue of its special role it is genuinely *sui generis*. So Oxford and Cambridge are taxonomically correct as well as organisationally fortunate to have *faculties* of philosophy.

What do you consider to be the proper method for metaphysics?

I've thought a lot about this because I disagreed with logico-linguistic methods. Firstly, I agree with Franz Brentano that theoretical philosophy should adhere to the same general kind of method as natural science, which is abductive, or inference to the best explanation. To take account of the special nature of metaphysics however I think that within this remit metaphysicians should adopt a three-stage method. You can call the stages Gather, Sift, and Sort. The first phase consists in gathering or listing (putative) entities, as varied as possible, from anywhere: everyday experience, the sciences, philosophy, fiction. This gives you a wide range of data with which to work. The sifting stage consists in what metaphysicians always naturally do anyway, which is consider which of these entities exist and which do not, and of those that exist, whether any are more fundamental than others. Obviously this gathering and sifting activity cannot take place in a vacuum, since disputes about what there is and what is fundamental are going on all the time in metaphysics. Also it would be wrong to suppose the sifting stage is simply a matter of keeping some entities and rejecting others as they come to attention. Any metaphysician has to be prepared to stick his or her neck out and tender some broad speculative hypotheses. My own broad speculative hypothesis is a Naturalism that considers all objects are spatiotemporal with causal powers, and so rejects abstract entities, non-spatial minds, and supernatural entities like God. I am also strongly inclined to nominalism, although some assays of universals allow them spatiotemporality and causal powers.

The final Sort stage, towards which all metaphysics should strive, though rather little gets that far, is *systematization*, in which things are sorted into a system of fundamental categories and their interrelationships are made clear. Analytic philosophy in the twentieth century has tended to be un- or anti-systematic, partly in order to concentrate on detail, and partly perhaps for fear of relapsing into the kind of loosely grounded speculation of the German idealists. But metaphysics cannot remain forever unsystematic, so it is as well to acknowledge the need for system provided it is not pursued at the expense of good philosophizing at the previous stage. Of course in real life the three stages are not neatly separated in this way, but the principle of their separation is worth bearing in mind.

You can find a beautifully clear statement of the primary goal for philosophy which agrees in fundamentals with mine in a very unexpected place, namely at the beginning of G. E. Moore's (unattractively titled) *Some Main Problems of Philosophy*. Moore writes, "it seems to me that the most interesting and important thing which philosophers have tried to do is this; namely: To give a general description of the *whole* of the Universe, mentioning all the most important kinds of things which we *know* to be in it, considering how far it is likely that there are in it important kinds of things which we do not absolutely *know* to be in it, and also considering the most important ways in which these various kinds of things are related to one another." (p. 1) The goal Moore highlights in these 1910-11 lectures fits Aristotle, Aquinas and Christian Wolff much better than the caricatured myopic method of analysis usually associated with his philosophy. Moore does not even reject systematization, despite his familiarity with the mischief it had caused in Hegel, because Hegel's *aim* was legitimate even if his execution was faulty. Moore was not alone. Samuel Alexander wrote in S*pace, time and Deity*, "Philosophy, by which I mean metaphysics, differs from the special sciences, not so much in its method as in the nature of the subjects with which it deals. [...] What is the relation of these different orders of existence to one another? [...] What is the primary form of being, and how are different orders of being born of it? [...] Metaphysics is [...] an attempt to describe the ultimate nature of existence if it has any, and these pervasive characters of things, or categories." (pp. 1–2)

What do you consider to be the most neglected topics in contemporary metaphysics, and what direction would you like metaphysics to take in the future?

Arising from the answer to the previous question I think that modern metaphysicians have badly neglected classification in general and categories in particular. For most of the history of metaphysics, metaphysicians have attempted to establish and defend a system of categories: think only of Aristotle and Kant. But modern metaphysics has ignored categories because the assumption has been that these can be read off semantics (consider the vanilla fourfold classification of entities into things, properties, relation and states of affairs which uncannily resembles the division of expressions into names, one- and many-place predicates, and sentences). Much of twentieth century metaphysics was either done in the shadow of mathematics, and so unquestioningly assumed classification could easily be dealt with as applied set theory, or eschewed theorizing about classification altogether on the assumption that natural language provided its own classifications. But neither mathematics nor linguistics nor the dictionary can do our work for us. The briefest of acquaintance with the deep and fraught issues of biological taxonomy and systematics should dispel any idea that classification can be left to take care of itself. The last metaphysicians to take categories seriously in the twentieth century were my heroes Alexander and Whitehead. In 1929 Whitehead wrote, "Philosophy will not regain its proper status until the gradual elaboration of categor[i]al schemes, definitely stated at each stage of progress, is recognized as its proper objective. [...] Metaphysical categories are not dogmatic statements of the obvious; they are tentative formulations of the ultimate generalities." (p. 8) That is even more apt now than it was then, since despite the progress of philosophy, the crucial role of categories as an indispensable framework for system has been neglected these eighty years.

The other area where I think metaphysicians need to change is in becoming more willing to apply metaphysics to specific domains and not simply engage in "pure" metaphysical theory. Not only does this give metaphysicians areas in which they can test their theories, it also helps in the entity-gathering, and last but not least, can help to convince the outside world that metaphysics is not esoteric and irrelevant but the most widely relevant of all disciplines. Certain areas of application are familiar to philosophers: mathematical objects, the abstracta assumed in logic and semantics, the increasingly strange entities posited by physics, the species and genes of biology, societal collectives, and humans with all their idiosyncrasies. But the net can be cast much more widely, to include engineered artefacts, geographical features, the ontology of the arts and sport, medicine, business and industry, history and politics. Nothing is foreign to metaphysics: all objects are in its purview. People across the academic world pay lip-service to interdisciplinarity, but tend to remain within their narrow disciplinary boundaries, out of disinterest or fear of embarrassing themselves in a world of specialists. The problem with that kind of false modesty is that it leaves the borders of disciplines unguarded, to be crossed by intellectual brigands. It's surely better for specialists to tentatively reach out to their neighbours despite the potential for misunderstanding than for charlatans to pre-empt their efforts. I am a great believer in the potential for philosophy in general and metaphysics in particular to facilitate informed and relatively jargon-free communication across specialist divides. All it takes is goodwill on all sides.

Let me illustrate how metaphysics can interact with special disciplines with an example that happens to be quite dear to me: music. What ontology do we need to suppose in order to give an adequate "assay" of music? This is difficult because it requires us to furnish adequate frameworks encompassing sound both as a physical phenomenon and as a perceptual phenomenon, as well as the aspects of music which consist in our taking some combinations of tones as consonant and others as dissonant. From a naturalistic and nominalistic point of view we have to start with the concrete production and reception of musical tones, their sequences and combinations. In all this the tonal qualities and relationships among sound play a crucial part, and indeed the formal ontological relationships of part-whole, sequence, and the quantitative relationships of higher and lower, louder and softer, and many more all play together in a highly complex way. This calls out for a rich ontology of physical and phenomenal qualities, quantities and relations congenial to a nominalist, which means taking dependent tropes and their compounds very seriously. From this nominalistic point of view and in the light of empirical knowledge about varying versions, editions and performances of musical pieces, we can safely predict that there will be radical vagueness and uncertainty surrounding just that concept which holds so many ontologists of music paralysed in its glare like rabbits in car headlights: the Romantic idea of a work of music. Platonists and other realists about works struggle to explain the variations: nominalists have no problem. Historically, incidentally, music and trope theory are connected: one of the earliest modern proponents of tropes in ontology was the psychologist-philosopher Carl Stumpf. He wrote a massive two-volume work *Tonpsychologie* in which he investigated the psychology underlying the perception of music. Stumpf's

Verschmelzung (fusion) theory of consonance is now discredited, but he was asking the right questions.

This observation prompts the last complaint I have about modern analytic metaphysics, which is that too much of it is conducted in the scientific spirit of "latest is best", as if there had not been two and a half millennia of the cleverest people thinking about similar problems, from Thales to David Lewis. Too many metaphysicians start with very recent work and rush on to the next iteration. Metaphysicians should be more humble about the present, more knowledgeable about the past, and less prone to fashion. Fashion in philosophy is wholly insidious: it not only encourages a butterfly approach to hard problems, but lets the good fall into desuetude along with the bad. While history is no substitute for theory, in a subject as difficult as metaphysics, it pays to be aware of the spread of alternatives. One of my favourite ways to approach a topic is to bounce my own considerations off the well-framed views of an historical figure, even if only a relatively recent one such as Meinong, Ingarden, Whitehead or Wittgenstein. The works of the great philosophers of the past are there to help us, because philosophy rarely refutes a view without residue. But help can also come from the history of other disciplines: the French botanist Michel Adanson (18th C) applied family resemblance concepts to classification a century and a half before Wittgenstein, while the English mathematician William Kingdon Clifford (19th C) formulated an algebra of space which is only now gaining the recognition it deserves in explicating spatial concepts. We are too puny to afford pride in metaphysics, so should accept help wherever we can get it.

15

Barry Smith

Julian Park Professor of Philosophy
University at Buffalo, USA

Why were you initially drawn to metaphysics (and what keeps you interested)?

My first encounter with metaphysics was triggered by one of my grammar school teachers in Bolton, England, who lent me his copies of Wittgenstein's *Tractatus* and Russell's *Introduction to Mathematical Philosophy* after I had expressed an interest in applying to read for the then newly established joint degree in Mathematics and Philosophy in Oxford. I did not, at that stage, have more than a foggy idea about what studying philosophy might involve, but I was immediately taken by the *Tractatus*, and by what I would later formulate as the goal of finding ways to represent reality in formal, structured ways analogous to those of mathematics. I have remained faithful to this goal ever since, and it provides a unifying thread along a meandering journey from Wittgenstein and Russell, through Frege and Dummett to Ingarden, Husserl and Brentano, and from there to a new terrain of applications of metaphysical ideas in areas outside philosophy.

It was the Polish philosopher Roman Ingarden whose work first made clear to me what 'metaphysics' might mean. I encountered Ingarden by accident after chancing upon a copy of his *time and Modes of Being* on the Bodleian library shelves. This short book, long since out of print, is a translation of portions of Ingarden's four-volume defense of metaphysical realism entitled *The Problem of the existence of the World*. The latter is, I believe, one of the few great works of metaphysics to be published in the twentieth century. However – not least due to the fact that it was published originally in Polish and then, in extended form, in German, and to the fact that it is still available in English only through the fragments compiled in *time and Modes of Being* – it is a work which, outside Poland, has been almost entirely neglected.

Ingarden enjoyed for a time a certain following in the English-speaking world for his *The Literary Work of Art*, a work which was read primarily for theoretical contributions of a sort once of interest to students of literature. But Ingarden's own reasons for writing this book were strictly philosophical. Its subtitle is: *An Investigation on the Borderlines of ontology, Logic and Theory of Literature*, and its goal was to provide a supplement to the defense of metaphysical realism advanced in *The Problem of the existence of the World*. Roughly, the latter provides an account of what the real world would have to be like if different forms of realism and idealism were to be true. According to one important sub-family of idealisms the real world would be a configuration of intentional objects, processes and states of affairs of the sort that are represented in a work of literature. In *The Literary Work of Art* Ingarden provides a description of a world of this sort, demonstrating how different such a world would be from the world we know through scientific investigation.

I was immersed in Oxford overwhelmingly in logic and in the philosophy of mathematics (most memorably in lecture courses given in the Mathematics Institute by Michael Dummett on Frege, on axiomatic set theory, and on the intuitionistic differential calculus). The still predominantly linguistically oriented Oxford analytical philosophy of the day I found much less exciting. Against this background, Ingarden's writings provided me with the first glimpse of a tradition of philosophizing that was both friendly to realism and marked by a philosophical rigor at least comparable to that of mathematics. It was also refreshingly free of any overarching concern with niceties of language. I moved in stages from Ingarden to his teacher Husserl and from Husserl to his teacher Brentano. Along the way I learned to appreciate the work of other realist followers of Husserl such as Adolf Reinach (inventor, in 1913, of a remarkably sophisticated version of speech act theory) and to distinguish these realists phenomenologists from Heidegger and other progressively more zany 'Continental' thinkers in the broadly phenomenological tradition initiated by Husserl.

I take metaphysical realism, or any metaphysical realism worth believing in, to be consistent with both scientific and common-sense realism. Hence my interest in the work of Roland Omnès and of other proponents of the 'consistent histories' school in quantum mechanics, for whom the 'quasi-Newtonian' physics governing common sense reality is (after taking account of a negligibly small probability of error) logically inferable from the equations of quantum mechanics. Hence, too, my interest in the so-called 'ecological psychology' of J. J. Gibson and Roger Barker – an approach to empirical psychology based on the direct realist view that we are engaged, in our perceptions and actions, not with sense data or other figments of idealist philosophers' imaginations, but rather with concrete objects in the world of everyday reality.

Against this background, and seeking a formal means to translate Gibsonian ideas into a form which would allow them to be used as the basis of a more adequate semantics for natural language, I discovered the work of the former philosopher Patrick Hayes, and specifically his two papers entitled "Naïve Physics Manifesto" and "ontology for Liquids" published in a volume on *Formal Theories of the Common-Sense World* which appeared in 1985.

These papers opened up for me what artificial intelligence researchers were then beginning to refer to as 'formal ontology' – inadvertently employing a term coined by Husserl in his *Logical Investigations*. In 1993 I was invited by Nicola Guarino, one of the leaders in this new field, to work with his formal ontology group in Padua, Italy. Formal ontology in the sense of Hayes and Guarino is a subdiscipline of computer science in which metaphysical ideas and the technology of first-order logic are applied by software engineers, for example in order to provide a basis for programming robots with the rudiments of common-sense. Collaborating with practitioners of this new discipline provided a valuable boost to my interest in ontology, since it gave first indications that I might enjoy a practical utility.

What do you consider to be your most important contributions to metaphysics?

2.1 "Truth-Makers"

My work on Brentano, Husserl, Ingarden and their followers led to a more general interest in the philosophy of Central Europe at the turn of the last century, and I collaborated closely in various endeavors relating to the Austrian and Polish schools of philosophy with Kevin Mulligan and Peter Simons. The three of us had already founded the Seminar for Austro-German Philosophy in 1977 upon completing our doctoral studies in Manchester. Kevin, here, played the signal role of convincing Peter and myself of the importance of Husserl's 3rd Logical Investigation, "On the Theory of Wholes and Parts", and of Husserl's application of the term 'formal ontology' to designate a formal discipline analogous to, though in essential ways different from, logic. Peter, in turn, showed us how to meld Husserlian formal ontology with the formal approach to the theory of parts and wholes (or mereology) he had learned from Czesław Lejewski (then Professor of Philosophy in Manchester, and a student of the great Polish logician-ontologist Stanisław Leśniewski).

In 1980 the three of us began to apply Husserl-inspired ideas on formal ontology to the development of a correspondence theory of truth broadly in the spirit of Russell and the *Tractatus*. This led in 1984 to our paper "Truth-Makers," which did much to spark the renaissance of interest in truthmaker-based approaches to the theory of truth which continues to this day. It also led to an alliance with Australian realists such as David Armstrong, also interested in truthmaking, and in the potential for a theory of truthmaking to provide new arguments for a realist theory of universals.

"Truth-Makers" proposes an account of truth which supplements the work of Tarski by asserting, for certain kinds of logically simple true empirical sentences, the existence of a real relation which obtains between the relevant truthbearer and some truthmaking portion of reality.

	Not in a Subject *Substantial*	In a Subject *Accidental*
Said of a Subject *Universal, General*	*Second Substances* man, ox	*Non-substantial universals* knowledge, running
Not said of a Subject *Particular, Individual*	*First Substances* this man, this ox	*Individual Accidents* this knowledge, this run

Figure 1: The Aristotelian Ontological Square

At the heart of the doctrine is Aristotle's so-called 'ontological square' (Figure 1), and more specifically the idea of what Aristotelians call 'individual accidents'. The "Truth-Makers" paper defends the view that such individual accidents are the principal truthmaking ingredients of reality: they are that, in reality, to which the verbs of simple empirical sentences correspond. Our approach to truthmaking thus has a certain connection to Davidson's theory of events. Unlike Davidson, however, we recognized the need to quantify not only over those individual accidents which correspond to event verbs such a 'runs' or 'swims' or 'eats', but also over those which correspond to state verbs such as 'knows' or 'owns' or 'loves'.

2.2 "Against Fantology"
Individual accidents in this broad sense were, we argued, neglected by analytic philosophy because they did not fit well with the Fregean function-argument approach to logical grammar. I attempted much later, in my "Against Fantology" (delivered at the Wittgenstein Conference in Kirchberg in 2005), to use this idea as the basis for a new view of the history of analytical metaphysics in terms of the pernicious influence of the doctrine according to which, in Russell's terms, "all form is logical form". According to this view, Frege-inspired metaphysicians from Russell and the early Wittgenstein to David Armstrong have seen the key to the ontological structure of reality as being captured syntactically in the 'Fa' (or, in more sophisticated versions, in the 'Rab') of first-order logic. Because predicate logic has maximally two syntactically different kinds of basic referring expressions—'F', 'G', 'R', etc. on the one hand, and 'a', 'b', 'c', etc. on the other—the fantologist sees himself as being allowed to infer that reality itself must consist of maximally two correspondingly different kinds of entity: the general (properties, concepts, sets) and the particular (individual things or objects). This leaves no room in the fantological ontology for individual accidents (tropes, moments, particularized qualities) such as pains or debts. Such fantological thinking amounts to what Luc Schneider has referred to as the 'ontological diagonal', since it recognizes only two of the four corners of the Aristotelian ontological square. Davidson took one small step away from fantology in recognizing the need for a category of individual occurrents ('events') in addition to the category of individual things. "Against Fantology" argues that we need to go one step further and admit also what I would now call dependent continuants, in addition to the individual things (independent continuants) upon which they depend. Dependent continuants include qualities, roles, capabilities and functions; they include information objects such as the representations of genetic structures we find in sequence databases; and they include debts, ownership and authority relations, and many of the other individual relational entities which form the glue which holds together social reality.

"Against Fantology" contains also a proposal to counteract the effects of fantological thinking by introducing a minimal adjustment to the standard syntax of first-order logic, effectively by reducing substantially the allowed substituends for 'F' in 'Fa' and for 'R' in 'Rab' so that they would be confined only to predicates and relational expressions of the highest possible generality, almost all of them binary relations such as 'is identical to' (or '='), 'is part of', 'is an instance of', and other relations incorporated into the RO Relation ontology (see below). At the same time the range of the constant and variable terms 'a', 'b', 'c', ..., 'x', 'y', 'z', ... is broadened tremendously to include not only individual things, individual events, and individual qualities, but also the universals or types which such individual entities instantiate. The syntactically reformed predicate logic would then consist of atomic formulae such as:

$=(x, y)$,	for:	x is identical to y,
Part(x, y),	for:	individual x is part of individual y,
Inst(x, y),	for:	individual x instantiates universal y,
Inhere(x, y),	for:	individual quality x inheres in individual thing y,
Is_a(x, y),	for:	universal x is a subkind of universal y,

and so forth.

The result is comparable to the vocabulary of set theory in the sense that there, too, we have a restricted number (two) of primitive relational predicates: $=$ and $\in$. But while the language we are proposing has a vocabulary structurally very similar to that of set theory, it differs radically in that the formal tie of set-theoretic membership itself emanates from the fantological stable.

2.3 "On Drawing Lines on a Map"

Moving gradually towards applying formal-ontological theories to domains outside philosophy, I began collaborating in the early 1990s with David Mark and his colleagues in the National Center for Geographic Information and Analysis in Buffalo. Drawing not only on formal ontology but also on the work of linguists and other cognitive scientists, Mark and I embarked on an empirical study of the ontologies of geographic space underlying the cognition of human subjects, including comparative studies involving the speakers of multiple languages.

One output of this interaction was a new way of understanding the distinction between what we can loosely think of as the 'natural' boundaries of a lake or an island and the artificial boundaries marking, for example, rectangular states and provinces such as Utah or Saskatchewan. Geographers had until that point been disposed to call the latter 'abstract' or 'conceptual'. To the extent that they reflected on them ontologically at all, they preferred to view them as mere fictions, and thus as not really a part of the furniture of reality. In a paper entitled "On Drawing Lines on a Map" published in 1995, and since much cited by geographers and others, I propounded an alternative, realist view, resting on a distinction between what I called 'fiat' and 'bona fide' boundaries, the former being illustrated by the borders of real estate parcels or postal districts, the latter by entities such as planets and apples, which have borders or boundaries in their own right, independent of any drawing of borders by cognitive beings such as ourselves. Fiat boundaries and the fiat objects which they bound are, I argued, not only full-fledged denizens of reality, but also surprisingly pervasive not just in the geospatial realm but also for example in clock- and calendar-induced partitioning of regions of time. The drawing of fiat boundaries plays an important role, too, in medicine, for example in the anatomy of brain regions and in the definition of terms such as 'elevated blood glucose' or 'hypertension' or 'anemia' or indeed 'leg'.

In 2000 I published with Achille Varzi a paper in which we sought to show that, where bona fide physical discontinuities can be axiomatized in classical topological terms, fiat boundaries require for their understanding a non-classical topology, in which the distinction between open and closed regions can no longer be made – hereby drawing in turn on mereotopological ideas on boundaries developed by Roderick Chisholm, who drew in his turn on Brentano's *Philosophical Investigations on Space, time and the Continuum*.

"Searle and de Soto: The New ontology of the Social World"
The ontology of geography led to work on the ontology of social objects, and to a series of debates with John Searle concerning his *Construction of Social Reality*. These debates turned on Searle's naturalistic view of social objects as being, like presidents and cathedrals and parcels of real estate, physical objects which *count as* entities with special social attributes in certain special kinds of contexts. Social objects such as debts, claims, ownership rights, and collateralized debt obligations do not admit of such an analysis, since there is typically no physical object which *counts as* (for example) a debt. Such objects thereby fall outside the limits of Searle's Naturalism, and their absence leaves a problematic hole in his social ontology.

While engaging with Searle I began to read the work of the Peruvian economist Hernando de Soto, whose *The Mystery of Capital* contains a treatment of the ontology of the social world that is in interesting ways complementary to that of Searle. For de Soto it is entities such as title deeds, stocks, shares and insurance policies which play the central role in structuring the ontology of social reality. The full title of de Soto's book is *The Mystery of Capital: Why Capitalism Triumphs in the West and Fails Everywhere Else*, and it presents the formula for what Bill Clinton has called 'the most promising anti-poverty initiative in the world'. de Soto's idea begins with the fact that we in the West have in almost all areas reliable and systematic ways of keeping track of ownership rights; it is this, de Soto argues, which explains why we have been able to harvest and augment the world's resources to a more successful degree than elsewhere when measured, for example, in terms of prosperity, longevity, and security.

This is because in the Western world property rights are recorded in *documents*, and these documents, where publicly registered and reliably maintained, allow the same piece of land or house or factory to serve simultaneously a double purpose – of providing food or shelter or productive services, and of providing collateral for further investment. In even the poorest countries, vast numbers of people have parcels of land which they farm, houses in which they live, and even factories in which people are employed in manufacturing goods. But their claims to land and buildings are tenuous at best because there is no framework of property title. de Soto's strategy, accordingly, a strategy that has been successfully applied in many third-world countries, is to develop very simple forms of legal title in order to allow the poor to enjoy the same benefits of collateral (and a variety of other benefits such as insurance and legal electricity supply) which are enjoyed in the developed nations of the West as a matter of course.

de Soto hereby awards to *documents* a crucial role in the social order, analogous to the role awarded by Searle to speech acts. Speech acts, we might say, suffice as a basis for claims and obligations in small, village-based societies in which everyone knows (and so knows how much he can trust) everyone else, and in which memories are long. As societies grow, and as markets become extended, verbal promising and the swearing of oaths give way to complex edifices of documents and document systems – encompassing bank statements, passports, driving and marriage licenses, bills and receipts, degree certificates and tax forms, as well as stocks and shares – all of which form part of the fabric of developed societies at every level, but which are still lacking in the undeveloped world.

In 2003 I organized with my Buffalo colleagues a conference entitled The Mystery of Capital and the Construction of Social Reality in which de Soto and Searle presented their views on social reality, and since then I have worked with de Soto on applying ideas pertaining to the ontology of documents in support of his work in developing countries sponsored by the United Nations-sponsored Commission on the Legal Empowerment of the Poor and by other bodies.

Interestingly, the document-based social reality of Western societies is becoming even more complex and sophisticated with the growth in importance of new kinds of digital documents and of new ways of handling the digital social objects which such documents bring in their wake, above all in the domain of banking and finance. At the same time, as we know, this new kind of sophistication brings also new kinds of hazards, where the value for example of collateralized debt obligations can no longer reliably be determined because, as de Soto shows (2009), there is no adequate documentary basis for determining which securities form their ultimate collateral.

What do you think is the proper role of metaphysics in relation to other areas of philosophy and other academic disciplines, including the natural sciences?

Metaphysics, I can well imagine, will continue in its present role within the discipline of philosophy. As concerns relations to the natural sciences, however, I envisage a new role for the sub-discipline of ontology, including a gradual spinning off of ontology from its philosophical home – in a way roughly analogous to the way in which other sciences have spun off from philosophy in earlier epochs – and it is with the fate of the new science of ontology so conceived that I shall concern myself in what follows.

There was a time, familiarly, when all university scientists working in the field of what we now call 'psychology' were employed as professors in departments of philosophy. Psychology made its first step towards its current status as an independent, scientific discipline when Wilhelm Wundt established the world's first psychological laboratory at the University of Leipzig in 1879. My present view is that ontology is currently taking similar steps towards establishing itself as a discipline in its own right.

The rationale for this development turns on the astonishing success of ontology in the extra-philosophical world, where it now forms a central part of a strategy for coping with the problems which arise when bodies of data developed independently for different purposes need to be harmonized, aligned or integrated, as when large financial companies or hospital systems merge, or military forces or disaster relief agencies from different countries need to coordinate their plans, or public health organizations need to aggregate data pertaining to epidemic outbreaks spanning multiple geographic areas.

To serve this strategy, multiple ontological research laboratories have been established in scientific institutions throughout the world, and many industrial and government organizations are developing and using ontologies for the representation and integration of their data and information. There are multiple ontology journals, and multiple national and international conferences in ontology, including an annual ontology Summit held in the US National Institute of Standards and Technology. There is an International Association for ontology and Its Applications, and a (US) National Center for Ontological Research (based in Buffalo) and National Center for Biomedical ontology (based in Stanford, Buffalo and the Mayo Clinic). Progress towards the establishment of ontology as an academic discipline, on the other hand, has been slow, in part because many of the philosopher-ontologists who would help to form its core are reluctant to leave what they see as the safe confines of traditional metaphysics. There is, in consequence, an acute shortage of trained ontologists relative to the large number of programs seeking to hire persons with ontology expertise.

It is especially in data-intensive areas of the life sciences such as biochemistry and computational genomics that the new ontology has yielded its most impressive results. Here ontologies are being used in hundreds of projects throughout the world to describe biological and clinical data in algorithmically useful ways that are designed to help biologists and clinical scientists address the increasingly urgent challenges they face in finding ways to make sense of each other's data. In 2002 I established in Leipzig the Institute for Formal ontology and Medical Information Science (IFOMIS), the world's first institute of bio-ontology, with the goal of applying formal-ontological methods in addressing these challenges.

There is a long-standing tendency for each biological research group to use its own guidelines for terminology and categorization. Their data is thereby siloed, and opportunities for harvesting valuable information from cross-organism comparisons are thereby lost. To address this problem a group of biologists studying different so-called 'model organisms' – which is to say organisms, such as mouse or fly, studied for purposes of understanding human health and disease – joined together in 1999 to create what they called the 'Gene ontology' (GO), a 'controlled structured vocabulary' designed to create a common terminological framework to be used by all model organism databases.

The GO consists of a hierarchically organized set of some 30,000 biological terms – such as 'induction of cell death' or 'cardiac muscle development' – together with semi-formal definitions. The ontology is used in multiple ways. Most prominently it serves the manual annotation of experimental results reported in the scientific literature, whereby teams of professional biocurators tag data about, say, gene and protein sequences to terms from the GO. This strategy makes the data that is presented in scientific publications not only more easily searchable by both humans and machines but also – because data pertaining to different species, including *home sapiens*, are annotated using the same terms – more easily comparable and integratable for purposes of research.

The GO was very quickly able to establish itself as a valuable tool of biomedical research, and the GO is today, when measured in terms of both numbers of users and of reach across species, the world's most successful ontology. There exist over 11 million annotations relating gene products described in major databases of molecular biology to terms in the GO, and data related to some 180,000 genes have been manually annotated in this way.

Unfortunately, initial versions of the GO were logically poorly structured, and its definitions were often circular ('hemolysis' was defined as 'the causes of hemolysis') or worse (the 'part-of' relation used in defining the hierarchical organization of the GO was provided simultaneously with four distinct and logically incompatible definitions). Responding to these problems I organized in Leipzig in May 2004 a workshop on the topic of "The Formal Architecture of the Gene ontology" in which the leading figures of the GO community participated, above all Michael Ashburner, Professor of Genetics in Cambridge and Suzanne Lewis of Berkeley National Labs. My own talk at the meeting was entitled 'STOP!' (short for: 'Smart Terminologies through Ontological Principles'), and it consisted primarily in the recital of a long list of logical and ontological errors in the GO, together with simple recipes for fixing these errors using methods familiar to students of logic and philosophy.

Fatefully, the meeting resulted in a productive collaboration between Ashburner and Lewis and myself which continues to this day. It led to an ambitious program of ontology reform, which in 2005 became institutionalized as the 'OBO Foundry' (http://obofoundry.org), whose goal is to establish a suite of interoperable, high-quality, logically well-formulated Open Biomedical Ontologies to be used in the annotation of biological and biomedical data and to provide effective guidance to biologists and others engaged in ontology creation.

Because this goal has been embraced by some thousands of biologists and bioinformaticians, its realization is allowing a kind of virtual experimentation, in which representations of complex biological systems are able to live side by side with representations of disease processes in individual humans in such a way that the two are brought together within a single, logically well-articulated ontological framework, which will incrementally allow biological hypotheses generated on the one side to be tested by reference to the clinical data that is being collected about patients on the other.

This goal of a logically formalized biological ontology was anticipated by the clinician/logical positivist J. H. Woodger in 1937. And it was anticipated, too, by Ingarden, with his theory of organisms as structures built out of relatively isolated causal systems on multiple levels of granularity in *The Problem of the existence of the World*. Its coherent realization today draws on first-order logic and its contemporary offspring, as well as on a number of recognizably philosophical ideas pertaining to continuants and occurrents, universals and particulars, dependent and independent entities, dispositions and functions. But the work involved in contemporary biological and biomedical ontology is in various ways distinct from the work of the philosopher. First, it involves an obvious focus on practical applications; second, it involves a large component of human interaction between ontologists and biologist users, who must be taught to understand each other's needs, and who must be taught to overcome the manifold difficulties involved in large-scale cross-disciplinary ontology coordination; third, the support which ontologies provide to scientists rests upon their being incorporated into the computational artifacts used by scientists to reason with their data; traditional philosophical concerns must therefore be tempered by concerns relating to computational tractability.

The establishment of the OBO Foundry has already led to the

creation of several new ontologies, including the OBO Relation ontology (RO) and the ontology for Biomedical Investigations (OBI). OBI is in large part a translation in ontological terms of those areas of the philosophy of science which relate to the design, execution and interpretation of experiments. It addresses an increasingly urgent need on the part of experimental biologists for a common controlled structured vocabulary which can be used to describe how given experimental results were achieved – for example in order to satisfy regulations governing approval of new drugs. The Relation ontology was first presented in a paper published in the journal Genome Biology in 2005, on which I served as co-author with seven biologists, a logician, and a database scientist. This paper has since been cited some 450 times and continues to be downloaded some 1,000 times each month. The Relation ontology forms one component of the Basic Formal ontology (BFO) upper level ontology framework which I and my colleagues have been developing since 2003, and which is being used in some 100 life science ontology projects, and also in ontology research sponsored by the US Army relating to the Universal Core data integration initiative of the US Federal Government (http://ucore.gov).

What do you consider to be the proper method for metaphysics?

I prefer to answer this question as it relates to the proper method of *ontology* in the sense outlined in the above, a discipline which will increasingly involve an empirical component. To see what this means, let us suppose (to take a very simple example) that we need to create an ontology that can serve as an effective framework for data integration in the field of infectious disease. Given two patients, both suffering from Dengue Fever, do we create an ontology which would bring it about that our database would recognize two instances of disease – two dependent entities – corresponding to the two human beings who are their bearers and to the one disease *type*? And if so, are these disease instances dependent *continuants*, which would endure through time, or dependent *processes*, which would unfold in time? Decisions on such questions determine how a principled ontology framework should be constructed that would enable the integration of the corresponding data. By comparing the success or failure of integration resulting from alternative ontology frameworks we can provide an empirical measure of the quality of the underlying ontology. Disputes formerly resolved (or not resolved) through philosophical argument can be tackled in a way which involves, at least in part, a variety of empirical testing. BFO has been subjected to such empirical testing since its inception, and it has been refined over time in light of the utility of specific ontological choices to its biologist users.

What do you consider to be the most neglected topics in contemporary metaphysics, and what direction would you like metaphysics to take in the future?

I hope that my answer to this question is by now clear. The most interesting future direction for metaphysics is to transform itself into a discipline which can support the new, empirical science of ontology.

Literature

Brentano F., 1976, *Philosophische Untersuchungen zu Raum, Zeit und Kontinuum* (ed. by S. Körner and R. M. Chisholm), Hamburg: Meiner. English translation by B. Smith as *Philosophical Investigations on Space, time and the Continuum*, London: Croom Helm, 1988.

de Soto, Hernando 2000 *The Mystery of Capital: Why Capitalism Triumphs in the West and Fails Everywhere Else*, New York: Basic Books.

de Soto, Hernando 2009 "Toxic Assets Were Hidden Assets", *Wall Street Journal*, March 25.

Guarino, Nicola 1992 "Concepts, Attributes, and Arbitrary Relations: Some Linguistic and Ontological Criteria for Structuring Knowledge Bases", in R.P. van de Riet and R.A. Meersman (eds.), *Linguistic Instruments in Knowledge Engineering*, Elsevier Science Publishers,195-211.

Hobbs, J. R. and Moore, R. C. (eds.) 1985 *Formal Theories of the Common-Sense World*, Norwood: Ablex.

Husserl, Edmund 1970 *Logical Investigations*, English translation by J. N. Findlay, 2 vols., New York: Humanities Press.

Ingarden, Roman 1964 *time and Modes of Being*, Springfield, Ill.: Charles Thomas. English translation by Helen R. Micheja of extracts from Roman Ingarden, *Spór o istnienie swiata* (The Problem of the existence of the World) vol. 1, 2nd rev. ed., Warsaw: PWN 1961. (First Polish edition 1947.)

Ingarden, Roman 1973 *The Literary Work of Art: An Investigation on the Borderlines of ontology, Logic, and Theory of Literature*, Evanston: Northwestern University Press, 1973.

Mulligan, Kevin, Simons, Peter M. and Smith, Barry 1984 "Truth-Makers", *Philosophy and Phenomenological Research*, 44, 287-321.

Mulligan, Kevin, Simons, Peter M. and Smith, Barry 2006 "What's Wrong with Contemporary Philosophy?", *Topoi*, 25 (1-2), 63-67.

Omnès, Roland 1999 *Understanding Quantum Mechanics*, Princeton: Princeton University Press.

Reinach, Adolf 1989 *Sämtliche Werke*, critical edition with commentary by Karl Schuhmann and Barry Smith, 2 vols., Munich / Hamden / Vienna: Philosophia.

Schneider, Luc 2010 "Revisiting the Ontological Square", in Antony Galton and Riichiro Mizoguchi (eds.), *Formal ontology in Information Systems. Proceedings of the Sixth International Conference (FOIS 2010)*, Amsterdam: IOS Press, 73-86.

Searle, John R. 1995 *The Construction of Social Reality*, New York: Basic Books.

Smith, Barry 1995 "On Drawing Lines on a Map", in Andrew U. Frank and Werner Kuhn (eds.), *Spatial Information Theory* (Lecture Notes in Computer Science 988), Berlin: Springer, 475-484.

Smith, Barry 2003 "ontology", in Luciano Floridi (ed.), *Blackwell Guide to the Philosophy of Computing and Information*, Oxford: Blackwell, 155-166.

Smith, Barry 2005 "Against Fantology", in Johann C. Marek and Maria E. Reicher (eds.), *Experience and Analysis*, Vienna: HPT&ÖBV, 2005, 153-170.

Smith, Barry 2008 "Searle and de Soto: The New ontology of the Social World", in Barry Smith, David Mark and Isaac Ehrlich (eds.), *The Mystery of Capital and the Construction of Social Reality*, Chicago: Open Court, 35-51.

Smith, Barry 2008 "ontology (Science)", in C. Eschenbach and M. Gruninger (eds.), *Formal ontology in Information Systems. Proceedings of the Fifth International Conference* (FOIS), Amsterdam: IOS Press, 21-35.

Barry Smith, Michael Ashburner, Cornelius Rosse, Jonathan Bard, William Bug, Werner Ceusters, Louis J. Goldberg, Karen Eilbeck, Amelia Ireland, Christopher J Mungall, The OBI Consortium, Neocles Leontis, Philippe Rocca-Serra, Alan Ruttenberg, Susanna-Assunta Sansone, Richard H Scheuermann, Nigam Shah, Patricia L. Whetzel, Suzanna Lewis, "The OBO Foundry: Co-ordinated Evolution of Ontologies to Support Biomedical Data Integration", *Nature Biotechnology*, 25 (11), November 2007, 1251 -1255.

Barry Smith, Werner Ceusters, Bert Klagges, Jacob Köhler, Anand Kumar, Jane Lomax, Chris Mungall, Fabian Neuhaus, Alan Rector and Cornelius Rosse 2005 "Relations in Biomedical Ontologies", *Genome Biology*, 6 (5), R46.

Barry Smith and David M. Mark,
http://www.geog.buffalo.edu/ncgia/ontology/
SmithMarkIJGIS2001p591_s.pdf
Geographical Categories: An Ontological Investigation", International Journal of Geographical Information Science, 15: 7 (2001), 591–612.

Smith, Barry and Searle, John 2003 "The Construction of Social Reality: An Exchange", in Laurence Moss and David Koepsell (eds.), *Searle on the Institutions of Social Reality*, Oxford: Blackwell, 285-309.

Smith, Barry, Vizenor, Lowell, and Schoening, James 2009 "Universal Core Semantic Layer", *ontology for the Intelligence Community*, George Mason University, Fairfax, VA, CEUR Workshop Proceedings, vol. 555.

Smith, Barry and Varzi, Achille 2000 "Fiat and Bona Fide Boundaries", *Philosophy and Phenomenological Research*, 60: 2, 401–420.

Woodger, J. H. 1937 *The Axiomatic Method in Biology*, London: Cambridge University Press.

16

Michael Tooley

Professor of Philosophy, and Distinguished College Professor
University of Colorado at Boulder, USA

Why were you initially drawn to metaphysics (and what keeps you interested)?

Some people have philosophical thoughts, and begin asking philosophical questions, at a rather young age. I think, for example, of one of my grandsons, Anthony. As I mention in the dedication of the book that I recently co-authored with Alvin Plantinga, *Knowledge of God*, Anthony, at the age of seven, discovered, entirely on his own, a version of the argument from evil. Anthony, at the time, knew nothing about my views on religion. Nor did he know that anyone had ever had any doubts about the existence of God. But one morning, when Anthony was with us, I had been reading something about creationism in a newspaper, and in a frustrated tone of voice, I said to my wife Sylvia, "I wonder how many dinosaurs were on the Ark?" It turned out that Anthony had recently been exposed to the story of Noah's Ark, and he said, "If there were a good God, he wouldn't have drowned all of those animals, would he?"

When I was young, I was exposed to many such stories, but they seemed to occasion no critical reflections in me: I happily believed them all, without question. Not a very promising start for a philosopher!

I did, during my high school days, develop a strong interest in mathematics and physics. Growing up near Toronto, when I graduated from high school, I went to the University of Toronto. There one chose a major as soon as one entered the University, and I decided to major in mathematics, physics, and chemistry. At that point, though I was extremely interested in mathematical problems, I do not believe that I had ever entertained a single critical thought, and philosophy was for me a completely unknown discipline.

At one point, however, I was talking to a friend whom I grew up with, and who, unlike me, was an intellectual, and read very widely. He recommended a book by Bertrand Russell – *Marriage and Morals* – which I read. As I did so, I realized for the first time in my life that one could ask why one believes various things. When I did that, it quickly became apparent to me that I really had no evidence at all for many of the most important things that I believed. Having realized that, I was somehow able immediately to set those beliefs aside, thinking that I would return to them if, upon further investigation, I found that there were good reasons for thinking that they were true.

My life had, in a mere day or two, changed dramatically. Before I read Russell's book, I had been a Christian; by the time I finished, I was an unbeliever. More importantly, I now found myself having critical thoughts about many things, and deeply interested in questions – especially in the area of ethics – that I had never really thought about before. I was very much on the road to becoming a philosopher.

I was still, however, in love with mathematics and physics. But shortly thereafter, I met another undergraduate, who was majoring in philosophy. His name was Danny Goldstick, and I would sometimes see him in the hallways, talking with his classmates about philosophy. Danny had the view that one could *prove* things in philosophy, and I sometimes listened to him as he offered proofs to his fellow students – for example, a proof that determinism was true, or a proof that absolutely every possibility that one could imagine, no matter how complex or strange, would be realized at some point in space and time. (Think of the concrete possible worlds of David Lewis, but view them, not as isolated from one another, but as somehow parts of a single, very large world.)

Danny made philosophy look extremely exciting, and the result was, when I was in the first week of my third year as a student in mathematics and physics, I decided to change my major, and switched to philosophy.

Philosophy at the University of Toronto at that time, however, turned out to be almost entirely the study of the history of philosophy. I had some really excellent teachers – including David Gauthier, who impressed me deeply – but aside from one or two courses, when one was studying philosophy at that time at the University of Toronto, one never quite made it into the 20th century.

There was one other person there, however, who had a major

philosophical influence on me, and that was Barry O'Neill. Barry was studying mathematics and physics, but he was also very interested in certain parts of philosophy, especially the work of Rudolf Carnap. So he and I read some Carnap together, including parts of Carnap's *Logical Foundations of Probability*. This exposure to Carnap's ideas has had a major impact on my views of how one should approach a variety of philosophical issues, including some in metaphysics, as I shall indicate later.

Upon graduating from the University of Toronto, I went on to Princeton for graduate study, and there I found myself in a very different, and very exciting world. Now I was being exposed to contemporary philosophy, and I was learning much more about how to do philosophy.

At Princeton, I had a number of really excellent teachers from whom I learned a great deal, but there were two who especially affected, in major ways, the future course of my philosophical life. One was C. G. Hempel, from whom I took a course in philosophy of science. I was deeply impressed by Hempel's great clarity of mind, and by the rigorous way in which he approached philosophical problems. But Hempel also introduced me to a number of fascinating philosophical problems that were very relevant to my later work as a philosopher. Especially important in this regard were, first, the problem of the meaning of theoretical terms; secondly, Goodman's New Riddle of Induction, and the problem of justifying induction; and, thirdly, the problem of giving an account of the nature of laws of nature.

In the term paper that I wrote for Hempel's class, I attempted, quite preposterously, both to answer Goodman's New Riddle of Induction, and to offer an account of laws of nature. As regards those two problems, my idea concerning laws of nature appeared the more promising, and so I more or less decided at that point that I would write my dissertation under Hempel on the problem of giving an account of laws of nature.

The account that I had in mind was a very positivistic account, being essentially a certain sort of regularity theory in which whether a given cosmic generalization expressed a law of nature, or was merely accidentally true, was determined by exactly what types of actual events fell under the generalization in question.

The following semester, however, I took a seminar from Walter Kaufmann, two of whose books in philosophy of religion I had read as an undergraduate, and both of which had impressed me deeply. As a result, I wound up doing a dissertation in philosophy of religion, rather than in philosophy of science. But my exposure to questions in Hempel's philosophy of science course, and especially ones concerning laws of nature and explanation, had generated a strong and enduring interest in metaphysics.

What do you consider to be your most important contributions to metaphysics?

The main topics in metaphysics on which I have worked have been laws of nature, causation, the nature of time, and the existence of God. As regards laws of nature, I started thinking once again about that topic in 1973, and when I did so, my thinking was very influenced by David Lewis's paper "How to Define Theoretical Terms", since given that it was possible to offer a realist, or non-reductionist interpretation of theoretical terms, it was clear that one should consider the possibility that the correct account of laws of nature is a non-reductionist one. Consequently, rather than attempting to refine the reductionist account of laws of nature that I had formulated as a graduate student studying with Hempel, I decided to consider the prospects for a non-reductionist account.

In doing so, my views in philosophy of mind probably played an important role. For I was attracted to property dualism, and if one is a property dualist, one is committed to the view that there are at least some *basic* laws of nature that connect quite complex neural states to simple, emergent, phenomenal properties. The idea of such laws leads rather naturally to certain thoughts. One is that if our world had been slightly different in certain ways, the specific, complex neural states that appear to be causally necessary for experiences involving specific phenomenal properties might never have existed. So there might never have been an experience of, say, the purple variety. But when one considers such an altered world, it is tempting to think that if *that* world had been different in certain ways – so that the relevant complex neural state did arise – then there would have been experiences of the purple variety. But what would make such a counterfactual true? Presumably, such a counterfactual cannot be true unless there is a law connecting the complex type of neural state in question to the property of qualitative purpleness. But if that is so, then it must be possible for even *basic* laws of nature to be uninstantiated.

A closely related thought is this. If it is true that, had life on earth been destroyed earlier by some catastrophe, there would have been uninstantiated basic laws of nature, what is the likelihood that, in the world as it is, *all* laws linking neural states as causes to qualitative properties of experiences as effects are instantiated? Upon reflection, this does not seem very likely. For one thing, how likely is it that the limited ranges of complex neural states that humans and other actual organisms are capable of exhaust the totality of complex neural states that are causally relevant to qualitative properties of experiences? This, it would seem, is not at all likely. But if that is right, uninstantiated basic laws of nature are not only logically possible, but very likely as well.

In any case, if basic uninstantiated laws of nature are possible, laws of nature cannot be cosmic regularities of any sort. What, then, can they be? A natural answer, which Fred Dretske, David Armstrong, and I arrived at, around the same time, is that laws of nature are irreducible, second-order relations among universals.

Thus conceived, non-probabilistic laws of nature, if not uninstantiated, entail the existence of corresponding regularities, while probabilistic laws determine the probabilities of relevant events, so what one has is a governing conception of laws of nature, and there are a variety of arguments that strongly support, I believe, the conclusion that our ordinary conception of laws of nature is a governing conception. But to show that a certain concept is our ordinary concept still leaves it an open question whether there is anything in the world that corresponds to that concept. So is there any reason for holding that there actually are governing laws of nature?

Here my initial line of argument was a purely negative one, namely, that if metaphysically strong, governing laws of nature are not logically possible, then it is reasonable to believe that the probability of the existence of exceptionless, cosmic regularities that subsume an infinite number of events is infinitesimally close to zero. This follows, for example, from Laplace's famous rule of succession, which says that for any family of properties that contains only two members, the probability that a given object has a particular property belonging to that family, given only the information that n other things have that property, is equal to $\frac{n+1}{n+2}$. It is also possible, however, to prove similar negative results, dealing, first, with probabilistic laws, and secondly, with the possibility of there being some law or other, probabilistic or non-probabilistic, falling within a given range. The overall result is that if strong, governing laws of nature are *not* logically possible, then one can never be justified in believing that any non-governing, reductionist-style law obtains.

On the other hand, advocates of a governing conception of laws of nature typically argue that one can justify the belief that there are governing laws of nature via an inference to the best explanation. I do not think that this is the right way to proceed, since I agree with Bas van Frassen's view that inference to the best explanation cannot be a fundamental inductive principle. What one has to do, it seems to me, is to work with the notion of logical probability, and I now believe that, when this is done, one can show that if governing laws of nature are logically possible, then information about relevant events can raise the probability of the existence of such laws arbitrarily close to one.

Given the virtues of a non-reductionist account of laws of nature, I next turned to consideration of the idea of a non-reductionist approach to the concept of causation. In the case of laws of nature, it had been a simple matter to set out a theory of laws of nature that provided the basis for theoretical-term definitions of nomological relations. This was not so, however, for causation, where arriving at a satisfactory theory was very challenging.

Consider, for example, the ideas that enter into Hume's reductionist account: a cause and its effect are contiguous, both spatially and temporally; a cause precedes its effect; cause and effect exhibit a constant conjunction. On reflection, none of these seems satisfactory. As regards the first, while a number of philosophers, including Wesley Salmon, have viewed it as a necessary truth that causal processes are continuous, one can vividly imagine scenarios in which a cause and its effect are spatially separated, or temporally separated, or both, and where there are no causally intervening events. Moreover, there are no arguments, I believe, that show that such apparent possibilities give rise to a contradiction. So it would seem that neither spatial nor temporal contiguity or continuity should enter into a general, analytical theory of causation.

What about temporal priority? Here there are at least two problems. First, it seems that one can also vividly imagine situations that involve temporally backward causation – most commonly in the form of scenarios involving time travel into the past – and while it may turn out that backward causation involves a contradiction, any such contradiction cannot lie, surely, at the surface – as it would if temporal priority were part of the very analysis of causation.

Secondly, there is a fundamental philosophical question concerning what account is to be given of the relation of temporal priority. Is it a basic and unanalyzable relation? Is it to be analyzed in terms of tensed concepts? Or does its analysis involve some concepts from physics, such as increase in entropy, or the expansion of the universe? These types of accounts are all open to serious objections. What then should be done? One traditional idea, going back to Leibniz and Kant, is that the relation of temporal priority should be analyzed in terms of causation. But this possibility would be immediately excluded if one incorporated the relation of temporal priority into one's analytical theory of causation.

Of Hume's suggestions, that leaves one with only 'constant conjunction' – which one can interpret as the claim that any cause and its effect must fall under some law, and where one can expand the idea of constant conjunction to include falling under either a non-probabilistic law or a probabilistic one. That this alone cannot give one a satisfactory theory is clear from the fact that some worlds that intuitively involve a clear direction of causation contain only laws that are temporally symmetric. In addition, however, there are strong arguments that focus upon conceivable situations where the totality of facts concerning (1) the non-causal properties and relations between things, (2) the ultimate powers and propensities of things, (3) causal laws of nature, and (4) the direction of time, do not serve to fix how events are causally related, since there may be two or more possibilities concerning the causal relationships that are present that are compatible with the totality of such facts. But if this is so, then it seems that causation must be an irreducible relation between events, and while this does not entail that events can be causally related without falling under any law, the latter view is the simplest account of why it is that causal relations do not logically supervene upon the totality consisting of non-causal states of affairs plus causal laws.

My solution to the problem of formulating an analytical theory of causation turned upon the following idea. Suppose that one assigns different *a priori* probabilities to events of type S and events of type T. If one somehow learns that there are laws of nature that entail that an event of type S occurs when and only when it is accompanied by an event of type T, one knows that one must equate the *a posteriori* probabilities of events of types S and T, but that information does not provide any guidance concerning precisely how the probabilities should be adjusted to make them equal. Contrast this with being given, instead, the information that there are laws of nature that entail that events of type S are both causally sufficient and causally necessary for events of type T. Once again, one knows that one must equate the *a posteriori* probabilities of events of types S and T, but now, I claim, there is a clearly correct view concerning the *a posteriori* probabilities – namely, the *a posteriori* probabilities of events of types S and T should both be equated with the *a priori* probability of events of type S.

This basic idea can be expanded into a full theory, both of causal laws and of the relation of causation. The resulting theory, moreover, enables one to make sense of what appear to be genuine possibilities, including, first, the possibility of there being causation in very simple worlds – such as worlds with only a single particle; secondly, the possibility of situations where causal relations are underdetermined by the totality of non-causal facts; and thirdly, the possibility of a world just like our own except for having causal processes running in the opposite direction. The compatibility of the theory with these apparent possibilities provides good reason for thinking, I suggest, that it captures our ordinary notion of causation.

As in the case of laws of nature, so, too, in the case of causation, it is one thing to set out a satisfactory analysis of a concept, and another to provide reason for thinking that the world contains states of affairs answering to that concept. But the fact that my theory of causation entails that if certain types of events are causally related, then certain relations obtain between the *a priori* probabilities and *a posteriori* probabilities of those types of events, means that the hypothesis that two types of events are causally related entails testable consequences, and this in turn enables one to confirm or disconfirm the relevant causal hypothesis. So a non-reductionist account of causation does not entail, as some philosophers have claimed, that causal hypotheses cannot be confirmed or disconfirmed.

With an account of causation in hand, I next went on to consider the idea of a causal analysis of temporal priority. In exploring that idea, I considered competing accounts of temporal priority, including the view that the earlier than relation is to be analyzed in terms of tensed concepts, and this in turn led me very quickly into the more fundamental question of the correct theory of the nature of time.

Most tensed theories of time incorporated theses that seemed to me untenable, such as, first, the idea that the tensed concepts of past, present, and future are basic and unanalyzable; secondly, the thesis that the earlier than relation can be analyzed in terms of tensed concepts; and thirdly, the thesis that tenseless quantification is less basic than tensed quantification. These, and other common theses, seemed to me open to decisive objections. But the idea of a "growing block" view of reality, according to which past and present events are now real, but future events are not, was one that I found very appealing, and I saw that, given the key idea of a causal analysis of temporal priority, it was possible to set out a tensed, growing block view of time while rejecting the various untenable notions associated with common tensed views, such as the notion that tensed concepts are analytically basic.

But even if one can formulate a tensed view of time that avoids the objections to which most tensed views fall prey, is there any reason for thinking that our world is a tensed world, rather than a tenseless one, as many philosophers hold? In response to this question, most advocates of tensed accounts of the nature of time appeal to the phenomenology of experience, holding that one is directly acquainted with the flow of time. This route is not one that I find appealing, in part because I am not convinced that advocates of tenseless approaches to the nature of time – such as Hugh Mellor – cannot give an adequate account of one's experience of time. But, in addition, if this is a tensed world, then its being so surely does not depend upon the presence of conscious beings, and so it seemed to me that it should be possible to offer an argument that does not depend upon an appeal to phenomenology.

The argument that I developed was based upon my account of causation. It turned upon the question of what world would have to be like for it to be possible for it to contain causation, and what I argued was that the postulates of my analytical theory of causation could only be true in a world in which both the past and the present are actual as of a given moment, but the future is not.

The final area of metaphysics in which I am very interested, and that I have thought about in a reasonably sustained way, concerns the question of the existence of God. Of the arguments in that area, the most promising has always seemed to me to be the argument from evil. But the thesis that the existence of God is logically incompatible either with the existence of evil, or with certain types of evil, or with a certain quantity of evil, never seemed to me very plausible,, for while I am not inclined to accept the view that some evils are logically necessary either for greater goods, or to avoid still greater evils, the thesis that this is not the case certainly appears to be a substantive ethical claim, and I do not think that a version of the argument from evil that rests upon such a substantive ethical thesis can be effective. Consequently, it has always seemed to me that one should focus instead upon evidential, or probabilistic, versions of the argument from evil.

How should such a version of the argument from evil be formulated? First of all, and as William Rowe has argued, one should focus on concrete cases of evil. Secondly, the argument should not be formulated in axiological terms – that is, in terms of the goodness and badness of states of affairs – but, instead, deontologically, in terms of rightmaking and wrongmaking properties of actions. The starting point of the argument is then that, contrary to what is claimed by those who offer theodicies in response to the argument from evil, there are occurrences in our world – such as the Lisbon earthquake – where the known rightmaking properties of allowing that event, if any, are outweighed by the known wrongmaking properties. Then comes the crucial inductive step, of which the conclusion is not that it is unlikely that there is an unknown rightmaking property that outweighs the known wrongmaking properties, but, instead, and more modestly, that it is likely that the totality of wrongmaking properties, both known and unknown, outweighs the totality of rightmaking properties, known and unknown.

How is this inductive step to be justified? Here my view is that one can never arrive at a satisfactory evaluation of the inductive soundness of the argument from evil as long as one discusses that issue in an informal way. What one needs to do, instead, is to bring inductive logic to bear upon the inference. As a result, my approach is to appeal to Rudolf Carnap's structure description formulation of inductive logic, and I argue that when this is done, one can establish a very simple but powerful conclusion, namely, that given only the evidence that there are n events in the world, each of whose known wrongmaking properties outweighs its known rightmaking properties, the probability that there is an omnipotent, omniscient, and morally perfect person is less than $\frac{1}{n+1}$.

What do you consider to be the proper method for metaphysics?

The best way to tackle this question, I think, is to start by asking what the main activities are that philosophers engage in, and as regards the latter question, I would suggest that philosophy involves at least the following four central activities: (1) the analysis of fundamental concepts; (2) an inquiry into whether basic human beliefs are justified, and, if so, how; (3) the discovery and proof of important necessary truths; (4) the attempt to formulate a comprehensive, and intellectually plausible, synoptic view of reality.

As regards the first of these, I think it is crucial to ask, as the British empiricists did, first, whether some concepts are analytically more basic than others; secondly, whether, if this is so, some concepts are analytically basic; and thirdly, what the criterion is that delimits the class of analytically basic concepts.

With regard to the last of these three questions, I think it is very likely that it will be crucial to distinguish between logical concepts and descriptive ones, since it seems to me doubtful that a single criterion of analytically basic concepts can cover both logical concepts and descriptive ones.

Given an account of analytically basic concepts, the goal should then be to offer rigorous definitions of other important concepts in terms of them. In this task, we have a great advantage over earlier philosophers, in that we now know how to define theoretical terms in a non-reductionist way.

Next, as regards the task of justification, this is the activity that lies at the heart of epistemology. Nevertheless, it seems to me that it is crucial to metaphysics as well, in at least two ways. First of all, metaphysics has traditionally been concerned with the existence of various entities, such as God, immaterial minds, numbers, universals, and so on, so metaphysics must address the question of whether it is reasonable or not to believe that such things exist. Secondly, in offering analyses of metaphysically fundamental concepts such as those of causation and laws of nature, one cannot be content simply to provide analyses of those concepts: it is crucial to go on to ask whether anything in reality actually corresponds to such concepts.

As regards the discovery and proof of necessary truths, different methods will presumably be appropriate depending upon whether all *a priori* truths are analytic or not. If not, and there are synthetic *a priori* truths, then it would seem that one will have to appeal to some faculty of intuition, since the main alternative – that of some sort of transcendental argument – has not, I think, proved at all promising. In the case of analytic truths – and I am strongly inclined to believe that all necessary philosophical truths are analytic – the appropriate method is that of rigorous deductive proofs from clear definitions, each of whose *analysans* involves, ultimately, only analytically basic concepts.

Finally, as regards the development of a synoptic view of reality, I think that the starting point should be with a demonstration that all justified beliefs are either non-inferentially justified, or else inferentially justified on the basis of non-inferentially justified beliefs. If that foundational view is right, then one needs an account of the ground of non-inferentially justified beliefs, and here my view is, first, that the ground is a matter of direct acquaintance with instances of properties and relations, and secondly, that the only properties and relations with which one can be directly acquainted are ones that are immediately given in experience. Developing a synoptic view of reality is then a matter of constructing theories that can be shown to be probable relative to the totality of propositions concerning all of one's experiences, either by virtue of evidential relations, or by virtue of synthetic *a priori* propositions.

What do you think is the proper role of metaphysics in relation to other areas of philosophy and other academic disciplines, including the natural sciences?

Metaphysics is obviously an important part of a number of areas of philosophy, such as ethics, philosophy of mind, and philosophy of religion. Thus, in the case of ethics, two crucial metaphysical issues are whether a coherent account can be given of the idea of objective values, and, if it can be, whether the best synoptic view of reality will incorporate reference to objective values.

In the case of philosophy of mind, a number of metaphysical questions are absolutely central, including that of the nature of the mind, that of whether there are qualia with which we are directly acquainted, and that of what causal relations there are between mental states and one's body.

Finally, in philosophy of religion, central metaphysical issues include, for example, whether God exists, whether humans have immaterial minds or souls, and whether it is possible for humans to survive death.

I have mentioned above that metaphysics is dependent in important ways upon epistemology. Is there any dependence in the opposite direction? In contrast to its relation to other areas of philosophy, metaphysics does not seem to be part of epistemology in the sense of their being epistemological questions that just are metaphysical questions. Nevertheless, it does seem to me that epistemology is dependent upon metaphysics at crucial points. In particular, I think it turns out that whether there are satisfactory answers to central skeptical challenges turns upon whether the metaphysical idea of governing laws of nature is coherent. Thus, as I mentioned above, I think that one can show, for example, that one can be justified in believing that there are laws of nature if and only if the idea of strong, governing laws of nature is a coherent concept.

What about the relation between philosophy and the sciences? Aside from cases where synthetic *a priori* truths are relevant – cases about which I am rather skeptical – it seems to me that in constructing a synoptic view of the world on the basis of non-inferentially justified beliefs, philosophers must use *inductive* methods, and, moreover, that the methods in question are precisely those that scientists employ.

Given that this is so, one might expect that some metaphysical questions have been settled by science, and that seems to me so. One of the best examples of this is the question of whether humans involve immaterial minds or souls, where it seems to me that the science of psychology provides excellent grounds for concluding that our world does not contain any immaterial minds, of either a Cartesian or Thomistic sort.

But would not one also expect that *all* metaphysical questions concerning the existence of contingent entities and states of affairs that are not objects of direct acquaintance are then in principle questions that fall within the scope of science? This seems to me right, and so I would argue, for example, that such questions as whether there are strong, governing laws of nature, whether our world contains causation, non-reductionistically construed, whether God exists, whether there is an intelligent cause of the physical world, whether qualitative properties of experiences causally affect physical states of the brain, whether there is a physical, external world, and so on, are all questions that fall with the scope of *potential* scientific investigation and resolution.

But this does not mean that, as regards the relation between science and metaphysics, science rules. First of all, it may turn out that metaphysical conclusions rule out certain theories that scientists have seriously entertained. Here the most dramatic examples concern theories that involve particles traveling backward in time, or causal and temporal loops. Many metaphysicians think that it can be shown that both backward causation, and causal and temporal loops are logically impossible. If so, certain physical theories can be excluded on *a priori* grounds.

Secondly, scientists often think in terms of the simplest mathematical formulations, and ignore metaphysical questions. Consider, for example, a Newtonian world. In such a world it is natural to say that a force's acting upon a body *causes* the body to accelerate, where the acceleration is proportional to the force, and inversely proportional to the mass of the body. Mathematically, this is typically expressed in the form '$F = ma$'. This formulation is very compact and convenient. But notice that the idea of causation, which was part of the informal statement, has disappeared. A serious question then arises as to whether causation would be present in a Newtonian world, or whether only what is represented in the mathematical formulation of the theory would be real. Metaphysicians are much more likely than scientists to be alive to such issues.

Thirdly, scientists almost always think in terms of observations described by sentences about observable physical objects, and so the existence of a physical world is taken for granted. Philosophers who think seriously about non-inferentially justified beliefs, on the other hand, are often attracted to the idea that all justified belief is based upon beliefs that are justified via direct acquaintance with purely subjective states of oneself, and if one adopts that view, it becomes clear that the existence of a physical world, which scientists take for granted, itself needs to be investigated.

Finally, given such a focus on a more fundamental level of observation, involving direct acquaintance, the question inevitably arises as to how the qualitative aspects of one's experience, with which one appears to be directly acquainted, fit into a synoptic view of reality. A natural answer is that, first of all, neural states of one's brain give rise to experiences with the qualitative properties in question, but, secondly, those qualitative states of one's brain then causally affect one's behavior. But if this view is right, then physicists, in considering only interactions involving the fundamental particles and fields of physics, are not considering all of the states of affairs that can causally affect those fundamental physical particles and fields, with the result that physics, as presently practiced, appears to be necessarily incomplete.

It may be, of course, that the natural view is mistaken, and that either experiences do not involve any irreducible, qualitative properties, or else, although experiences do involve such properties, the latter have no effects upon the stuff of physics. The point here, however, is simply that physicists appear not to consider this possibility at all, whereas metaphysicians, given their commitment to constructing a synoptic view of reality, are very likely indeed to address this question.

What do you consider to be the most neglected topics in contemporary metaphysics, and what direction would you like metaphysics to take in the future?

Interest in metaphysics has grown enormously in recent years, and if one looks back over the history of philosophy, I think one will find relatively few clearly formulated metaphysical questions that are not being seriously considered today. But I do think there are three important weaknesses that are very widespread in contemporary metaphysics.

First of all, there seems to me to be insufficient focus upon issues of analysis, and, in particular, upon the questions, first, of what the criterion is, in the case of descriptive concepts, of analytically basic concepts; secondly, of whether certain concepts are or are not analytically basic; and, thirdly, if they are not, how they can be analyzed. Thus, in the philosophy of time, defenders of tensed approaches to the nature of time typically help themselves to the tensed concepts of past, present, and future, without offering any analysis of those concepts. But given standard empiricist criteria of when a concept is analytically basic – formulated in terms of such notions as direct perception, direct awareness, or direct acquaintance – it follows that, at the very least, the concept of the future cannot be analytically basic. How, then, can that concept be analyzed? A natural answer, to put it roughly, is that the future is by definition what is later than the present. This general sort of analysis is fine, but given this type of analysis, one cannot then go on to hold – as most tensed theorists do – that the relation of temporal priority can be analyzed in terms of tensed concepts. Moreover, this sort of analysis of the concept of the future is not, it turns out, a viable option at all if one is a presentist. This in turn leads to a decisive objection to presentism, but one that is rarely noticed: the concept of the future cannot be analytically basic, but a presentist cannot offer any analysis of that concept.

There are a multitude of other areas of metaphysics where no satisfactory analyses have been offered of crucial concepts. Thus, in the case of mereology, no analysis of the part-whole relation in terms of analytically basic concepts has been offered. Similarly, in the metaphysics of persistence, no satisfactory analysis of what it is to endure has been given, while in the theory of action, the same is true of the concept of libertarian free will.

Secondly, in metaphysics, as in most areas of philosophy, philosophers appear generally not to be aiming at anything much beyond suggestive arguments that render a given view 'plausible'. I think that, as philosophers, we should aim much higher. If a metaphysical thesis is, if true, contingently true, and cannot be justified by direct acquaintance, then one should, as a philosopher, attempt to provide the type of support for it that scientists attempt to offer for scientific theories. If, on the other hand, a given metaphysical thesis is one that, if true, is analytically true, then one should attempt to offer a proof that is as rigorous as the proofs that mathematicians offer.

One thing that stands in the way of offering rigorous proofs is the failure to offer analyses of crucial concepts. Consider, for example, the dispute in mereology concerning the principle of unrestricted composition, according to which every specifiable set of entities has a mereological sum or fusion. In the absence of a satisfactory analysis of the part-whole relation, it seems unlikely that this issue will be resolved. But given an analysis of the part-whole relation, the prospects for proving or disproving the principle of unrestricted composition might be very good.

Finally, in metaphysics, as again in most areas of philosophy, I think that there is a failure to take seriously the possibility that proofs of central, very simple philosophical theses may turn out to be very difficult, complicated, and lengthy. Consider, for example, the thesis that a cause is always earlier than its effect. The brevity of this thesis may tempt one to think that if this proposition is true, a proof will not be too complicated, or too difficult to find. But if one considers the case of mathematics, it seems clear that such an assumption may very well be false. Consider, in particular, two of the most famous recent theorems in mathematics: the four color theorem, and Fermat's Last Theorem. In both cases, the proposition to be proved is a very simple one, but the proofs are very difficult. Thus, the four color theorem, as proved in 1976 by Kenneth Appel and Wolfgang Haken, involved considering 1936 special maps that were shown by a combination of hundreds of pages of hand analysis plus computer calculations to have certain properties, while in the case of Fermat's Last Theorem, the proof developed by Andrew Wiles (and in the final stage, his student Richard Taylor) is more than 100 pages in length, required seven years of work to find, and involved a number of sophisticated mathematical ideas developed by many mathematicians.

In short, I think that future progress in metaphysics requires, first, that one formulates a criterion for analytically basic concepts, and then offers analyses of fundamental metaphysical concepts in terms of analytically basic concepts; secondly, that given such analyses, one attempts to offer rigorous proofs of any propositions that, if true, are necessarily true; thirdly, that in searching for such proofs, one takes seriously the admittedly daunting possibility that such proofs may be as complicated and as difficult to find as many proofs are in the case of mathematics; and fourthly, that, in the case of metaphysical propositions that, if true, are only contingently true, and that cannot be justified by direct acquaintance, one should seek to adhere to the standards that scientists embrace in attempting to confirm a scientific theory.

17
Peter van Inwagen

The John Cardinal O'Hara Professor of Philosophy
The University of Notre Dame, USA

Why were you initially drawn to metaphysics (and what keeps you interested)?

When I was starting out in philosophy, when I was, so to speak, beginning to be a philosopher, I should have described my interests as centered not on "metaphysics" but on certain philosophical problems: the problem of free will and determinism, the problem of fictional existence, the nature of modality. As time passed, however, I began to use the term 'metaphysics' to tie the members of this rather diverse set of problems together. (As I became interested in further problems—the nature of material objects and their relations to their parts, the problem of identity across time, the problem of nominalism and realism—, I continued to use the word 'metaphysics' as a general term to tie the problems I was interested in together. I do not think that I became interested in these further problems because someone had classified them as belonging to 'metaphysics'.) But why did I use *that* word? This is a hard question to answer because it is not at all clear what it means to classify a philosophical problem as metaphysical. I had long been aware that 'metaphysics' and 'metaphysical' were problematical terms, but I did not fully appreciate how problematical they were till a few years ago when I began to write the article "Metaphysics" for *The Stanford Encyclopedia of Philosophy*.

Even when I had not seriously thought about any other philosophical problem than the problem of free will and determinism, I described my interest in that problem as "metaphysical." (Or perhaps I said, "I'm interested in the *metaphysical* problem of free will and determinism"—implying that there was more than one philosophical problem that could be called 'the problem of free will and determinism' and that I was interested in the one that was

metaphysical.) I said this because I believed that determinism—
the thesis that only one future is consistent with the present state
of things and the laws of nature (or the laws of physics)—was a
metaphysical thesis and that any problem that essentially involved
determinism was therefore a metaphysical problem.

But what did I mean by saying that determinism was a metaphysical thesis? That would be hard to say. I think it's clear what
the, as one might say, phenomenology of my choosing that term
was. Most other writers on the problem of free will and determinism did not think of determinism in the very abstract way that
I did—or so at least it appeared to me. *They* were not thinking
in terms of "the laws of nature" or "the laws of physics." *They*
had not had scientific educations—not even the first few stages
of a scientific education that I had had. *They* had never had to
answer examination questions like, "An artillery piece is fired at
an elevation of 37 degrees. The muzzle velocity of the shell is 2000
meters/second. What will the position and velocity of the shell
be ten seconds later? (Neglect air resistance and the rotation of
the earth.)." *I* could see that these examination questions had
answers—as, of course, examination questions should. *I* could see
that (neglecting air resistance and the rotation of the earth, to
be sure), Newton's laws of motion and assumption that the acceleration due to gravity near the surface of the earth is a given
that does not vary from case to case jointly implied that the elevation of a gun and the muzzle velocity of a shell fired from it
were together sufficient to *determine* the position and velocity of
the shell at any moment between the moment the gun was fired
and the moment of impact.

determinism, as I saw determinism, was a generalization of and
abstraction from the fact that certain questions have answers—the
questions about the evolution of physical systems that constitute
such a high proportion of the exercises that one finds at the ends
of the chapters in physics textbooks. (That is to say: the author
of the text gives the student some numbers that describe the state
of a system at one time and expects the student to produce some
numbers that describe its state at some later time.) The generalization, however, and the abstraction are extreme, and their
extremity takes one outside science. In making this generalization one quantifies over laws of physics and the physical quantities
that occur in them—over *real* laws of physics, God's-eye laws of
physics, which may well be radically different from any of those
principles that scientists and engineers of the present day use to

grind out numbers that characterize the behavior of projectiles and planets and protons. And quantifying over real, God's-eye, laws of physics is not something that is done "within" the science of physics or within any other science. It was because my approach to the problem of free will and determinism had this sort of "feel" that I described it as 'metaphysical'. (As opposed to what? Well, as opposed to 'psychological', 'linguistic', 'commonsensical', 'ethical'—all words I used to describe the approaches to the problem of free will and determinism that I found in the work of various other writers.)

The preceding two paragraphs were an attempt to describe what was in my mind when I said that the determinism I was interested in was "metaphysical" determinism. (Other philosophers might use the word 'determinism' as a name for—say—the thesis that human action is determined to occur by the agent's desires and beliefs at the moment just prior to that action. That sort of thesis wasn't . . . well, metaphysical enough to engage *my* refined interest.) Perhaps this attempt was successful and perhaps not, but it was certainly not much help with the question, What did I *mean* by calling the kind of determinism I was interested in "metaphysical" determinism. After all, that question has an answer only insofar as I did mean something by 'metaphysical', and it's not now evident to me that there was anything much I meant by the word—or anything much beyond this: a philosophical thesis is metaphysical if (i) it can't be assigned with confidence to any other part of philosophy, and (ii) it involves a very high level of abstraction.

And what, if anything, do I mean by 'metaphysics' now? I have no interesting answer to this question. For an extended exploration of the question 'What does "metaphysics" mean?' (and for some difficulties I now see in an earlier attempt of mine to answer this question), see the article in *The Stanford Encyclopedia of Philosophy* that I mentioned above.

What keeps me interested in the questions I *call* metaphysical (beyond the interest each of them has for me *individually*, in and of *itself*: I just *am* interested in the problem of identity across time; I just *am* interested in the question whether there are abstract objects), is that the attempt to answer them seems in every case to involve a certain kind of thinking (there is a certain kind of thinking such that, in every case of a question I call metaphysical, when I attempt to answer that question I find myself engaging in that kind of thinking). It seems, moreover, that *only* the questions I call metaphysical call for that kind of thinking. I will attempt to describe the nature of this kind of thinking in my answer to the question, "What do you consider to be the proper method for metaphysics?". Here I want to say something that is not about its nature but about what it is like to engage in it. I will do this by contrasting it with another kind of philosophical thinking that I have some experience of. Most of my philosophical thinking that is not about metaphysics belongs to Christian apologetic. (Which does not of course imply that none of my apologetic thinking is metaphysical thinking—that would be false.) This thinking could be looked upon as being in the service of "applied philosophy." (When apologetic is done by a philosopher, it is generally fair to describe it as applied philosophy.) It is the kind of thinking one does when one is defending an ethical or political or aesthetic or religious position that one considers particularly important against some reasoned attack by an opponent of that position. A good example of the kind of thinking I have in mind can be found in my papers "Non Est Hick" and "Critical Studies of the New Testament and Users of the New Testament." If Christianity is not the illusion most philosophers suppose it to be, what I have done in these and other essays of the same type may well be—depending on how good it is and whom it has reached—more important, perhaps vastly more important, than my work in metaphysics. But it is clear to me from my own experience of engaging in the kind of thinking that goes into these essays that that thinking does not engage the full resources of my mind. And that is not what I would say of the kind of thinking on display, for good or ill, in *Material Beings* or the essays collected in *ontology, identity, and modality*. Only when I am thinking about matters like "the special composition question" or Lewis's modal ontology or Putnam's criticisms of Quine's ontological method do I feel that my mind is fully awake. (I do not identify myself with my mind; I am not saying that *I* am fully awake only when I am engaged in metaphysical thinking. One in fact doesn't want one's mind to be fully awake any very high proportion of the time—if for no other reason, because when one's mind is fully awake, one's capacities for interacting with other human beings in all sorts of important ways will be asleep. If the Good Samaritan's mind had been fully awake when he was on the road from Jerusalem to Jericho, he would have been too wrapped up in his own thoughts even to have noticed the man who had fallen among thieves.) And this sort of thinking is addictive. I hope that when I am no longer able to do it, I shall be aware of this fact and able gracefully to stop trying to it. Till then, however, I have no choice but to continue indulging my addiction.

Having re-read what I have just written, it occurs to me that it may well be that I call a question metaphysical just in the case that my attempt to answer it involves the kind of thinking I have been trying to describe.

What do you consider to be your most important contributions to metaphysics?

I think I did as much as anyone to undermine the view that was the consensus on the problem of free will in the middle sixties when I began graduate studies in philosophy. This view was that the problem of free will was a solved problem. And the solution was 'compatibilism': the thesis that free will and determinism are compatible (because 'X was able to do otherwise' means something conditional, something along the general lines of, 'X would have done otherwise if X had chosen to do otherwise').

I think also that I left the problem of free will and determinism *clearer*, more precisely stated, than I found it. (It saddens me that those now working on the problem of free will and determinism are, or a significant proportion of them are, engaged in simply throwing all that hard-won clarity away. If one examines a really clear piece of writing on the problem of free will and determinism—for example, David Lewis's great essay, "Are We Free to Break the Laws?"—and the kind of thing that makes up no small part of what is written about free will and determinism today, the contrast is astonishing.)

I attach some importance to my defense of an "abstractionist" modal ontology—and particularly to my reply to David Lewis's charge that anyone who claims so much as to *understand* the language in which abstractionists frame their modal ontology is in effect claiming to possess magical powers of understanding.

I think that I did as much as anyone to create "the problem of material constitution." And I was certainly the philosopher who brought the "Special Composition Question" to the attention of the philosophers who were working on material constitution (despite the fact that I was not the first philosopher to formulate the question).

I think that I have had some important things to say about the identity of things and persons across time. I think that some of the things I have said about the concept of a temporal part and about the psychological-continuity theory of personal identity are worth paying attention to.

I believe I am responsible for metaphysicians' having come to think in terms of a distinction between 'ontology' and 'meta-ontology'—ontology being the discipline that asks the question 'What is there?' and meta-ontology being the discipline that asks the question, "What are we asking when we ask 'What is there?'?"

What do you think is the proper role of metaphysics in relation to other areas of philosophy and other academic disciplines, including the natural sciences?

I think that philosophy in general, and metaphysics in particular, have very little to offer to the natural sciences. (Philosophy and metaphysics are none the worse for that—just as sociology is none the worse for having nothing to offer to astrophysics.) In making this statement, I mean the phrase 'the natural sciences' to be understood in its strictest sense—I mean 'the natural sciences' to refer to the kind of research that leads to publications in journals of molecular biology or paleontology or condensed-matter physics. It is, however, a commonplace that not all scientists are content to communicate information about their work only in the pages of such journals—only to their peers, only to specialists in their own and closely related disciplines. According to Bouwsma, Wittgenstein once said (in conversation), "This is the age of popular science, and so cannot be the age of philosophy." I think that this characteristically gnomic statement means something like this: This is an age in which popular science plays a role in the general intellectual life of our species that had been played in an earlier age by philosophy (and in a still earlier age by theology). If this is true—and I think it is—, its truth is at least partly explained by two facts: that in the present age, scientists can expect that large numbers of people will listen to what they say on any subject they care to talk about, and that much of what appears under the rubric 'popular science' is, to all intents and purposes, philosophy. And this philosophy, the philosophy that infuses many works of popular science, is, I make bold to say, *radically amateur* philosophy, the philosophy of writers who do not know that there is such a thing as philosophy. (These writers no doubt know that there is something *called* 'philosophy' but they are unaware that this thing has any bearing on what they are trying to say—or perhaps a few of them do know that they are doing this thing called 'philosophy' but assume that, being scientists, they will automatically and without any resources beyond the furnishings of their own minds, be able to do it better than its official practitioners.) I have never seen any philosophical work by scientists (Galileo is the sole exception I am willing to allow) that is of much philosophical interest. And this judgment certainly applies to the attempts of scientists to discuss metaphysics. The attempts of scientists to address large questions outside their own disciplines (but informed by their knowledge of their disciplines) in work addressed to the general public would certainly be much better for some knowledge of what philosophers have had to say about those and related questions.

If metaphysics has nothing to offer the sciences, the sciences—the fruits of the real work of scientists and not their amateur attempts at philosophy—have a great deal to offer metaphysics. Many scientific discoveries are not only relevant to metaphysics but of inestimable metaphysical importance (one might cite the discovery by cosmology that the physical universe had a beginning in time, or the discovery by high-energy physics that material things are ultimately composed of things that are not themselves composed of smaller things—and yes, I know what McCall, Ladyman, and Ross have to say about that thesis). Nevertheless, the exploitation of this important resource for metaphysics (and more generally for philosophy) has been entirely the work of scientifically literate philosophers.

I would also note that, quite apart from the *discoveries* of physics (and the other sciences), many metaphysicians could learn a great deal by carefully studying the way in which the writers of physics textbooks introduce such concepts as "velocity," "acceleration," "mass," "force," "momentum," "energy," "work," "power," and "heat."

I do wish that my colleagues in literature and the social sciences would stop trying to do metaphysics (well, it's generally *anti*-metaphysics that they're trying to do). The scientists, philosophical amateurs though they may be, at least have at their disposal a fund of propositions that can serve as premises in metaphysical arguments. The *littérateurs* and the social scientists, however, have no such fund on which to draw. (I do think that literature and the social sciences are of signal philosophical relevance. But their relevance is to ethics and political philosophy and—of course—aesthetics, not to metaphysics or anti-metaphysics.)

It has long been a complaint of mine that the philosophy of mind suffers from the failure of philosophers of mind to pay sufficient attention to the metaphysical issues their statements involve them in. When I try to read through—as an interested outsider—the course of various debates in the philosophy of mind, I often find them difficult to follow. (That's the polite way of putting my point. The less polite is: I constantly find myself saying, "What does that even *mean*?") In a typical work in the philosophy of mind, concepts—and more often than not, they're metaphysical concepts—are pulled out of the air with no attempt to provide them with any definition or analysis. I will provide two examples of what I'm talking about.

Philosophers of mind like to talk about 'states'—mental states, physical states, what-have-you states. And when you ask a philosopher of mind what a 'state' is, the reply is generally either a blank stare or something along the lines of, "Well, *you* know—*states*. Please, none of your metaphysician's ontological quibbling. We philosophers of mind know what we mean when we talk about mental states and physical states, and if you don't, that's *your* problem." I insist on ontological quibbling, however. I insist on asking whether a state is an *attribute* (or a *property*, *quality*, *characteristic*, or *feature*). These are abstract objects, things that exist in all possible worlds and which are without causal powers. And the answer to this question I insist on asking (when any answer is given) is usually something like, "Well of course that's not what states are. A person's mental states exist only when he or she is *in* them, and they're constantly causing and being caused by other states." And then I have to ask, "But what is there for a state to *be* but a property? Aunt Milly's mental and physical states aren't *substances*, are they?—that is, things that belong to the same ontological category as Aunt Milly herself?" It is rare for the conversation to get as far as this, but if it does, I'm told (I paraphrase), "Well, they're neither substances nor attributes, they're *states*. Don't expect the things we talk about in the philosophy of mind to fit into the neat *a priori* categories you metaphysicians dream up." And my rejoinder is, "I don't see any reason to believe that there are any things with the combination of properties you assign to 'states.' It looks to me as if the very idea of a thing that has those properties makes no sense. All the stuff you say about or in terms of 'states' looks to me as if it's *not even false*." (A closely related point: don't get me started on the radical ontological—and even logical—confusions that infect what philosophers of mind say when they start talking about "qualia.")

My second example is the psychological continuity theory of

personal identity. But I have had a great deal to say about this subject already. I refer the interested reader to my essay, "Materialism and the Psychological Continuity Account of Personal identity" (*Philosophical Perspectives, Vol. 11: Mind, Causation, and World* (1997), pp. 305-319).

What do you consider to be the proper method for metaphysics?

William James has said, "Metaphysics means only an unusually obstinate attempt to think clearly and consistently." While this will hardly do as a *definition* of metaphysics, it is not a bad statement of the only *method* we metaphysicians have. A fuller attempt to answer this question can only take the form of a series of footnotes to this statement—can only be an attempt at a statement of what a metaphysician's obstinate attempt to think clearly and consistently should involve.

Bas van Frassen, an avowed enemy of metaphysics, seems to believe that the method of metaphysics (insofar as a pseudo-discipline can have a method) is that of "inference to the best explanation." As scientists are said by some to survey a set of empirical data and then try to come up with a theory that is the best explanation of those data, metaphysicians, van Frassen maintains, (think they) proceed by surveying some set of data (I will not attempt to say what these data might be) and then attempting to construct theories that explain them. These metaphysicians (so they suppose) then proceed to compare the theories they have constructed to explain one of these sets of data with an eye to discovering which one *best* explains them. (What the standards of comparison are, I will not attempt to say.) And it may be that van Frassen is right to say that this is what some metaphysicians (think they) are up to—and right in his unflattering comparison of the fruits of their labors with those of the labors of physicists and geologists and microbiologists. van Frassen errs, however, in supposing that this "method" (I agree entirely with his low opinion of its fruits) is essential to metaphysics, and I am doubtful whether it is very commonly employed by philosophers who call themselves metaphysicians. Like many people who offer unflattering diagnoses of the ills that afflict some field of human endeavor, van Frassen has fallen in love with his diagnosis and applies it indiscriminately and uncritically. "You're one of the people he's applied it to, right?" Very perceptive, Reader. But if I use my own work as an example, at least I'm in a position to have an informed opinion concerning the method of the person I'm using as an example. van Frassen has written:

> When interpreting scientific theories, we see much careful attention to the empirical aspect, and the relationship of the empirically superfluous parameters introduced to the observable phenomenon. That is why the Cartesian theory of vortices should receive considerably more respect—I'll say the same about Bohm's particles—than e.g., Peter van Inwagen or David Lewis' mereological atoms. Mere observance of correct logical form does not make a theory genuinely valuable: in Tom Stoppard's phrase, it can be coherent nonsense.
> -("Replies to Discussion on The Empirical Stance," Philosophical Studies, Vol. 121/2 (2004), pp. 171-192. The quoted passage is on p. 181.)

If I understand what van Frassen is saying, he thinks that the "mereological atoms" that occur in a certain metaphysical theory of mine—the theory presented in *Material Beings*—are "there" for some metaphysical reason: that they are a "metaphysical posit," that I have *postulated* them because, in my view, postulating them aids in explaining some set of data I have set out to explain. In fact, however, the mereological atoms are there because, rightly or wrongly (wrongly, Ladyman, *et al.* would say), I thought that the physicists said that matter had an atomic structure. Feynman has said:

"If in some cataclysm all scientific knowledge were to be destroyed and only one sentence passed on to the next generation of creatures, what statement would contain the most information in the fewest words? I believe it is the atomic hypothesis (or atomic fact, or whatever you wish to call it) that all things are made of atoms—little particles that move around in perpetual motion, attracting each other when they are a little distance apart, but repelling upon being squeezed into one another. In that one sentence, you will see there is an enormous amount of information about the world, if just a little imagination and thinking are applied." *The Feynman Lectures on Physics*, 3 Vols. (Reading, Mass.: Addison-Wesley, 1963-65), Vol. I, p. 2

Feynman, of course, is talking about atoms in the modern, chemical sense. In that sense, "atoms" are not what van Frassen calls *mereological* atoms—but Feynman would certainly not have objected to the statement that, just as "all things" (all things that are present to the senses or that can be seen through an optical microscope) are "made of (chemical) atoms," so chemical atoms are made of electrons and protons and neutrons (and perhaps photons), and protons and neutrons are made of quarks (and perhaps gluons). And there are good empirical reasons to suppose that electrons and quarks (and photons and gluons) are not "made of" anything (or, if you like, that they are not represented by the "standard theory" of elementary particles as made of anything): that they are (represented as) mereological atoms. And there is good reason to think that future physical theories, successors to the standard theory, if they do not postulate electrons and so on, will postulate partless things (little vibrating "loops of string," perhaps—but little loops of string that neither have proper parts nor are made of a stuff called string.) It is as certain as anything in this area can be that no physics descended from present-day physics is going to represent the physical world as consisting of continuous, homeomerous Aristotelian matter or as consisting of "gunk." Physics is (pretty clearly) always going to be "atomistic" in *some* not entirely empty sense. Physics is always going to have to find *some* sense for statements like, "The matter—the *stuff*— that was in this test tube after the reaction is the same matter that was in it before the reaction—albeit in a different form." And this sense, when spelled out, is (pretty clearly) always going to involve phrases of the form 'same Xs' where 'Xs' represents a plural count-noun. So what I am I *supposed* to do when I'm constructing a metaphysical theory about the identities of physical objects across time—a theory that involves the notion of "same matter"? Adopt an *Aristotelian* understanding of "same matter"? No, I simply borrowed the current scientific account of "same matter" (and perhaps registered my conviction that any future scientific account of "same matter" will be like the present-day account in being—in a very broad sense—atomistic). In sum, the mereological atoms are present in my metaphysical theory simply because I believe what the physicists tell me about matter—or at any rate, I believe what I *believe* they've told me. Even if I've misinterpreted them, even if my understanding of them is as feeble as Ladyman *et al.* think it is, my mereological atoms are not present in my metaphysical theory for a metaphysical reason. van Frassen thinks that they are only because he has brought to his reading of *Material Beings* a theory about what metaphysicians think they are doing—a theory that tells him that that's what I'm doing.

Whether or not this is fair to van Frassen, I do, as I have said, agree with his contention that trying to construct theories that explain some set of data is not going to yield any metaphysical conclusions of any interest. But then what method or methods *should* metaphysicians employ? I would not presume to dictate to other metaphysicians how they ought to proceed—or not beyond urging them to make an unusually obstinate effort to think clearly and consistently. But I'll say a few things about what I try to do when I'm doing (what I call) metaphysics.

First, in metaphysics (and I would say, in all parts of "core" philosophy: metaphysics, epistemology, the philosophy of language, the philosophy of mind, and philosophical logic) all words and phrases should be used in their ordinary senses or else explicitly defined. (As I said earlier, physics texts can provide some very instructive examples of good, precise definitions.) Definitions should satisfy the following formal requirement. They should be in "Chisholm style": the *definiendum* should be a sentence—normally an open sentence or a sentence schema—and the *definiens* a sentence containing the same free variables or schematic letters. In metaphysics, all terms of art should be connected to ordinary language by a chain of Chisholm-style definitions. (What I mean is that such a chain of definitions should be possible in principle, implicit in one's text and easily extracted from the text. One may certainly introduce one's terms of art more informally if one is confident that the reader will be able to see how to construct the chain of definitions. There's no call for unnecessary formality. But in borderline cases it's always better to err on the side of pedantry—for recall Russell's definition of a pedant: 'A man who cares whether what he says is true'.) Similarly, one's arguments should be formally valid—though not necessarily presented in a form that is explicitly so. To say this is not to imply that there are proofs in philosophy as there are proofs in mathematics. It is simply to recommend a trick that will ensure that one is at least *aware* of all one's premises.

While we are on formal matters, I insist that in core philosophy one be scrupulous about use and mention. Every metaphysician must understand "Quine Corners" or "quasi-quotation marks" and use them when they are appropriate. (In my experience, about eighty per cent of the philosophers who use Quine Corners use them impressionistically, without actually understanding how they work.)

Following these simple rules will enable the philosopher at least to produce what van Frassen has called coherent nonsense. In my view, it's much better to write coherent nonsense than to write incoherent nonsense. The reason is simple: if nonsense is logically coherent, it's much easier to see that it's nonsense and to see *why* it's nonsense than it is if the nonsense is logically incoherent. For example, if a philosopher's sentence contains a gross use-mention confusion, a reader of the text in which it occurs may suspect that there was some meaningful thesis that the author was *trying* to express—and may find, after re-writing or attempting to re-write the sentence without the use-mention confusion, that there was really no idea there at all. If the author had taken the trouble to write *coherent* nonsense, the reader would have been spared that task.

But these matters—important though they are—are of merely formal significance. What can I say that is more substantive? I would say that my own method in metaphysics (insofar as I have one) is this:

One should consider those theses that one *brings to* philosophy—theses that (so one supposes) practically everyone, oneself included, accepts, or theses (so one supposes) that have been endorsed by disciplines other than philosophy and in which one reposes a high degree of confidence (economic history, it may be, or microbiology or algebraic topology). One should try to discover what the metaphysical implications of those theses are. If, for example, one wants to know whether there are universals, what one should *not* do is this: collect a set of data ("This thing here is red and that other thing over there is also red") and attempt to discover whether those data a best explained by a "theory" that "posits" universals; what one *should* do is to ask whether the theses that one brings to philosophy *logically imply* the existence of universals (one will, of course, have provided a careful definition of 'universal').

Note that this "method" (better: this piece of methodological advice) has implications for the epistemology of metaphysics. It implies that the epistemological problems or questions that confront metaphysicians—those of them who employ this method—fall into two groups: questions that are raised by the things they believed before they came to metaphysics, and questions that are raised by their beliefs concerning the logical implications of those things. (For example: How can one determine whether the existence of the real numbers is a logical implication of the statement that there are bodies whose behavior is governed by the law of universal gravitation?) The questions in the first group are profoundly difficult, but they are not questions that confront metaphysicians because they are metaphysicians: they confront metaphysicians only because, outside or prior to philosophy, they believe what most people believe. (Obviously, therefore, the metaphysician who employs this method will be, in Strawson's words, a "descriptive" rather than a "revisionary" metaphysician.) The questions in the second group are no doubt difficult—some of them are difficult—, but there does not seem to be any good reason to regard them as intractable.

It is important to realize that I have *not* recommended the following method: Treat the theses we accept before we come to metaphysics as data that it is the business of metaphysics to explain; construct metaphysical theories that explain those data; compare these theories and find the one among them that best explains those data. (The so-called Quine-Putnam Indispensability Argument is an example of this method at work.) No, I'm recommending only that metaphysicians try to discover the metaphysical implications of—the metaphysical theses that are *logical* implications of—the things they believe on non-metaphysical (and, more generally, non-philosophical) grounds.

There is another method, or another methodological idea, that has, I believe, profoundly influenced my own work. But I find this "idea" very difficult to formulate verbally. My best attempt is along these lines:

Let your investigations be centered on general theses, not particular examples. If an otherwise attractive general thesis seems to have counterexamples, try to explain them away. If it is in conflict with particular things we are inclined to say, try to explain the fact that we are inclined to say these things away. Look at the particular theses about things in the light of the general theses you find attractive.

This methodological idea played a central role in the development of the theory I presented in *Material Beings*. In that case, it took something like this form:

Do not begin your investigation of the metaphysics of material objects by asking, e.g., whether there are tables and chairs. Begin by considering possible alternative answers to the Special Composition Question. If the best answer seems to be one that implies that there are no tables or chairs, try to explain the fact that "We all think there are tables and chairs" away. Ask yourself whether there really *is* such a fact as this.

But *Material Beings* is a special and very difficult case. (Many philosophers believe the book to be an essay in revisionary metaphysics. And many who are not guilty of that misreading would be hard-pressed to find a way to regard it as an example of "trying to discover the metaphysical implications of things we all believe." I do so regard the book, but I cannot defend this view here.) Instead I will give a relatively simple example of the method I am recommending, an example drawn from philosophical logic rather than metaphysics. (It can be more briefly stated and raises fewer side issues than any example I can think of from metaphysics.)

According to standard sentential logic, the argument-form '$\sim p \mid\!\!- (p \rightarrow q)$' is valid. Many philosophers say that this fact implies that '$\rightarrow$' does not represent the 'if-then' of "ordinary" English conditionals ("'is'-'is'" conditionals, as opposed to "'were'/'did'-'would be'" conditionals). If it did, they contend (the example, of course, is my own), the following argument would be valid:

Marseilles is not the capital of France

hence, If Marseilles is the capital of France, Kim Jong-il is the illegitimate son of President Truman.

And if this argument were valid, 'If Marseilles is the capital of France, Kim Jong-il is the illegitimate son of President Truman' would be true—which it obviously isn't. And how do they know this? Well, they ask themselves whether this sentence is true, and they discover within themselves a conviction that it isn't. In my view, according to the methodological principle I'm recommending, this isn't what they should be asking. They should, rather, be asking themselves what general logical principles they think govern 'if-then' (and 'or' and 'it is not the case that' and the other little English words and phrases that are in some sense supposed to correspond to the connectives of sentential logic). I would ask them to consider the following argument:

Marseilles is the capital of France

hence, Either Marseilles is the capital of France or Kim Jong-il is the illegitimate son of President Truman

Marseilles is not the capital of France

hence, Kim Jong-il is the illegitimate son of President Truman.

And I would ask them whether they would concede that it was valid. Most of them would, although a few of them wouldn't. Let me address only those who would. I would proceed to ask them whether the principle of "Conditional Proof" applies if the "conditional" in question is an "ordinary" 'if-then' conditional. And this is a relevant question, for if it does apply, then (in virtue of the above argument's validity), the argument

Marseilles is not the capital of France

hence, If Marseilles is the capital of France, Kim Jong-il is the illegitimate son of President Truman.

is valid. I don't in fact know what "they" would say, but *I* can testify that I find it much easier to believe that 'If Marseilles is the capital of France, Kim Jong-il is the illegitimate son of President Truman' is true (I mean, who *cares* what truth-value that bizarre sentence has?—isn't that a *paradigm case* of a "don't care"?) than I do to believe that Conditional Proof is not valid if the "conditional" in question is the 'if-then' conditional. In other words—and this is the point of the example—I do not proceed simply by considering a particular 'if-then' sentence with a false antecedent and asking myself whether it's true. I proceed by considering some argument-forms that involve 'if-then' (and 'either-or' and 'it is not the case that': the ordinary-language analogues of Addition and Disjunctive Dilemma) and asking myself whether I think those argument-forms are valid. In other words, I consider the question whether the conditional 'If Marseilles is the capital of France, Kim Jong-il is the illegitimate son of President Truman' is true only in the light provided by my consideration of much more general logical questions.

And I recommend considering the question whether there are tables and chairs only in the light provided by consideration of much more general ontological questions.

What do you consider to be the most neglected topics in contemporary metaphysics, and what direction would you like metaphysics to take in the future?

Only a few years ago, I should have said that meta-ontology was the most neglected topic in metaphysics (I mean of those that don't deserve to be neglected). Happily, this is no longer the case. I hope that the current lively debates about meta-ontology (such as those on display in the recent collection *Metametaphysics: New Essays on the Foundations of ontology*) will continue and deepen.

I hope that in the coming decade, metaphysicians will devote considerably more time than they so far have to the topic of the relative merits of constituent and relational ontologies.

Constituent ontologies are ontologies that affirm the existence of attributes (properties, qualities, characteristics, features) and which, moreover, treat these objects as being in some sense "constituents" of the substances (individuals, particulars) that have them (exemplify them, instantiate them, exhibit them). The theory that individuals are "bundles" of qualities is a paradigmatic example of a constituent ontology—for if x is a bundle of ys, those ys must in some sense be constituents of x.

Relational ontologies are ontologies that affirm the existence of attributes but which treat the "having" relation as in no way like the whole-to-part relation—as not even remotely analogous to that relation or to any mereological relation. According to the advocates of relational ontology, the binary relation "having" that Mars and a socialist banner bear to the quality redness is as abstract, as bloodless, as purely external, as the variably polyadic relation "are numbered by" that the moons of Mars and the epics of Homer bear to the number two. It is an axiom of relational ontology that the only "constituents" of any substance (individual, particular) are its parts, its parts in the strict and mereological sense; and, further, that any proper parts a substance (individual, particular) has are "smaller" members of the same ontological category: smaller substances (smaller individuals, smaller particulars).

Many metaphysicians have endorsed and have worked within a constituent ontology. Many metaphysicians have endorsed and have worked within a relational ontology. But an examination of the relative merits of constituent ontologies (on the one hand) and relational ontologies (on the other) is a neglected and important topic.

I also hope that some metaphysicians will turn their attention to the question of the implications a relational ontology for the philosophy of mind. For a first attempt at an investigation of this question, see my essay, "A Materialist ontology of the Human Person" in the collection *persons: Human and Divine* (Oxford: 2007) that Dean Zimmerman and I edited.

18
Dean Zimmerman

Professor of Philosophy
Rutgers University, USA

Why were you initially drawn to metaphysics (and what keeps you interested)?

My first college course, the summer after high school, was an introduction to philosophy in which we read Richard Taylor's *Metaphysics*. The topics in Taylor's book — the mind-body problem, freedom and determinism, fatalism, time and change, causation, God — struck me as deep, difficult, and profoundly important. These were the themes that had captured my interest in the science fiction I had read in junior high, in the apologetics by C. S. Lewis I had read in high school, and in the "serious" literature I would read as a college English major. As my undergraduate studies continued, I gradually realized that I didn't want merely to write and think about philosophical problems indirectly, as they cropped up from time to time in the fiction of Camus, Malraux, Dostoevsky, Thomas Mann, Charles Williams, or Walker Percy. If they, or their characters, could ask — and try their best to answer — questions about God, free will, time, and so on, why couldn't we still do these things? That's what Richard Taylor had seemed to be doing. Although I retaineqd my English and French majors, I found myself taking more and more philosophy courses until, before I knew it, I turned into a philosophy major as well.

Fortunately, by this time (c. 1983) metaphysical topics were once again on the front burner in (so-called) "analytic philosophy" — including in the small philosophy department at the university in my hometown, where I was a student: Mankato State University, now Minnesota State University. Epistemology and metaphysics were my favorite topics. (Earnest and hopeful attempts to understand Wittgenstein and the writers of "semiotics" ended in failure.) My teachers (mainly Hal Walberg, the late Ron Rickers, Ron Yezzi, and Robert Wallace) were very impressive in the classroom, and generous with their time outside of it. They all seemed to agree that Russell, Quine, and Chisholm were three of the most important figures in 20th century philosophy, so I read a lot by them. Quine's brilliance and impeccable style impress me still; but, ultimately, Russell and Chisholm have done more to shape the way I approach philosophy in general and metaphysics in particular.

My teachers advised me to go to Brown. The Brown philosophy department then included Felicia Ackerman, Roderick Chisholm, Jaegwon Kim, Martha Nussbaum, Ernest Sosa, and James van Cleve. (I also drove to Yale seminary twice a week one winter to take two classes with Robert Merrihew Adams.) I expected to study epistemology, but Chisholm's seminars were mostly metaphysics while I was there. His winsome Socratic style, and his warm encouragement of our best efforts to refute him, won me over immediately; and soon I, too, was doing mostly metaphysics. Chisholm directed my thesis on mereological essentialism, and the committee was, for me, a metaphysical dream team, with Kim and van Cleve on board as well. My undergraduate professors had given me excellent advice.

For those of us who entered philosophy in the 1980s, it was as if the anti-metaphysical movements that began in the late '30s — first logical positivism and then the "ordinary language philosophy" practiced by Wittgenstein and J. L. Austin — had never happened. My teachers in Mankato had conveyed the impression (correct, I believe) that these movements were historically important but brief episodes in the history of the subject, and that the problems and methods of late 20th century metaphysics — what I found in Chisholm, Thomas Nagel, Saul Kripke, Alvin Plantinga, David Armstrong, David Lewis, Peter van Inwagen, Jaegwon Kim, etc. — were not all that different from those of Aristotle, Aquinas, Descartes, Berkeley, or Hume. The impression was confirmed at Brown, where Chisholm frequently appealed to Thomas Reid, the Austrian school (Brentano, Meinong, and others), and the pre-positivist analytic philosophers (mainly Russell and Moore); and van Cleve made Locke, Leibniz, Berkeley, and even Kant(!), seem like the most natural conversation partners for contemporary philosophers.

Later on, I was to discover that, outside philosophy departments in the Anglophone world, and almost everywhere in Continental Europe, it was widely believed that, "since Kant", philosophers had somehow discovered that metaphysics was impossible. From within philosophy departments, however, things looked very different. It appeared that what philosophers had been doing, at least since mid-century, was proving that the proofs of the impossibility of metaphysics were bad. Today, philosophers who believe in the impossibility of *Kant* greatly outnumber those who believe in the impossibility of metaphysics.

Why are philosophers in other departments (religious studies, theology, anthropology, Cultural Studies, English...) so eager to pronounce last rites over metaphysics? At least part of the answer must be the kind of motivation that lay behind the critiques of metaphysics given by Kant, Wittgenstein, and the logical positivists: Metaphysical problems seem never to go away, and long-dead metaphysical views come back to life with alarming regularity, hardly the worse for wear. If, after a hundred generations, we have made little progress in our attempts to solve a set of problems, it would be nice to think that there are really no problems there to be solved. The alternative — that we're just not very good at solving these sorts of problems — is much harder on the ego. There may be principled reasons to be suspicious of the practice of metaphysics; but much anti-metaphysical sentiment seems to me to be borne of little more than intellectual hubris, unwillingness to accept that some problems may be too hard for the human mind to solve in a truly conclusive way.

Which raises the second part of this question: "What keeps me interested in metaphysics" — especially when the subject does not admit of the kind of progress one can hope for in some other fields? Partly, it's a matter of temperament, I suppose: a metaphysician must be the sort of person who can work hard developing arguments that almost invariably fail to convince a solid majority of those whose opinion should matter. Apparently I have the temperament for that — I've certainly seen plenty of my arguments rejected by people I greatly respect; but I soldier on.

One factor that makes soldiering on seem not so bad is the conviction that the grass is not much greener elsewhere in philosophy. Should I, instead, take up ethics, hoping to be part of the generation that finally proves utilitarianism's truth (falsehood)? Would philosophy of language be safer? At least philosophers of language have achieved unanimity about, say, direct reference theories of proper names, and externalism about meanings more generally. (Oops! Spoke too soon....) Perhaps I'd be safer in philosophy of mind, where at least all the experts finally agree that a broadly physicalist conception of the mental is the only reasonable option. (A small but growing number of philosophers of mind no longer subscribe to the weak-tea, supervenience formulations of physicalism that had become the "party line".) The problems of metaphysics are on the same spectrum of insolubility as the hardest philosophical problems in other subfields. I suspect that there's a historical reason why we have been left with the hardest ones, why there appears to be more progress in other areas: metaphysics used to be the default location for *all* the most intractable questions; but, as metaphysicians succeed in developing conceptual tools that afford some traction on an issue, we give the set of problems and the tools to a newly minted science or philosophical subdiscipline. That means metaphysics is left with the most stubborn problems — but not because metaphysicians have never made progress on any of the issues they've tackled. (I'll say a little more to substantiate this claim in answer to question three.)

Another thing that makes metaphysics personally rewarding — despite the surprising fact that a consensus has not coalesced around my own opinions — is the friendships I have enjoyed with fellow metaphysicians. My admiration for many of my metaphysical heroes only grew upon meeting them; being able to count Chisholm, David Lewis, David Armstrong, Alvin Plantinga, Robert Adams, and Peter van Inwagen as teachers, mentors, colleagues, and friends has been a tremendous honor. And my friendships with "younger" (now mostly, like myself, middle-aged) metaphysicians have been among the deepest I have enjoyed. My papers would be much worse, had I not been able to try out ideas on Ted Sider, John Hawthorne, and many other dear friends (including, now, many former and current students) who are metaphysicians of the first water. In good company, the hunt can be pleasurable even when the quarry is elusive.

What do you consider to be your most important contributions to metaphysics?

I seem destined to play the role of "that one guy who still defends X", where X is some outmoded view, unpopular since at least the 1930s. presentism, mereological essentialism, endurantism, substance dualism, sense data, non-Humean causal powers, theism... I find all these doctrines attractive, and at least as defensible as their main competitors. Their unpopularity seems to me to be not so much due to conclusive refutations as to shifting intellectual fashions. If I'm right about that, they belong back on the table; and the fact that they're unfashionable just means that they are even more deserving of the best case I can make for them.

As a result, I suppose I'm bound to look like something of a dinosaur. But I'm a great admirer of Russell, Moore, C. D. Broad, C. J. Ducasse, H. H. Price, G. F. Stout, D. C. Williams, C. A. Strong, and other metaphysicians who flourished in the '20s and '30s; so if I were to be thought of as, basically, a throwback to their era, I would feel that I'm in good company.

Most of my work in metaphysics, so far, falls under one of three heads: the nature and persistence conditions of material objects, the nature of persons (in particular, whether they are material objects or something else), and the debate between the A-theory of time and the B-theory of time.

Obviously, the first two issues are closely connected. One of my first goals was to show that mereological essentialism — the view that objects do not, and cannot, gain or lose any parts — can be motivated (at least as a principal governing some kinds of physical objects) by considering (a) the presuppositions behind our use of mass terms and (b) the possibility of "atomless gunk" — stuff that has parts within parts *ad infinitum*, and no smallest bits. "Matter" is one very general mass term, and in some phrases (e.g., "the matter now constituting my body"), it seems to be used to refer to portions or parcels of matter. The possibility of the atomless case suggests that these portions cannot be construed as sets or pluralities, but must be (potentially scattered) individuals. The principal papers in which I explore the metaphysics of matter and other portions of stuff are (Zimmerman, 1995, 1997a, 1997b)

"The matter that now constitutes my body will eventually be widely scattered, though *I* will not be widely scattered." If that sentence is true, then there is such a thing as the matter that now constitutes my body, and it is not identical with me. The persistence conditions of the matter now in my body would seem to be: no gain or loss of any parts that are bits of matter (conditions that approximate the doctrine of mereological essentialism). Admitting that I am a physical object located exactly where the matter is now located would require coincident, intrinsically indistinguishable physical things. Quite a few of my papers try to make this position harder to maintain, sometimes by attacking the doctrine of temporal parts — a metaphysics of persistence through time that would make it easier to see how two physical objects could completely coincide at one time but differ in their total histories (Zimmerman, 1998b, 1998c, 1999). "Material People" (Zimmerman 2003) surveys a wide range of options for the metaphysics of persons. Several papers go to town on particular authors who defend a metaphysics of coincident physical objects (Zimmerman, 2002, 2009). More recently, I have begun to explore the question what I must be like, if I am not identical with this "gross physical body"; and to argue for a dualism of material and mental substances on the basis of the sort of property dualism defended by David Chalmers and many others. My case for substance dualism in (Zimmerman 2010) turns upon three propositions: that the right account of the vagueness of macrophysical objects such as brains and human bodies is that their vagueness is a matter of "semantic indecision"; that property dualism requires fundamental laws about phenomenal states; and that objects the vagueness of which is a matter of semantic indecision are the wrong sorts of things to enter into fundamental laws of nature.

My papers on time defend the idea that there really is a deep metaphysical difference between A-theories of time and B-theories of time: the A-theorists posit objective distinctions between past and present, and present and future; while the B-theorists do not. Most of my efforts in the philosophy of time have been expended in the attempt to understand what "objective" means in this context, and to work out the best A-theoretic account of the nature of the differences between things and events that are past, present, or future (Zimmerman, 1998b, 2005, 2006, forthcoming).

I sometimes suspect that my most important contributions to metaphysics, at least so far, have actually been more practical or social in nature. I've found the metaphysics scene to be friendly and downright fun. People help one another out (usually by delivering a devastating counterexample) and encourage one another (which is especially important after receipt of the devastating counterexample). I have devoted a lot of time and energy to collaborative projects that are intended to protect and amplify this positive vibe — including organizing about 14 conferences or workshops (with eight more planned for the next three years). I like to think that, by frequently bringing people together to discuss one another's work in cooperative and relatively noncompetitive settings (well, noncompetitive by philosophical standards), I've helped to foster the healthy sense of camaraderie enjoyed by those of us in the relatively small world of analytic metaphysics.[1]

Chisholm and David Lewis left their mark on several generations of metaphysicians. They impressed us by their eagerness to submit their work, before publication, to the most searching criticisms we could provide in seminars, talks, workshops, and correspondence. They wanted to get things right, and had no stomach for evasion. Both Chisholm and Lewis made deliberate efforts to mentor and promote the work of younger philosophers (and not just those who were their own students). I hope that, by convening numerous fruitful metaphysical workshops, I have helped promote some of the communal scholarly virtues they stood for.

What do you think is the proper role of metaphysics in relation to other areas of philosophy and other academic disciplines, including the natural sciences?

The boundaries of metaphysics are difficult to plot. One thing seems clear enough: ontology has always been central to metaphysics. Since ontological questions arise in every discipline, it is a good place to start when explaining metaphysics' relations to other fields.

ontology comprises all attempts to think clearly about what it is to exist, and (some would say, more generally) what it is to *be*. A theory of existence and being must not only tell us whether there *are* things that do not *exist*; it must answer the question whether the categories of existing and being exhaust the objects about which we can talk and think. Must we countenance objects that are "beyond being and nonbeing" — like Meinong's round square, which neither *is* nor *exists*, yet manages at least to be round (and, of course, square as well)? ontology also includes "The Theory of Categories". Here, the goal is to catalogue and to chart the important relations holding among highly abstract kinds of thing (classifications only slightly less general than *Being*

---

[1] In the early years of my annual "Metaphysical Mayhem" workshops, I was bringing a group of younger metaphysicians together; the Mayhem gave us a chance to help one another and also to meet one or two senior figures each summer. Nowadays, the Mayhem is a biennial, week-long seminar for about 25 grad students coming from departments all over the U.S.; and again, the goal is to foster collaboration among geographically separated younger scholars, and to introduce them to senior professors they wouldn't otherwise meet (the leaders of the seminars). (Starting summer 2010, Michael Rota and I will be hosting a similar, but longer, workshop in philosophy of religion at the University of St. Thomas, in Minnesota.)

and *Existing*); and to describe properties and relations that apply to extremely wide ranges of things. Though we have only had the label "ontology" since the 18th century, it subsumes concerns that were central to philosophy since its inception. Aristotle's theory of categories included substance, quantity, relation, place, time, position, state, action, and being acted upon; subsequent generations of metaphysicians have added to and subtracted from his list. Other notions sufficiently general to belong to ontology include: property, accident and e, necessary and contingent existence, fact, state of affairs, event, and the parthood relation.

Every serious academic discipline has a subject matter about which one can raise ontological questions — metaphysics rears its head whenever a scholar in another field of study starts asking sufficiently abstract questions about the kinds of things he or she is studying. The student of literature might be led to ask: "What *are* fictional characters, anyway? Do they *exist*? If so, is their existence contingent or necessary? And what are they like? Are they like unexemplified properties, or more concrete things made out of words, or what?" The physicist might start to wonder: "Does space-time exist? Is it an entity in addition to particles, fields, and whatever other phenomena stand in spatiotemporal relations?" Or she might ask herself: "How should I think about the multi-dimensional phase space so useful to contemporary physics? Is it a real thing, a manifold with parts that actually exist; or is it just a handy way of talking about the possible states of the much simpler, four-dimensional space-time manifold?"

Questions about the ontological status of a given subject matter are often the kind of thing only a metaphysician could love, with little relevance to the bulk of what goes on in the study of literature, physics, or what have you. Occasionally, though, failure to get clear about the fundamental nature of the objects of study can throw a discipline off course. Berkeley's ontological questions about the "fluxions" of early calculus revealed a deep confusion in this new part of mathematics, a confusion that had to be resolved before the method could be given a firm basis. Ontological questions about the nature of dispositions seem to have played a role in the demise of doctrinaire behaviorism in psychology. In all of the sciences, causal claims are made. But causation is notoriously puzzling; and because causal claims are made about phenomena from so many different domains, exploration of the nature of causation belongs, at least in part, to ontology. The special sciences, in particular, make use of causal notions that call out for some careful attention. What are the kinds of things or properties or states that serve as causes and effects in economics, for instance? Some schools of economic theory claim the others start off on the wrong foot, due to faulty ontological assumptions; and for all I know, they are right.

So one way in which metaphysics connects with other academic disciplines is by helping them to get straight about the ontology of their subject — at the very least, to see what the options are, and to help determine whether choice of ontological scheme might make some difference to the way theories are developed in that field.

Metaphysicians have much to gain from the effort to fashion an ontology adequate to knowledge in a wide variety of fields. A system of ontological categories aspires to universality — nothing should be without a kind under which it falls, and every kind should be given some general characterization. Propounding an ontology adequate to physics or literary studies or psychology serves as a test of the completeness of one's theory of the categories. Here is an example of how one might find oneself altering one's ontology to make room for the subject of some other field: Some metaphysicians suppose that everything is either concrete and contingent or abstract and necessary. To make sense of fictional entities, one might be forced to accept the existence of a further category: the abstract contingent things.

Not all of metaphysics falls neatly under the heading of ontology, though most problems of metaphysics have an ontological aspect to them. I suspect that the presence of problems that are not closely tied to ontology — e.g., the compatibility or incompatibility of freedom with determinism — is due to the fact that metaphysics is the great dumping ground for outstanding problems with no proper home of their own. Problems for which no successful, empirically-driven method of inquiry has so far been developed are often left at our doorstep, when no other subfield of philosophy wants them.

Looking at the scope of "metaphysics" in older textbooks and systematic treatises, I can see an explanation for this arrangement; not that long ago, "metaphysics" seems to have meant little more than "all the deepest, darkest problems of philosophy, with the exception of ethics and (maybe) logic". It was the vaguely demarcated center of philosophy, from which portions broke off to become more specialized subfields of philosophy or, in the most successful cases, autonomous sciences. As philosophical study of knowledge became more specialized, it became the independent enterprise of epistemology (or "criteriology", as the neo-scholastics called their version of it); when philosophical study of the mind became more specialized, it broke away to become "philosophy of mind"; and so on. Metaphysics is connected to most of the sciences in a similar way. The questions of physics, before the scientific revolution, were typically pursued by metaphysicians using largely a priori methods. One can admire the cleverness of medieval arm-chair arguments for or against the thesis that, after a projectile is thrown, it is the air that pushes it along; while nevertheless being grateful for the day when such questions could be taken from metaphysicians' hands. In the late 19th century, psychology and cosmology were still routinely classified alongside ontology as two of the principal subcategories of metaphysics; soon, they, too, were on their own. The founders of the special sciences — e.g., psychology, linguistics, sociology, economics,... — have almost always been philosophers or philosophers-without-portfolio, making metaphysical distinctions and giving recognizably philosophical arguments as they laid the groundwork for a new discipline. When philosophers find ways to think about a certain domain that allow for the formulation of testable hypotheses, the domain may gradually come under the purview of an autonomous science whose practitioners need something other than mere philosophical expertise. We should be grateful to be rid of some metaphysical questions when this happens. There are always plenty left! From this point of view, metaphysics is not so much the garbage heap where unanswerable questions are dumped; it is the place where all sorts of intransigent problems have been kicked around in hopes that, eventually, successful strategies for answering them will emerge — as they frequently have.

Sometimes attempts to establish a new science are abortive. The assumptions underlying a protoscience may turn out to be false; think of phrenology, for example. And sometimes it is tempting to lay at least some of the blame on a lack of metaphysical or philosophical savvy on the part of the founders. To take a somewhat outdated example: the theoretical underpinnings of Alfred Korzybski's General semantics (a once popular "non-Aristotelian" discipline for understanding and controlling our "semantic reactions") exhibit philosophical sloppiness which raised suspicions about its therapeutic value. Anthropology provides a more controversial example. I am not qualified to judge whether the following story is correct, but it's what one hears from some critics of the discipline, both within and without; and, if the story is even roughly accurate, anthropology provides a good example of the interplay between metaphysics and the attempt to found a new scientific discipline: Apparently anthropology is showing every sign of unraveling as an autonomous academic field with its own methods and subject matter (there seems little disagreement about this, even from within anthropology). The founders posited a category, "human nature", in virtue of which all societies made up of members of the species *Homo sapiens* would inevitably follow similar trajectories, passing through the same stages. The second generation of anthropologists rejected many of the earliest anthropologists' fundamentally metaphysical assumptions about human nature; but, instead of searching for better, more stable categories to comprehend the phenomena they wished to study, they embraced extreme forms of philosophical relativism that made the search for firmer ground seem misguided. Eventually, the desire to find some kind of theoretical underpinnings led many to the adoption of whatever philosophical trends blew over from Continental Europe — none of which provided a stable foundation for a genuine *science* of anthropology. According to this 'just-so story' of the failure of anthropology, it can be traced, first, to ontological assumptions (about whether *human nature* is a natural kind, one that constrains the ways in which human societies can evolve) that turned out to be false; and, second, to principled opposition to (sound) metaphysics (or at least sound philosophy) when these assumptions were called into question.

What do you consider to be the proper method for metaphysics?

There is often supposed to be something especially undisciplined about metaphysical disagreements; I guess we metaphysicians are thought to be further away from knowing the proper method for settling our disputes than philosophers in other subfields. But the central problems of metaphysics seem to me to arise for the same kinds of reasons as the central problems of ethics, philosophy of mind, philosophy of language, etc. "Proper method" for dealing with our problems seems to me to be no more or less principled than in other subfields of philosophy; and the amount of disagreement after our methods are implemented may be somewhat greater. To the extent that it *is* greater, the fact may be attributed, at least in part, to metaphysics' habit of giving away its problems when metaphysicians begin to develop promising strategies for solving them.

The philosophical impulse — which can lead even ordinary people, unspoiled by the teachings of philosophers, into thinking philosophically — springs from the discovery of apparent inconsistencies or tensions among beliefs we already have. In response to such discoveries, a person can distract herself with backgammon or horror movies or some more worthwhile pursuit. But, given the leisure, one surely ought to try to pinpoint the sources of such problems and, if possible, eliminate them. Many of the apparent inconsistencies that have bothered us, generation after generation, have for one reason or another been handed over to metaphysicians to sort out. And I have nothing specific or original to say about a general method for tackling all such problems in metaphysics (and philosophy more generally). I can think of nothing better to do than to recite some of Russell's maxims on the subject:

> In every philosophical problem, our investigation starts from what may be called "data," by which I mean matters of common knowledge, vague, complex, inexact, as common knowledge always is, but yet somehow commanding our assent as on the whole and in some interpretation pretty certainly true. ... We are quite willing to admit that there may be errors of detail in this knowledge, but we believe them to be discoverable and corrigible by the methods which have given rise to our beliefs.... There is not any superfine brand of knowledge, obtainable by the philosopher, which can give us a standpoint from which to criticize the whole of the knowledge of daily life. The most that can be done is to examine and purify our common knowledge by an internal scrutiny, assuming the canons by which it has been obtained, and applying them with more care and with more precision. -(Russell, 1914: 72-74)

I would not pretend that Russell gives us much more here than: (i) condemnation of appeals to special philosophical insights, *if* they lead to rejection of large parts of our "common knowledge"; and (ii) the admonition to think harder than we normally do about what we take ourselves to know, and the kinds of evidence we take ourselves to have for it. If Russell's advice is on the right track, however, there can be little excuse for doing philosophy that does not trace back to some apparent conflict among ordinary "prephilosophical" beliefs. I suppose I would be willing to grant that there are beliefs that have some positive epistemic standing for me, even though they pertain to a specialized subject matter that only a philosopher could love; but whatever reason I have for believing them couldn't be enough to give them leverage over significant bodies of "common knowledge".

I will say a few things, also unoriginal, about proper method with respect to metaphysics' hard core: ontology. Basically, I accept Quine's methodology — as have so many other metaphysicians, after reading "On What There Is" (Quine, 1948). Quine's "criterion of ontological commitment", as a recommendation for proper method in ontology, can be separated from the anti-metaphysical elements in his larger philosophical perspective (indeed, in his 1939 paper, "A Logistical Approach to the Ontological Problem", one finds Quine's central doctrines about how to pursue ontological questions with little or no admixture of verificationism or anti-realism).

The apparently conflicting beliefs that can drive a person to ask ontological questions are beliefs about the existence of this or that kind of thing — where the kinds in question are quite abstract, like *event*, *substance*, *property*, or *proposition*. We seem frequently to be talking about things that, if they really existed, would pose problems — their existence would conflict with other things we believe. In order to sort out our conflicting beliefs about such *"entia non grata"*, as Quine called them, we have to decide whether we think they exist (in which case the other things we believe must be false or misleadingly expressed), or show how our talk that is ostensibly about the problematic entities doesn't really commit us to their existence.

Sorting out whether I should believe in the existence of this or that kind may be the beginning of ontology, but it has long been a communal enterprise. We are, in effect, comparing notes to see how others have dealt with the same difficulties about existence. One thing we find is that we don't all start out believing the same things. Where some metaphysicians feel tension or conflict between the existence of such-and-such kind of thing and some other conviction they have, others will lack the conviction that creates the tension, and consequently see no difficulty in accepting the existence of a such-and-such. Thus we wind up with differences in the "ontological commitments" of the "theories" held by metaphysicians.

I follow Peter van Inwagen in taking "Quine's criterion of ontological commitment" to be really "a name for the most profitable strategy to follow in order to get people to make their ontological commitments — or the ontological commitments of their discourse — clear."

"The strategy is this: one takes sentences that the other party to the conversation accepts, and by whatever dialectical devices one can muster, one gets him to introduce more and more quantifiers and variables into those sentences. ... If, at a certain point in this procedure, it emerges that the existential generalization on a certain open sentence F can be formally deduced from the sentences he accepts, one has shown that the sentences that he accepts, and the ways of introducing quantifiers and variables into those sentences that he has endorsed, formally commit him to there being things that satisfy F." (van Inwagen, 2001: 28)

universals provide one of the stock examples of a category of thing to which some philosophers have been ontologically committed, while others have sought to avoid such commitment. I will focus on this case; but I believe very similar things could be said about controversies over the existence of all sorts of other ontological kinds: e.g., numbers, sets, propositions, composite objects made from any old collection of parts, distinct parts for each subregion an object fills, distinct temporal parts for every subperiod throughout which an object exists, etc. In each of these cases, problems arise about what such things would be like, if they existed; their existence conflicts with other things that many of us, at least, find ourselves believing. And one way to make the felt conflict go away would be to deny the existence of the entity in question — if only we could get away with it without giving up too many other things we take ourselves to know.

The problem of universals begins in reflection upon several of Russell's "matters of common knowledge" that do not fit well together. Distinct things can have properties, features, or attributes in common. Conifers, for example, have four important features in common. The most natural way in which to introduce quantifiers and variables into that sentence implies that there are four things, namely *features* — or, as they're usually called in philosophical contexts, *properties* — that these trees have in common. But features or properties fit ill with other things many of us are prone to believe. Here is a (mostly ancient) line of thought that appeals to some fairly natural things to think about the world and that makes it hard to see how there could be such things as properties.

Surely a thing is either in space and time, or it is not; but whichever one says about features or properties, they behave strangely. If two trees can have the same property, and if the property is in space and time, where could it be other than right there where the trees are? But in that case, features are a kind of thing that can occupy several locations at once. That's not such a trick for physical objects, which can have different parts in different locations — the legs of the table are down there, the top of the table is up here.... But could the common feature be spread around in all its instances like a physical object, with a part of it in one tree, and a different part in another? If only a part of it is present in each instance, features have begun to behave like a scattered collection of physical objects — e.g., like the artwork in a private collection, pieces of which may be loaned out to different museums. A scattered collection of objects can be radically different at the different places where it exists — in one place, the art collection is statuesque; in another, it is picturesque. So the many parts of the one property only constitute a common feature of all the trees that have it if the parts... well, if they have a feature in common! If having a common feature was supposed to *constitute* similarity among the things that have it, the idea that a feature is scattered, a different part for each instance, has gotten us nowhere. So common features, if in space and time, are instances of things that can be in many places at once without having different parts at those places. That seems odd; one would have thought that a thing is never closer to or further away from *itself*. Perhaps that thought is wrong, and will have to be given up; but it is a strange enough conclusion to justify thinking about the other alternative: that properties are things that cannot, strictly speaking, be said to have locations in space and time. Some people will stop right there, doubting that *anything* exists outside of space and time. Even if one is not so confident about the restriction of everything that exists to the spatiotemporal, how could we know about non-spatiotemporal things, given that all causal transactions seem to occur between events in space and time? Things outside space and time could have no impact upon us.

This, then, is one familiar sort of problem about universals. It arises because, at least to some people, the following four things *seem* true, or at least to have considerable plausibility, enough plausibility so that conflicts among them seem worth calling a *problem*: (i) there are features that things have in common; (ii) it is in virtue of having features in common that things resemble one another in a single respect; (iii) nothing can be in many places at once, except by means of distinct parts in distinct places; (iv) nothing exists outside of space and time. One is doing ontology as soon as one tries to find a way to make these compatible (by resisting the little argument I gave) or to decide which is false.

The standard, Quinean approach to ontology says there are two appropriate responses to this sort of puzzle: either search for a "paraphrase" of the problematic statement about conifers and their features that does not appear to imply that features exist, yet still seems to say everything important that one intended to convey by the original claim; or, absent such a paraphrase, give up one of the other principles with which the existence of features would conflict. Consider the second approach: One might, for example, give up the idea that it is fundamentally in virtue of the shared feature that things resemble one another; it is rather because the different parts of the feature resemble one another — and then one could deny that this resemblance is, in turn, a matter of sharing a feature, giving up (ii). One might decide that there's nothing wrong with saying that a thing can move closer to itself, rejecting (iii); or that we can know about things outside space and time, rejecting (iv). But one needn't give up these principles if one takes the first approach: Deny that there *are* such things as features. And of course that is just the strategy nominalists have been pursuing for hundreds of years.

Quinean methodology in ontology faces numerous challenges. In fact, judging by the contents of a recent book on *Metametaphysics* (Chalmers et al., 2009), it is virtually under siege! But it still seems to me to be the way of true ontology, and a mere formalization of the forms of reasoning ontologists have been engaged in all along, with respect to the existence of all kinds of categories of entity.

One traditional challenge to Quine's method is to reject his identification of both "there is..." and "there exists..." (and "for some...") with the backwards "E" of first order logic. But one reason for rejecting the equation is, as Quine pointed out, bootless: Quite a few philosophers have, with Meinong, distinguished between *existing* and *being*.[2] Some of these neo-Meinongians are willing to say that, if conifers have four features in common, then there *are* features (they "have being"); but they then go on to

---

[2] Few go the further step with Meinong, to admit objects "beyond being and non-being".

deny that features *exist*. Quine's response seems spot on: We can make this metaphysician a present of the word "exist", and put the original puzzle entirely in terms of "being". It's not just that I'm inclined to doubt whether there *exists* anything that can move closer to itself, or lies outside of space and time; I'm just as dubious about whether there *is* any such thing.[3]

Other challenges to Quinean methodology try to make the dialectic dissolve into triviality by claiming, for one reason or another, that "existence is easy". Proponents of this strategy say: "*Of course* there are properties (or numbers, sets, propositions, arbitrary composites, temporal parts, etc.) — their existence is a trivial consequence of our ability to talk about them." But being told that it's easy to exist does not yet tell me how a thing can move closer to itself or exist outside of space and time. (I believe similar things can be said with respect to all the other traditional *entia non grata*. They make their way into ontological discussions because their existence seems to conflict with things many of us find ourselves believing; the conflicts go away if we can maintain that there are no such things, but they do not go away simply on the assumption that the existence of such things is somehow automatic or easy.) So, easy existence doesn't, by itself, explain *why* the conflicts between belief in universals and other things I believe should be thought to be unproblematic.

The old-fashioned ordinary-language anti-metaphysicians probably qualify as using an "existence is easy" strategy; they would try to calm us down, to help us stop worrying about the apparent conflict among the original beliefs, by repeating ("in a plonking tone of voice") all of the problematic sentences ("There *are*, after all, features conifers have in common, aren't there?", "Things *do* resemble one another in virtue of common features", "A thing is located just where it is; it could hardly move closer to or further away from itself, could it?", "Everything is located *somewhere* in space and time") and then denying that there is any conflict. I have nothing to say to this sort of anti-metaphysician (of whom there are, mercifully, fewer and fewer).

Today's easy existence philosophers are prepared to offer more by way of argument than the ordinary language philosophers were.

---

[3] A neo-Meinongian philosopher who makes the being-existence distinction may, for all I have said, be right: perhaps it is right to say that, although there *are* properties, properties don't *exist*, only concrete objects exist. My point is that, even if I were to concede this much, the distinction does not provide any immediate help diagnosing the problem posed by (i)-(iv).

Still, even the recent easy existence literature has not helped me to figure out how to make the problem of universals go away. I cannot hope to survey all the latest attacks upon Quinean method; they come from many radically different angles.[4] But I'll mention a couple of popular strategies, and say why I decide to stick with Quine.

Some will say, for example, that there are these things called *conceptual schemes*, and that all talk about what exists is relative to a scheme. Relative to the *feature-friendly scheme* there are things shared in common by many trees; while relative to the *physical-objects-only scheme*, there are no such things. But, the schemers will say, there is no absolute, scheme-independent fact of the matter about whether there are features. A more prosaic version would multiply *languages* instead of schemes, alleging that the philosophical proponents and opponents of features-as-existing-things are simply trying to lay down stipulative rules for two languages in which "there is" means different things.[5] In the

---

[4] For example, I shall not discuss, beyond this note, the easy existence views of Hale and Wright. According to them, an equivalence relation like *precisely the same color as*, holding among a number of, say, red objects, guarantees the existence of the universal *redness*. The argument I gave, and called "the problem of universals", turns me into what they call an "anxious metaphysician" — someone who worries whether the world provides objects of the right sort to be referred to by *redness*. Hale and Wright point out that, if one is the sort of metaphysician who accepts an abundant theory of universals, one is likely to think that "the color of those objects" refers to something so long as they all resemble one another with respect to color; and if one is the sort of metaphysician who accepts a sparse theory of universals, one is likely to worry about whether "the color of those objects" refers to something even when they all resemble with respect to color (Hale and Wright, 2009: 209). True enough. But I would add that arguments like the one generating the problem of universals can turn one into a nominalist; in which case, one is *really* likely to be an anxious metaphysician, who doubts whether "the color of those objects" refers to something. If the premises generating the problem of universals are reasonable, and the argument form is valid, then the anxious metaphysicians have good reason to be anxious; in order to calm us down, Hale and Wright should have to wade into the muck of metaphysics, showing what is wrong with one or another step in the reasoning that created the problem of universals — but that does not seem to be part of their program. So, after reading Hale and Wright, I am left with my anxieties.

[5] For invocations of linguistic and conceptual relativity along these lines, see (Carnap, 1950), (Putnam, 1987), and (Sosa, 1990). Hirsch's quantifier variance account of ontological disagreements (Hirsch, 2009) is a version of the anti-Quinean strategy that appeals to relativity-to-language; but I should mention that Hirsch is selective about the ontological kinds for which he will invoke relativity-to-language; in particular, he exempts properties and other

feature-friendly would-be language, existence is easy, at least for features; in the other, existence is harder, and features trivially fail to have it. (There may be disagreement amongst proponents of this strategy over whether the metaphysicians succeed in *speaking* the languages they are trying to create.)

But do these strategies really help to resolve the puzzlement that sucked me into the problem of universals in the first place? I'm being told that there is one way of talking or thinking that makes the existence of properties trivial and obvious; and another that rules them out. Which way was I talking or thinking when I ran that argument, the line of thought that made them seem problematic? Either (a) I was using the feature-friendly scheme or language, or (b) the physical-objects-friendly one, or (c) some mixture of the two.

Take option (a): suppose I was implicitly being feature-friendly all the way through. For the easy existence schemer to be of any help with the problem of universals, she must think that at least one of principles (ii), (iii), and (iv) is unproblematically false relative to the feature-friendly scheme or language. (ii) ("Things are similar in virtue of shared features") will likely be a feature-friendly truism, so presumably one or both of the latter principles must come out false when a feature-friendly version of the argument is stated: "A thing cannot move closer to itself", or "Nothing is outside space and time". But these seemed at least initially plausible to me, despite my (*ex hypothesi*) use of a feature-friendly scheme or language from within which the sentences express falsehoods; how does the existence of a possible language or scheme that assigns meanings to them in a way that makes them true undermine their initial plausibility for me, the (allegedly) feature-friendly speaker and thinker?

Let us try option (b): I was implicitly thinking and talking in a physical-objects-only way throughout the argument. In that case (i) and, presumably, (ii) were both false, since physical-objects-only ways of thinking and talking imply something I would then express by saying "There are no such things as features". How does the schemer propose to take the sting out of the fact that I have to reject these truisms? The bare possibility of a language or scheme that can interpret the words in (i) and (ii) so that they express truths is hardly relevant (one could invent a language in

---

abstracta. I hope what I say engages with the views of anti-Quineans like Carnap who *do* make the existence of properties relative to a language.

which (i) and (ii) mean "There are four apples on the table" and "We eat apples").

In order to make either strategy (a) or (b) helpful to me, when I confront the problem of universals, the schemer must suppose that the language or scheme I am *not* using is somehow very close to the one I'm actually using — it's a near miss, and intimations of this other interpretation are, the schemer must suppose, making me think that false sentences are true in my mouth. Am I able to *understand* the alternative language or scheme, now that the scheming philosopher has made me aware of its existence? I should think so. After all, it is so close to mine that its implications are bleeding over into my actual reasoning; it's as though I am *almost* speaking or thinking in this other way already. But suppose that I can easily step into the alternative language or scheme, without encountering any conceptual hurdles; this leads to problems for the schemer — especially for the second sort of schemer, according to whom I was thinking in a physical-objects-friendly way while giving the argument.

If I can understand the feature-friendly scheme or language, then I can ask what the terms for features in that language refer to when they occur in true sentences; or ask what users of the scheme would be thinking about when they use terms which, as they would say, "refer to features or properties" (though "refer" may mean something different when they say it). If, while still speaking a language recognizable as English, I can easily acquire the ability to talk and think about properties, I will likely retain my surprise that they can be multiply-located without having distinct parts, or that they can exist outside space and time. If I *cannot* very easily think or talk, while remaining an English speaker, about the referents of the terms of the feature-friendly language, why can't I? Why are people who use English barred from giving a semantics for this very similar language, the one we are almost speaking? If it is so alien that I cannot say anything about how its words work, is it really plausible to suppose that its nearness to my own language fools me into thinking that (i) and (ii) are true?[6]

One might also suppose that I was shifting from one language or scheme to the other in mid-argument; or that each sentence I used

---

[6] Objections along these lines are lodged against Eli Hirsch's brand of quantifier variance by Matti Eklund and John Hawthorne; see (Eklund, 2009) and (Hawthorne, 2006).

was ambiguous between feature-friendly and physical-objects-only interpretations. Since I don't, myself, feel the ambiguity, it is hard to know what to do with the suggestion that (i), (ii), (iii), or (iv) is unproblematically false on one disambiguation and unproblematically true on another. There are, of course, (possible) languages in which these words could be stipulated to mean different things, some obviously true and others obviously false. But I should need some serious argument to convince me that I wasn't speaking in a single language, English (a language that was fully capable of expressing my thoughts about conifers), when I considered these four sentences and found them to be in tension. Absent such an argument, option (c) just puts me back with the ordinary language philosophers who told me to stop worrying about it without telling me what went wrong.[7]

The easy existence philosophers are not without offensive weapons. They can make the Quinean uncomfortable by saying things like: "*Of course* there are features conifers have in common. Talk about your Russellian matters of common knowledge! How could anyone deny such a thing? Simply running through the argument that constitutes the problem of universals, and then asking, 'Do features *really* exist?', does not generate a context in which (i) or (ii) can sensibly be doubted. So denying (i) or (ii) is simply not an option as a response to the problem you've set up."

Even if this line of thinking is right, and the problem of universals cannot make it reasonable to doubt (i) or (ii), it does not tell us which of (iii) or (iv) is false, and why it seemed plausible in the first place. So a table-thumping insistence that, *of course, features exist*, does not immediately help with the problem of universals. And, although I'm a believer in universals myself, and do not see that rejecting (iii) is so bad, I shouldn't want to put too much weight on the claim that, because we seem always to be talking about properties, properties must exist. The Quinean holds that sufficiently troubling arguments can lead us to deny the existence of things we frequently say exist, including properties.

---

[7] Eli Hirsch suggests alternative languages that are, he thinks, relevant to explaining how some philosophical conundrums might arise from confusion about which language we are speaking — conundrums that have led Quinean metaphysicians to repudiate certain *entia non grata* as, strictly speaking, non-existent. I do not know that he would use this strategy to diffuse the apparent conflict among (i)-(iv), since he takes nominalism-vs.-platonism to be a genuine, substantive debate. In a full-blown defense of Quinean method, I should have to engage properly with his important work on the subject.

One option, in response to the problem of universals, is to admit that, strictly speaking, there are no properties; but the false things we frequently say by means of such talk are true enough for ordinary purposes. So long as the Quinean's proffered paraphrase to avoid commitment to something seems to pretty well capture the facts we were struggling to express, giving up the strict and literal truth of the thing we ordinarily say need not violate Russell's methodological maxims. Russell assumes that most of what we say and think is "vague" and "inexact", containing "errors of detail". Russell's recommended process of sorting and sifting and making more precise is likely to separate out closely related and easily confused propositions, one of which is true, the other of which is false. And the Quinean who says "strictly speaking, there are no features that things have in common", while giving a nominalist paraphrase of "Conifers have four features in common" is simply engaged in the process of sifting and making more precise.

What do you consider to be the most neglected topics in contemporary metaphysics, and what direction would you like metaphysics to take in the future?

I suppose I will simply be listing the topics and projects that *I* find most intriguing right now, but here are three:

Philosophical Theology: There are many metaphysicians who do a good deal of philosophy of religion; but we have tended to keep our discussions at a pretty high level of generality: mainly, we talk about traditional arguments for and against a generic "God of Western Theism". Gradually, some of us with religious convictions have become more interested in exploring issues specific to our particular brand of theism — a change probably due, at least in part, to some of Plantinga's "Advice to Christian Philosophers" (Plantinga, 1984). The result has been a growing body of work by analytic metaphysicians on the trinity, the incarnation, the atonement, and other doctrines.

The time seems to be ripe for the renewal of traditional philosophical theology. To do a respectable job of it, we need to find philosophically-oriented theologians to help us out; most of us analytic philosophers of religion are amateurs in theology, at best. Until recently, it has been almost impossible to find theologians who would take analytic philosophers seriously. Philosophy in seminaries and departments of theology or religion has tended to be exclusively of a continental kind. I have heard that students of theology are still likely to be told by their professors that the entire discipline of analytic philosophy is a form of logical positivism, hostile to metaphysics and theology. This is far from the truth. Granted, if we were all positivists, there would be little reason for theologians to talk to us. But positivism has been dead for 60 years; the traditional problems of metaphysics have been among the hottest topics in analytic philosophy for about 40 years; and numerous notoriously religious philosophers have done a great deal of theology from within analytic philosophy while nevertheless being accorded the highest honors our profession can bestow (e.g., Alvin Plantinga, Robert Adams, William Alston, Marilyn Adams, Peter van Inwagen, Eleonore Stump... the list of prominent, well-respected Christian philosophers is surprisingly long). The myth that analytic philosophy is hostile to metaphysics and theology has survived for decades. But, given how glaringly false it is, I am hopeful that, within my lifetime at least, it may actually fade away. There is some evidence that the situation in seminaries, and in theology and religion departments, is changing, and that analytic philosophers of religion can finally find some theologians willing to be conversation partners. There are plenty of analytic philosophers interested in the project, as is evident from the contents of (Flint and Rea, 2009; and Rea and Crisp, 2009). So I am optimistic about the prospects for reinvigorating the traditional enterprise of metaphysically serious philosophical theology.

The Metaphysics of Qualia: Although there is a vocal (hopefully growing) minority in philosophy of mind defending "property dualism", insufficient attention has been paid to the metaphysics of these additional, fundamental, qualitative properties. What is their proper subject, the thing that exemplifies them? Me, or parts of me? Or parts of some peculiar intrinsically qualitative objects of experience, i.e. sense data? Philosophers like David Chalmers — those who accept property dualism for reasons having to do with the independence of the phenomenal and the physical — must be prepared to reopen the old debate about whether phenomenal states are to be analyzed in terms of relations to sense data or as a kind of "adverbial" state of the experiencing subject — an intrinsic modification of the experiencer, not constituted by a relation between the subject and something else — or in some other way. Chalmers himself is certainly interested in the question; and it has been explored seriously by Leopold Stubenberg, William Seager, John Foster, and Howard Robinson, among others. But there is plenty of work to be done here; and there are some historically important options for property dualists that belong on the table once again, but have yet to be recovered or rediscovered. Some of these forgotten metaphysical positions are to be found among...

The *"Lost Generation" of North American Metaphysicians*: "American Philosophy", as a name for a category in the history of philosophy, has become almost synonymous with the history of pragmatism. One wouldn't know it from reading most books with "American Philosophy" in their titles, but North America produced mostly idealists and realists throughout the 19th century and the early years of the 20th century; pragmatism was an important minority position, among philosophers, even in its heyday. I'll grant that the "big three" pragmatists — Pierce, William James, and Dewey — are among the most important figures of the period. And there is a sort of rationale one can give for focusing almost exclusively on them when telling the story of philosophy in the "New World": pragmatism is harder to view as the continuation of European philosophical movements than are American versions of idealism, realism, and Naturalism; and so pragmatism seems more distinctively "American". But the "big three" pragmatists had few important students (C. I. Lewis being the most noteworthy exception), and their influence (within philosophy) faded quickly; while the naturalists and realists of the period had wider networks, published much more, and their chief doctrines survived to merge with the British realism championed by Russell and Moore during the early days of "analytic philosophy". (It must be kept in mind that Russell and Moore were themselves quite serious about metaphysics, even though the "philosophy of analysis" they started soon became, for a time, anti-metaphysical.)

The story of American philosophy appears to me to go like this: the high tide of idealism gradually goes out during the 19th century, and the American scene is flooded with varieties of ("naïve" and "critical") realism much like the realism of Russell and Moore, though sometimes more "naturalistic" than theirs. The towering but lonely figures of Pierce, James, and Dewey sink without a trace into a sea of naturalists and realists; and it is the basic assumptions and orientation of the naturalists and realists that have come to be shared by the vast majority of metaphysicians, epistemologists, and philosophers of mind in English-speaking philosophy departments today. (I am prepared to believe that the pragmatists' impact *outside philosophy* may have been greater and more long-lasting than their impact within philosophy; I am only competent to comment on the latter.)

So, even if pragmatism is the closest thing we have to an entirely American contribution to philosophy, there is no excuse for telling the story of American philosophy as though the majority of the philosophy produced in North America during the last 150 years never existed. Many non-pragmatist philosophers were nearly as impressive as Pierce and James (I don't really know what to make of Dewey, so I'll leave him out of it). Royce and Santayana are an idealist and a realist who belong in the first rank alongside the great pragmatists, and it is true that they have not been entirely neglected within the field of American Philosophy (though they are usually mere foils for the pragmatists, and sometimes portrayed as pragmatists *manqués*). But there are numerous other important non-pragmatist philosophers from the period who are completely forgotten, but who had a major impact in their day and still repay serious study by metaphysicians. My personal favorites are Ralph Barton Perry and C. A. Strong; but there were many other excellent philosophers who flourished just before and after the turn of the previous century, especially among the "Critical Realists", a group that included Strong, Santayana, Arthur O. Lovejoy, Durant Drake, James Bissett Pratt, and Roy Wood Sellars. Borden Parker Bowne (the founder of Personalism) and W. T. Stace are two other once famous, now little-known figures who flourished in America (Stace was British-born, but held teaching appointments only in the U.S.). Many of these American opponents of pragmatism had metaphysical insights that could be appropriated in our day.

There is a British "lost generation" too: the metaphysicians of the first half of the last century, such as C. D. Broad, H. H. Price, G. Dawes Hicks, W. E. Johnson, and G. F. Stout, whose work has been largely screened off from us by the anti-metaphysical positivists and Wittgensteinians who dominated British philosophy during the 1930s and '40s. Broad's stock, at least, has gone up; the importance of his work in the philosophy of mind is more widely recognized than it was thirty or forty years ago. C. A. Strong is the American C. D. Broad, and deserves a similar revival. The gatekeepers of "American Philosophy" have little interest in the American realists of the period, so metaphysicians are the only scholars poised to recover Strong's important contributions to philosophy — including his highly original theory of sense-data as "essences" (Strong, 1920). The theory is an attractive one, much discussed in Strong's day, but forgotten for many years until it was finally reinvented (independently of Strong's work) by Mark Johnston (Johnston, 2004).[8]

References

Carnap, Rudolf. (1950) "Empiricism, semantics and ontology", *Revue Internationale de Philosophie* 4: 20-40

Chalmers, David, David Manley, and Ryan Waasserman, eds. (2009) *Metametaphysics: New Essays on the Foundations of ontology* (Oxford: Oxford University Press)

Eklund, Matti. (2009) "Carnap and Ontological Pluralism", in (Chalmers *et al.*, 2009), 130-56

Flint, Thomas and Michael Rea (2009) *Oxford Handbook of Philosophical Theology* (Oxford: Oxford University Press)

Hirsch, Eli. (2009) "ontology and Alternative Languages", in (Chalmers *et al.*, 2009), 231-59

Haslanger, Sally, and Roxanne Marie Kurtz, eds. (2006) *persistence* (Cambridge, Mass.: M.I.T.)

Hawthorne, John. (2006) "Plenitude, Convention and ontology", in Hawthorne, *Metaphysical Essays* (Oxford: Oxford University Press, 2006), 279-93

Johnston, Mark. (2004) "The Obscure Object of Hallucination", *Philosophical Studies* 120: 113-83

Plantinga, Alvin. (1984) "Advice to Christian Philosophers", *Faith and Philosophy* 1: 253-271

Quine, W. V. O. (1939) "A Logistical Approach to the Ontological Problem", *Journal of Unified Science (Erkenntnis)* 9: 84-89

——. (1948) "On What There Is", *Review of Metaphysics* 2: 21-38

Rea, Michael and Oliver Crisp. (2009) *Analytic Theology: New Essays in Theological Method* (Oxford: Oxford University Press)

Russell, Bertrand. (1914) *Our Knowledge of the External World* (London: George Allen and Unwin)

---

[8] I am grateful to Daniel Nolan and Ted Sider for comments that helped me improve at least two of my five answers.

Strong, C. A. (1920) "On the Nature of the Datum", in Durant Drake, et al., *Essays in Critical realism* (London: Macmillan), 223-44

van Inwagen, Peter. (2001) *ontology, identity, and modality: Essays in Metaphysics* (Cambridge: Cambridge University Press)

Zimmerman, Dean. (1995) "Theories of Masses and Problems of Constitution", *The Philosophical Review* 104: 53-110

———. (1997a) "Coincident Objects: Could a 'Stuff ontology' Help?", *Analysis* 57: 19-27

———. (1997b) "Immanent Causation", *Philosophical Perspectives*, Vol. 11: Mind, Causation, and World: 433-71

———. (1998a) "Criteria of identity and the 'identity Mystics'", *Erkenntnis* 48: 281-301

———. (1998b) "Temporary Intrinsics and presentism", in *Metaphysics: The Big Questions*, ed. by Peter van Inwagen and Dean W. Zimmerman (Oxford: Basil Blackwell), 206-219; reprinted, with Postcript, in (Haslanger and Kurtz, 2006), 393-404

———. (1998c) "Temporal Parts and Supervenient Causation: The Incompatibility of Two Humean Doctrines", *Australasian Journal of Philosophy* 76: 265-288

———. (1999) "One Really Big Liquid Sphere: Reply to David Lewis", *Australasian Journal of Philosophy* 77: 213-215; reprinted, with Postscript, in (Haslanger and Kurtz, 2006), 195-200

———. (2003) "Material People", in *The Oxford Handbook of Metaphysics*, edited by Michael J. Loux and Dean W. Zimmerman (Oxford: Oxford University Press), 491-526

———. (2002) "The Constitution of persons by Bodies: A Critique of Lynne Rudder Baker's Theory of Material Constitution", *Philosophical Topics* 30: 295-338

———. (2005) "The A-theory of time, the B-theory of time, and 'Taking Tense Seriously'", *Dialectica* 59: 401-57

———. (2006) "Can One 'Take Tense Seriously' and Be a B-theorist?" (a postscript to "Temporary Intrinsics and presentism"), in (Haslanger and Kurtz, 2006), 404-424

———. (2009) "properties, Minds, and Bodies: An Examination of Sydney Shoemaker's Metaphysics", *Philosophy and Phenomenological Research* 78: 673 738

———. (2010) "From Property Dualism to Substance Dualism", *Proceedings of the Aristotelian Society*, Supplementary Vol. LXXXIV

———. (Forthcoming) "presentism and the Space-time Manifold", *The Oxford Handbook of time*, ed. by Craig Callender (Oxford: Oxford University Press)

About the Editor

Asbjørn Steglich-Petersen is Associate Professor at the Department of Philosophy and History of Ideas at Aarhus University, Denmark. He received his Ph.D. in 2007 from the University of Cambridge, and has since published his work in journals such as *Mind*, *Philosophical Studies*, *The Philosophical Quarterly*, *Journal of Semantics*, *Synthese*, *Dialectica*, *British Journal for the Philosophy of Science*, and others. In 2009, he was awarded the Elite Young Researcher Prize by the Danish Ministry of Science, Technology, and Innovation.

Index

Ackerman, F., 198
Adams, R.M, 198, 200, 219
Adanson, M., 144
Alexander, S., 141, 142
Alston, W., 219
Anjum, R.L., 55
anti-realism, 16, 17, 209
Appel, K., 176
Aquinas, T., 91, 96, 141, 198
Aristotelian, 7, 39, 56, 98, 135, 148, 149, 189
Aristotle, 7, 39, 71, 84, 91, 96, 114, 124, 132, 135–138, 141, 142, 148, 198, 204
Armstrong, D.M., 41, 63, 135, 136, 148, 149, 165, 198, 200
Austin, J.L, 198

Baker, L.R., 1, 223
Banning, C., 124, 126
Barker, R., 147
Bealer, G., 75, 76
Beebee, H., 11, 52, 104
Benacerraf, P., 110, 111
Bennett, J., 31
Berkeley, G.., 198, 204
Bowne, B.P., 221
Brentano, F., 135, 140, 145–147, 151, 158, 198
Broard, C.D., 201, 221
Burge, E., 39
Burgess, J., 110–112, 119–121

Cantor, G., 137

Carnap, R., 22, 31, 71, 93, 163, 170, 222
Cartwright, N., 40
category, 71, 87, 94, 133, 149, 186, 195, 205, 207, 210, 220
causation, 7, 11, 12, 14, 16, 35, 40–46, 48–50, 56, 68, 72, 85, 89, 125, 127, 128, 164, 166–169, 171, 173, 174, 197, 204
Chakrabarti, A., 104
Chalmers, D., 31, 202, 212, 219, 222
Chisholm R., 9, 80, 151, 158, 190, 198, 200, 203
Clifford, W.K., 144
Cohen, B., 124, 126
conditionals, 40, 65, 73, 193
Crisp, O., 219, 222

Danto, A., 109, 120
de Soto, H., 151–153, 159
Descartes, R., 31, 91, 105, 116, 124, 198
determinism, 12, 51, 82, 129, 162, 179–181, 183, 197, 205
Dewey, J., 220, 221
Drake, D., 221, 223
Dretske, F., 127, 165
Ducasse, C.J., 60, 201
Duchamp, M., 109
Dummett, M., 40, 145, 146
Dworkin, R., 116

Einstein, A., 66, 112
Eklund, M., 222
existence, 3, 10, 13, 17, 21, 23, 27, 36, 43, 45, 46, 49, 65, 69, 82, 95, 104, 110, 112, 113, 118, 129–131, 135, 141, 148, 161, 164–166, 169, 171, 173, 174, 179, 191, 194, 195, 203–205, 209, 210, 212–217
experimental philosophy, 14, 88

Feynman, R., 188
fictionalism, 65, 114, 120
Field, H., 112, 120
Fine, K., 26, 30, 31, 118–120
Flint, T., 219, 222
free will, 12, 13, 15–17, 48, 51, 68, 82, 129, 175, 179–181, 183, 197
Frege, G., 23, 31, 145, 146, 149

Gallois, A., 63
Gauthier, D., 162
Gibson, J.J., 147
Goodman, N., 163
Guarino, N., 147, 158

Hacking, I., 40
Haken, W., 176
Hardin, L., 79
Hart, H.L.A, 42, 44, 51
Haslanger, S., 222, 223
Hawthorne, J., 90, 120, 200, 222
Hayes, P., 147
Hegel, G.W.F, 91, 124, 141
Heidegger, M., 64, 95, 96, 146
Hempel, C.G, 163, 164

Hicks, G.D., 221
Hinckfuss, I., 63
Hirsch, E., 222
Hitchcock, A, 109
Hitchcock, C, 43, 51, 52, 89, 127
Hofweber, T., 19, 21, 23, 24, 26, 29, 31, 32
Honoré, T., 42, 44, 51
Hume, D., 12, 61, 71, 166, 167, 198
Husserl, E., 135–137, 145–148, 158

identity, 3, 76, 77, 86, 89, 103, 104, 179, 181–184, 187, 223
Ingarden, R., 135, 144–147, 156, 158, 159
intuitions, 14, 15, 30, 45, 48, 70, 72, 77, 83, 105, 106
Inwagen, P.v., 179

James, W., 187, 220, 221
Johnson, W.E, 221
Johnston, M., 222

Kant, I., 30, 66, 81, 88, 91, 96, 101, 124, 142, 167, 198, 199
Kaufmann, W., 163
Kim, J., 39, 44, 51, 198
Knobe, J, 89, 90
Krasner, B., 124, 126
Kripke, S., 15, 198
Kurtz, R.M., 222, 223

Ladyman, J., 90, 185, 188, 189
Le Poidevin, R., 37
Leibniz, G.W., 71, 75, 88, 91, 135, 139, 167, 198

228 Index

Lejewski, C., 148
Lesniewski, S., 136
Lewis, C.I., 220
Lewis, C.S., 155, 156, 160, 197
Lewis, D., 2, 9, 36, 41, 42, 51, 56, 60, 61, 65, 85, 86, 110, 114, 117, 120, 125, 126, 162, 164, 182, 183, 188, 198, 200, 203, 223
List, C., 45, 51
Locke, J., 61, 115, 120, 198
Loewer, B., 125, 126
Lovejoy, A.O., 221
Lycos, K., 39

Maddy, P., 120
Manley, D., 31, 222
Maudlin, T., 125, 126
McGee, V., 125
McLaren, R., 125
McLaughlin, B., 125, 126
Meinong, A., 135, 144, 198, 203, 212
Mellor, D.H., 41, 169
Mellor, H., 35
Mencies, P., 39
Menzies, P., 41–45, 51, 52
Minkowski, H., 66
modality, 40, 55, 63, 64, 85–87, 89, 114, 118, 120, 121, 179, 182, 223
Moore, G.E., 141, 158, 198, 201, 220
Mulligan, K., 137, 147, 159
Mumford, S., 53

Nagel, T., 16, 125, 198
naturalism, 5, 73, 113, 120, 140, 151, 220
Nolan, D., 63, 65, 67, 69, 70, 73, 120

nominalism, 104, 106, 110–113, 115, 120, 121, 135, 140, 179
Nussbaum, M., 198

Ockham, 113, 135
Olson, E.T, 75
Omnès, R., 146, 159
ontological commitment, 136, 138, 209
ontology, 1, 2, 5, 9, 11, 12, 19–22, 25, 27, 31, 54–56, 69, 94, 96, 98, 101, 106, 109, 110, 117, 118, 135–139, 142, 143, 146–160, 182–184, 194, 195, 203–206, 209, 212, 222, 223

Paul, L.A., 51, 85–90, 125
Pearl, J., 43, 50, 52
Peirce, C,S., 10
Perry, R.B., 221
persistence, 16, 55, 76, 175, 201, 222
persons, 1, 2, 4–6, 11, 79, 86, 154, 183, 195, 201, 202, 223
physicalism, 24, 44, 46, 51, 138, 200
Plantinga, A., 161, 198, 200, 218, 219, 222
Platon, 7, 39, 54, 63, 75, 91, 120, 124
Popper, K., 36
Pratt, J.B., 221
presentism, 28, 175, 200, 223, 224
Price, H.H., 43, 50–52, 201, 221
Prior, A., 138

properties, 1, 3, 5, 10, 21–
    24, 27, 31, 49, 55,
    61, 65, 76, 85, 87,
    89, 96, 98, 104, 109,
    110, 114, 117, 118,
    133, 134, 139, 142,
    149, 164, 165, 167,
    170, 172–174, 176,
    186, 194, 204, 205,
    210, 211, 213, 215–
    219, 223
Puntel, L.B., 91
Putnam, H., 112, 120, 125,
    182, 192

Quine, W.v.O., 11, 55, 73,
    95, 112, 131, 135, 136,
    138, 182, 190, 192,
    198, 209, 212–214,
    222

Ramsey, F., 42
Rea, M., 89, 219, 222
Read, S., 40
realism, 5, 9, 16, 209, 220,
    223
reduction, 119, 121
reflective equilibrium, 8, 49,
    57, 117
Reichenbach, H., 71
Reid, T., 198
Reinach, A., 146, 159
Rodriguez-Pereyra, G., 103
Rosen, G., 109, 111, 114, 115,
    119–121
Ross, D., 185
Rowe, W., 170
Russell, B., 36, 50–53, 71, 124,
    145, 148, 149, 162,
    190, 198, 201, 208,
    210, 218, 220, 222

Salmon, W., 166

Santayana, G., 221
Scalia, A., 116, 121
Schaffer, J., 55, 123
Schneider, L., 149, 159
Searle, J., 151–153, 159, 160
Sellars, R.W., 40, 221
semantics, 10, 15, 24, 31, 46,
    69, 93, 94, 101, 136,
    137, 142, 147, 206,
    216, 222, 225
Sider, T., 200
Simons, P., 37, 135, 147, 159
Smart, J., 41
Smith, B., 135, 137, 145, 158–
    160
Sosa, E., 198
Spinoza, B., 31, 75
Stace, W.T., 221
Stalnaker, R, 65
Stout, G.F., 201, 221
Strong, C.A., 201, 221–223
Stump, E., 219
Stumpf, C., 143
supervenience, 14, 89, 119, 132,
    133, 200

Taylor, R., 176, 197
Thom, P., 40
time, iii, v, 3, 5, 6, 8, 10–12,
    14, 16, 20, 22, 24,
    27–30, 35, 39, 44, 46,
    50, 53–55, 57, 60, 63–
    68, 70, 71, 77, 79,
    80, 82, 85, 86, 88,
    89, 91, 92, 104, 109,
    116, 127, 129, 135,
    137, 139–141, 145,
    146, 150, 151, 153,
    157, 158, 161, 162,
    164–169, 173, 175,
    179–183, 185, 189,
    194, 197–199, 201,
    202, 204, 206, 211–

213, 215, 216, 218–
221, 223, 224
Tooley, M., 161

Unger, P., 77
universals, 11, 13, 16, 20, 22,
24, 58, 83, 87, 106,
135, 140, 148, 150,
156, 165, 171, 191,
210, 211, 213–218

vagueness, 143, 202
van Cleve, J., 198
van Frasseen, B., 65, 110, 111,
121, 166, 187–190
van Inwagen, P., 76, 77, 188,
198, 200, 209, 210,
219, 223
Varzi, A., 151, 160
Velleman, D., 29, 32

Warhol, A., 109
Wasserman, R., 31, 222
Whitehead, A.N., 91, 136, 142,
144
Wiles, A., 176
Williams, D.C., 197, 201
Wittgenstein, L., 71, 135, 144,
145, 149, 184, 197–
199, 221
Wolff, C., 96, 141
Wollheim, R., 109, 121
Wolterstorff, N., 121
Woodger, J.H., 156, 160
Woodward, J., 43, 52
Wundt, W., 153

Zimmerman, D., 195, 197, 201,
202, 223

www.ingramcontent.com/pod-product-compliance
Lightning Source LLC
Chambersburg PA
CBHW032003220426
43664CB00005B/131